Dr. Dimitropoulos and her team hav[illegible] [illegible]ge in the
areas of adolescent development an[illegible] [illegible]disorder
treatment. In doing so, they have [illegible] [illegible]ne with
cutting-edge scientific evidence and [illegible] [illegible]anual is
an absolute necessity for anyone pr[illegible] [illegible]ce, and
offers an invaluable foundation of be[illegible] [illegible]earchers
hoping to effectively work with patients ages 16–25.

Jocelyn Lebow, PhD, LP, *Consultant, Division of Integrated Behavioral Health, Department of Psychiatry & Psychology, Mayo Clinic School of Medicine*

This seminal book provides guidance on the evidence-base, theory and rationale for providing Family-Based Treatment (FBT) for Transition Age Youth (TAY) with eating disorders. Further background is provided on the critical differences between traditional FBT and FBT-TAY. In addition, this book includes a detailed step-by-step guide to providing this treatment. Every clinician caring for youth aged 16–25 years will want to read this book!

Jennifer Couturier, MD, MSc, FRCPC, *Child and Adolescent Psychiatrist and Medical Co-Director, McMaster Children's Hospital Eating Disorders Program; Professor, Department of Psychiatry & Behavioural Neurosciences, McMaster University*

This book offers a thoughtful and much-needed contribution to the evolving field of eating disorder treatment. What distinguishes this work is its careful balance of scientific rigor and clinical wisdom. The authors articulate the foundational principles of family-based care while demonstrating how these principles can be applied with greater developmental sensitivity for individuals navigating the transition to adulthood. By emphasizing collaboration with the young person alongside continued caregiver involvement, FBT-TAY reflects the realities of this life stage and honors the emerging autonomy of young adults without compromising the urgency of medical and nutritional recovery.

This book is a timely and important resource that advances both the science and practice of eating disorder care.

Dr. Karen Bernstein, *Associate Professor of Pediatrics, University of Illinois Chicago*

Family-Based Treatment for Transition-Aged Youth with Anorexia Nervosa

This book provides a comprehensive theoretical, empirical, and clinical account for the use of an adapted form of family-based treatment for transition-aged youth (FBT-TAY) aged 16–25 with anorexia nervosa.

In FBT-TAY, the treatment team prioritizes addressing the young person's concerns and challenges related to their developmental stage, such as solidifying their identity, educational or vocational aspirations, relationships, and future life goals. Therapy sessions incorporate discussions and interventions that are relevant and meaningful to the young person's developmental stage while recommending specific ways to appropriately engage parents/caregivers to support the recovery process. The book includes an introduction to FBT-TAY concepts and strategies with a detailed description of each phase of treatment, a review of the available data and scientific support for this intervention, and discussions of FBT-TAY application with patients in post-secondary education from diverse families, those without family involvement, and underserved areas.

This book provides a foundation to clinicians who seek a tailored approach of FBT to fit the needs of their transition-aged patients with anorexia nervosa, in a series of chapters authored by leading experts in FBT-TAY and clinicians in the eating disorder field.

Gina Dimitropoulos is a professor at the Faculty of Social Work, University of Calgary, and is cross appointed with the departments of psychiatry and paediatrics. She also holds the inaugural University of Calgary Research Excellence Chair in Transdisciplinary System-level Interventions for Equitable, Accessible Youth Mental Health Services.

Daniel Le Grange is an emeritus professor of psychiatry and behavioural sciences at University of California, San Francisco, and emeritus professor of psychiatry and behavioural neuroscience at the University of Chicago.

James Lock is a professor of child psychiatry and the director of the eating disorder program at Stanford University.

Kristen Anderson is a licensed clinical social worker and the co-founder of the Chicago Center for Evidence Based Treatment, a specialized eating disorders treatment program serving individuals with eating disorders across the lifespan.

Family-Based Treatment for Transition-Aged Youth with Anorexia Nervosa

A Framework for Working with Young People and Their Families

Gina Dimitropoulos, Daniel Le Grange,
James Lock, and Kristen Anderson

Routledge
Taylor & Francis Group
NEW YORK AND LONDON

Designed cover image: Getty Images

First published 2027
by Routledge
605 Third Avenue, New York, NY 10158

and by Routledge
4 Park Square, Milton Park, Abingdon, Oxon, OX14 4RN

Routledge is an imprint of the Taylor & Francis Group, an informa business

ISBN: 978-1-032-73264-0 (hbk)
ISBN: 978-1-032-70479-1 (pbk)
ISBN: 978-1-003-46335-1 (ebk)

DOI: 10.4324/9781003463351

Typeset in Times New Roman
by Apex CoVantage, LLC

This book is dedicated to young people and their families affected by eating disorders.

Contents

	List of Figures	*xi*
	List of Tables	*xii*
	Acknowledgements	*xiii*
	Introduction	1
1	What Is FBT-TAY?	25
2	Why Use FBT-TAY? The Scientific and Clinical Rationale	44
3	Overview of Late Adolescent and Young Development in FBT-TAY	52
4	Setting Up Treatment for FBT-TAY	65
5	Phase 1 – Session 1	85
6	Phase 1 – Session 2 (The Family Meal)	102
7	Remainder of Phase 1	111
8	Phase 2	126
9	Phase 3 – Emerging Adulthood, Relapse Prevention, and Termination of Treatment	138
10	Contextual Considerations in FBT-TAY	153

11 Post-Secondary Considerations 162

12 FBT-TAY for Diverse Families 174

13 FBT-TAY for Young People Without Family Involvement 188

Book Summary and Conclusions 198

Index *200*

Figures

5.1	Weight Log	87
5.2	Compensatory Log	87
5.3	Externalization Using a Venn Diagram	91

Tables

A Comparison of the Key Principles of the FBT-TAY and FBT 36

B Summary of the Key Content of FBT and FBT-TAY (in Dimitropoulos et al., 2018a) 37

C Taking a History 90

Acknowledgements

We would like to acknowledge the young people, families, therapists, trainees, and students who have inspired us over the last decade to conduct research related to transition-aged youth and the family-based treatment (FBT) for this age group. Building on Dr. Daniel Le Grange's and Dr. Jim Lock's leadership in the field, the four of us embarked on an exciting journey to write a book that examines the various ways we can developmentally and flexibly use FBT-TAY with older teens and young adults while staying true to the principles of the FBT model.

We would like to express our gratitude to a number of colleagues who worked tirelessly to support us with this book. This book would not have been possible without these individuals writing on the wide breadth of topics required to help set up the FBT principles, interventions, and phases of FBT-TAY. A huge thanks to Dr. Millie Austin, Heidi Vander Steen, Jessica Sauerwein, Sela Scott, Randesh Wijesundera, Jayden Lee, Nick Michael, and Manya Singh, for reviewing, writing, and updating the literature presented in this book. Dr. Millie Austin supported the review of the literature related to the development of FBT-TAY while mentoring other members of the team and writing some of the earlier chapters. Heidi Vander Steen wrote various sections of the work in the first few chapters, including, but not limited to, the prevalence, incidence, and multi-factorial nature of eating disorders and the unique developmental issues related to emerging adulthood. Jessica Sauerwein supported the literature review related to the family life cycle and emerging adulthood. Sela Scott strengthened several chapters in this book and supporting the written descriptions of the various models of care (e.g., AFT, residential care, ECHO), measures for eating disorders, and unique challenges and opportunities in applying FBT-TAY when young people do not have family available to support them. Randesh Wijesundera and Jayden Lee supported the chapters on diversity and post-secondary issues, as well as assistance with references and editorial support. Nick Michael provided support with the compilation of references for the chapter on diversity. We are also grateful to Manya Singh for all her support in writing, synthesizing, editing, as well as organizing the team. We would finally like to thank Drs. Jennifer Mooney and Ellie Vyver for lending their expertise as adolescent medicine specialists to this work.

Introduction

In this book, we present an evidence-informed model for working with transition-aged youth (TAY, ages 16–25; see Dimitropoulos et al., 2016, 2018; Wilens & Rosenbaum, 2013) with anorexia nervosa (AN) and their parents/caregivers and families. Building on the empirically supported family-based treatment (FBT) for adolescents with AN and bulimia nervosa (BN) (Le Grange & Lock, 2007; Lock & Le Grange, 2025), this book provides a comprehensive theoretical, empirical, clinical account of FBT for transition-aged youth (FBT-TAY) with AN. We illustrate a step-by-step description of how FBT-TAY may be employed with young people, from those presenting with AN for the first time to those in paediatric care requiring a transition to adult services, as well as those receiving care in non-specialized services and post-secondary institutions.

While there is no universal definition of TAY, it is a term often used in clinical and educational systems to describe those transitioning between older adolescence (ages 15–17) and young adulthood (ages 18–25; Wilens & Rosenbaum, 2013). Throughout this book, we use the terms "*TAY*" and "*emerging adult*" interchangeably, as they both describe the late adolescence to early adulthood life stage (e.g., Arnett et al., 2014; Dimitropoulos et al., 2016, 2018). Moreover, the term "*young person*" is used to describe "*adolescents,*" "*TAY,*" and "*emerging adults,*" as it encompasses the life stages of childhood, adolescence, and young adulthood (United Nations, 2019), while the terms "*clinician*" and "*therapist*" may be used interchangeably to describe healthcare practitioners who offer therapeutic support via FBT to young people. Adaptations to the key principles and clinical interventions of the foundational model of FBT are highlighted to show how they are used with young people in a variety of contexts including those living with their family, residing on their own, or living on college and university campuses. In this book, we use "*parents,*" "*caregivers,*" and "*families*" interchangeably, recognizing that there are many types of natural supports including one's family of origin, family of choice, or other supportive carer who may participate in FBT-TAY.

DOI: 10.4324/9781003463351-1

In this introductory chapter, we provide an overview of the AN literature – including onset, prevalence and mortality rates – moving on to discussing the challenges of transitions in eating disorder (ED) healthcare. We also highlight the key developmental considerations for young people, including brain development processes and cognitive challenges that may be impaired due to AN. Lastly, we briefly introduce a summary of FBT-TAY for young people, highlighting research that demonstrates the rationale for continuing to use family-based interventions to support young people with AN transitioning to adulthood or adult care. To conclude the introductory chapter, an overview of the purpose of this manual and its structure is included.

Anorexia Nervosa

AN is a psychiatric disorder characterized by persistent preoccupation with weight-loss, restrictive eating and excessive exercise. Diagnostic criteria, per the DSM-5, includes a severe restriction of energy intake leading to weight changes, an intense fear of weight gain and a distorted perception of one's body weight or shape (American Psychiatric Association, 2013). AN diagnosis includes two subtypes: restricting type (no bingeing or purging) and binge-eating/purging type. Onset of AN typically occurs during mid-to-late adolescence, with 40% of young people receiving a new diagnosis between 15 and 19 years of age (Jagielska & Kacperska, 2017).

AN is associated with severe medical consequences, psychosocial impairment, and psychiatric co-morbidity (Treasure et al., 2020), affecting an individual's cognitive, physical, emotional functioning, and quality of life. The medical difficulties with AN are often linked to restriction of energy intake, which has adverse implications for nearly every organ system in the body (Cass et al., 2020), including the metabolic (energy production), endocrine (hormone production), gastrointestinal (digestive system), neurological (brain system), haematological (blood system), and cardiology (heart system) systems. AN can also have repercussions on dental and musculoskeletal health, causing a loss of bone density which can lead to osteopenia, osteoporosis, and serious tooth decay and loss (Cass et al., 2020). AN impacts children, adolescents, and young people differently, due to the variation in developmental stage, physical growth, and psychological maturity among these broad age groups. Children and adolescents with AN experience severe growth disruption, with regard to height, bone mineralization, and puberty development (Downey et al., 2023; Neale et al., 2020); due to their underdeveloped organs, malnutrition, and weight loss, they often have a greater effect on physical development (Dalle Grave et al., 2021). Young people are found to be at a high risk of infertility, cardiac complications, and osteoporosis (Friars et al., 2023; Kimmel et al., 2016; Mehler & Walsh, 2016; Misra & Klibanski, 2011). These medical complications are significant and can have long-term deleterious effects on the body if AN remains untreated (Treasure et al., 2020).

AN is associated with the second highest mortality rate among all psychiatric disorders (Arcelus et al., 2011; Mehler et al., 2022; Van Eeden et al., 2021), with an overall standardized mortality ratio (SMR) of 5.9. SMR is a ratio that compares the observed number of deaths in a study population to the number of deaths that would be expected based on a larger, standard population and adjusted for factors like age or sex (Wolfe et al., 1990). Mortality causes in AN have been primarily linked to medical complications such as cardiac issues (Auger et al., 2021).

Malnutrition can lead to sudden heart failure in people with AN, due to the abnormalities of heart rhythms that increase risk cardiac arrest, as well as fainting or seizures.

Alarmingly, suicidality is highly prevalent among individuals with EDs, encompassing suicidal ideation, suicide attempts, and non-suicidal self-injury (Auger et al., 2021; Mereu et al., 2022; Smith et al., 2018). A meta-analysis by Arcelus et al. (2011) found suicide to be the leading cause of death in one in five individuals with AN. With regard to suicidality specifically for younger people with AN, Buhren and colleagues (2014) conducted a large multi-site randomized controlled trial (n=148) examining psychiatric comorbidity, suicidality, and self-harm in adolescents with first onset AN; the authors reported significantly lower rates of psychiatric comorbidity and suicidal ideation in adolescents compared to adults with AN (Buhren et al., 2014). The finding by Buhren and colleagues (2014) was later affirmed in a review by Smith et al. (2018), who reported a higher frequency of suicide attempts among young people in comparison to adolescents with AN. Nonethelesssss, suicidality and suicide are major clinical concerns in AN regardless of age.

Young people with EDs are also at heightened risk of developing co-occurring mental health conditions (Hambleton et al., 2022; Le Grange et al., 2012; Momen et al., 2020), with a high prevalence of comorbid mood disorders (Radon et al., 2022), major depressive disorders, anxiety disorders (Hambleton et al., 2022; Kerr-Gaffney et al., 2018), and substance use disorders (Devoe et al., 2021). Research suggests that individuals with AN binge-purge subtype (AN-BP) exhibit higher rates of borderline personality disorder (diagnosable only in those over 18 years of age), substance use disorders, and impulse control disorders (Danon et al., 2024; Devoe et al., 2021, 2022) compared to those with AN restricting subtype (AN-R), who more commonly present with obsessive-compulsive traits, anxiety disorders, and maladaptive perfectionism (Cassin &von Ranson, 2005). These distinctions likely influence treatment responsiveness and clinical outcomes (Hambleton et al., 2022). OCD symptoms moderated the dose level in FBT (Lock et al., 2005), and those with OCD appeared to do better in SFT compared to FBT (Agras et al., 2014). The presence of multiple mental health conditions further increases the risk of mortality; the SMR for individuals with AN is over five times higher in those with at least one psychiatric comorbidity (Kask et al., 2016). Psychiatric comorbidity has also been found to be a risk factor for suicidality in individuals with AN, particularly those with the binge-purge subtype due to the higher level of impulsivity and rates of psychiatric co-morbidity (Hambleton et al., 2022). At the same time, psychiatric co-morbidity other than OCD has not been found to moderate response to FBT and studies suggest that among adolescents, depressive and anxious symptoms abate with successful treatment of AN (Lock et al, 2005; Agras et al., 2014).

AN has been shown to diminish a young person's quality of life, including their mental, emotional, and social well-being (Brockmeyer et al., 2022; Sy et al., 2013). Young people with AN often struggle with feelings of isolation or loneliness, due to an avoidance of social events, increased distress over food in social situations, or withdrawal from friendships and family interactions, propelled by feelings of shame or embarrassment (Cardi et al., 2018). These disruptions to peer, family, and community connection may make it difficult for young people to fully engage in academic, extracurricular, and social activities that they enjoy (Brockmeyer et al., 2022). Furthermore, interpersonal difficulties or conflicts have been found to negatively impact treatment outcomes and increase ED behaviours (e.g., dietary restriction) (Cardi et al., 2018).

Ultimately, this leads to a reduced quality of life and severe impediments to personal growth and self-development (Brockmeyer et al., 2022).

Key Developmental Considerations for Transition-Aged Youth

Brain Development

During adolescence, there is a rapid shift in brain development and maturation, involving significant structural and functional changes (e.g., Andrews et al., 2021). This period is critical for the pre-frontal cortex, known for guiding executive functioning responsible for memory, decision-making, and impulse control (Friedman & Robbins, 2022; Peters & Naneix, 2022; Steinberg et al., 2013). Development of the pre-frontal cortex emerges in late adolescence, when adolescents are characterized as having difficulty with impulse control and seeing long-term consequences of decision-making (Merz et al., 2018; Partridge, 2010). These developmental vulnerabilities mean that young people with AN may not yet be able to envision the consequences of their ED on their lives in the future. As adolescents transition to young adulthood, impaired executive functioning comes at a time when young people are expected to begin making independent help-seeking decisions regarding their health and treatment engagement (Gutierrez-Colina, et al., 2022; Nelson et al., 2019). Furthermore, chronic starvation and malnutrition associated with AN have acute detrimental impacts on the brain during this stage of development (e.g., Barbosa, 2023; Kappou et al., 2021; Posner & Steinglass, 2024; Seitz et al., 2016), including reduced brain volume, cortical thickness, and function (Bohon et al., 2019). In addition, the maturation of cortico-striatal systems involved in emotional and behavioural self-regulation, cognitive flexibility, and learning and memory are all impaired during this critical period when young people experience prolonged starvation (Olivo et al., 2019; Via et al., 2023). The disruption of brain development may delay a young person's formation of complex reasoning, abstract thinking, and perspective taking, reducing their ability to accept that they are experiencing an illness detrimental to their health (Kappou et al., 2021; Olivo et al., 2019).

AN's Effect on Treatment-Seeking Behaviours in TAY

Individuals with AN have been found to have higher levels of cognitive inflexibility (difficulty shifting cognitive sets) than their peers, which leads to dichotomous thinking and difficulty adapting to change (Berthoz et al., 2022; Brockmeyer et al., 2022; Bohon et al., 2019; Kerr-Gaffney et al., 2021; Lock & Nicholls, 2020; Smith et al., 2018). The cognitive inflexibility associated with AN may contribute to disruption in decision-making capacity which can lead to delays in help-seeking, withdrawing from treatment, or low treatment engagement associated with a high reluctance to make necessary changes for recovery (e.g., Elzakkers et al., 2017). In addition, cognitive rigidity and inflexibility in individuals with AN may induce scepticism about treatment or difficulties accepting the idea of gradual weight restoration (Berthoz et al., 2022; Brockmeyer et al., 2022; Chen et al., 2016; Duriez et al., 2021; Miles et al., 2023; Tchanturia et al., 2013; Treasure & Schmidt, 2013). These inflexible cognitive processes are also exacerbated by a heightened intolerance of uncertainty among young people with AN (Sternheim et al., 2024). Intolerance of uncertainty refers to the propensity to perceive stimuli as uncertain and to react with a great sense of threat to situations that are ambiguous (Dugas et al., 1998; Carleton et al., 2007).

Individuals with EDs have also been shown to have relatively weak central coherence compared to their peers. Weak central coherence leads to excessively focusing on details rather understanding the "bigger" picture. This leads to challenges integrating information holistically or understanding the broader context of their disorder and its medical and psychological implications (Lock & Nicholls, 2020; Kerr-Gaffney et al., 2021; Tenconi et al., 2021; Tchanturia et al., 2014). Both weak central coherence and difficulties in set-shifting have been reported to predispose individuals to AN (e.g., Kerr-Gaffney et al., 2021; Treasure & Schmidt, 2013). While each of these cognitive patterns can create distinct challenges, they frequently present themselves simultaneously, creating substantial barriers for young people to adhere to treatment and therefore impede recovery processes. Additionally, prolonged starvation has been found to exacerbate these cognitive patterns (Berthoz et al., 2022). However, recovery has been shown to improve cognitive functioning, set-shifting, cognitive rigidity, and central coherence (e.g., Kappou et al., 2021; Keegan et al., 2020; Tenconi et al., 2021).

Emotional Difficulties

Individuals with AN often struggle to recognize, process, and manage emotions (Bryant et al., 2022; Miskovic-Wheatley et al., 2023; Kappou et al., 2021). Difficulties identifying emotions and emotional regulation can lead to maladaptive coping strategies such as reliance on AN behaviours. They are also found to experience heightened anxiety and emotional avoidance, making the recovery process more challenging. A growing body of research demonstrates that individuals with AN often experience an impaired awareness of bodily states, known as interoception deficits (Phillipou et al., 2022; Wollast et al., 2022). With interoception deficits, individuals may struggle with recognizing hunger, satiety, and physical discomfort; the disconnect of physiological needs may sustain disordered eating patterns. The challenges associated with inadequate emotion recognition and difficulties tolerating strong or negative emotions may necessitate parental or caregiver involvement in supporting young people in the engagement of behavioural changes and the treatment process.

Moreover, AN has a multifaceted emotional impact, frequently encompassing profound feelings of shame and embarrassment for the illness and that others are needed to support them (Kelly et al., 2014; O'Connor et al., 2019; Potterton et al., 2020; Troop & Redshaw, 2012). Young people may feel embarrassed with their struggle with AN and refrain from reaching out for help due to their age (Potterton et al., 2020). They may attempt to cope with their AN alone, leading to an increase in self-isolation and delays in seeking treatment. In these circumstances, parental/familial support can provide a crucial source of encouragement and understanding to reduce stigma of AN; this helps young people feel both less isolated and more comfortable seeking help for the AN.

TAY with AN

There are several key distinguishing factors of young people with AN to consider in the provision of services while caring for this population. The "family unit" must be defined broadly and by the young person; a wide range of supports may be helpful to include in treatment such as close friends, roommates, romantic partners, siblings, or extended family members. This is especially pertinent for young people who are not living with their family and cannot rely completely on parental/caregiver support, or who may benefit from an expanded support system. Tailored treatment approaches that account for these differences in this population is necessary for their successful recovery and well-being.

Importance of Parental/Caregiver Support

There is no evidence to suggest that parents or caregivers are to blame for the development and maintenance of AN (Le Grange et al., 2016). AN is a highly complex disorder, and research demonstrates there are concurrent biological, psychological, and environmental factors that likely contribute to the risk for AN; specifically, genetics, neurobiological factors, trauma, and societal pressures may all play a role in the onset of AN (Barakat et al., 2023; Varela et al., 2023). A plethora of research has underscored that parental/family involvement in treatment significantly aids recovery rather than perpetuating the AN (Austin et al., 2025; Cripps et al., 2024; Hilbert et al., 2017; Treasure & Nazar, 2016). Hence, families are well positioned to offer emotional stability and practical meal support and help young people rebuild trust in their own bodies and relationship with food (Jewell et al., 2016), all of which are critical factors for long-term AN recovery (Kenny & Lewis, 2023).

Perception of Illness

Families may play a critical role in addressing several aspects of AN that must be targeted in treatment. First, the ego-syntonic nature of AN means that young people often view their disordered behaviours – such as restrictive eating and excessive exercise – as aligned with their personal values, identity, or sense of control, leading to difficulties in perceiving the severity of their symptoms (Potterton et al., 2020). Potterton and colleagues (2020) report that due to the ego-syntonic nature of AN, family and friends often raise initial concerns of young people's eating behaviours to healthcare professionals, as young people do not initially perceive their emerging symptoms as problematic. They frequently describe relying on their family and friends to help them decide whether to seek help or alternatively elicit help to assuage the concerns of their family and friends, especially when plagued with ambivalence and low motivation to pursue care (Potterton et al., 2020). This highlights crucial areas where parental/familial support can help reframe young peoples' perceptions of their illness, facilitate help-seeking, and eating rehabilitation (Gregertsen et al., 2017; Roncero et al., 2013).

The Impacts of AN on Parents/Caregivers

Caregivers and families often face substantial economic, mental, and emotional challenges because of the illness and their ongoing efforts to support their child without proper professional support and resources (Dennhag et al., 2021; Maunder & McNicholas, 2021; Obeid et al., 2024). Financially, families frequently encounter expensive out-of-pocket costs for treatment, as well as loss of income due to reduced working hours or leaving their job to provide full-time support to their child (Obeid et al., 2024). Taking into consideration the chronic nature of ANs, parents/caregivers are vulnerable to experiencing caregiver burnout especially when supporting a young person who is reluctant to engage in care or when they receive limited support while their child is in treatment. Caregiver burnout is defined as a state of physical, emotional, and mental exhaustion experienced by caregivers, resulting from an intensive and prolonged period supporting a loved one with a chronic ED (Stefanini et al., 2019). Parents and caregivers are often overwhelmed by stress and anxiety while lacking time or finances to access therapeutic support for themselves (Streatfeild et al., 2021). They may also experience their relationships with other family members as strained due to the intense focus on the young person with AN. These difficulties have the potential to manifest into physical health challenges, such as sleep disturbances and fatigue (Stefanini et al., 2019; Wallis et al., 2017). The lack of adequate professional support for parents/caregivers of young people with AN is profound; limited access to Medicaid or financial support for caregiving responsibilities further reduces the quality of life for parents/caregivers and access to necessary AN treatment for the young person (Accurso et al., 2021; Egbert et al., 2024; Sauerwein et al., 2025). The importance of parental/caregiver empowerment is critical to combat the system-level and illness-related challenges that may undermine their capacity and confidence to support their child with an AN (e.g., Ciao et al., 2022; Egbert et al., 2024). Family-based treatment for transition-aged youth pays special attention to the needs of parents/caregivers addressing burnout, distress, and disempowerment.

Transitions in Care

Approximately 40% of young people with EDs and 68% of young people with AN develop a chronic illness course (Eddy et al., 2017; Filipponi et al., 2022; Lock et al., 2010; Treasure & Russell, 2011), persisting on average for 10 years (Filipponi et al, 2022), necessitating a transfer of care – a point-in-time shift in the responsibility of care from a paediatric to an adult provider (Santos et al., 2025; Toulany et al., 2022) – for individuals moving from paediatric to adult healthcare services. Transfer of care often coincides with other developmental transitions and major life events, making it a particularly high-risk period. Of particular concern is that young people with mental illnesses including AN often disengage with and under-utilize services that would otherwise improve their psychosocial functioning and quality of life (Broad et al., 2017; Davidson et al., 2012; Gulliver et al., 2010). Stigma, shame, or fear can also make it difficult for young people to remain engaged in care, and they may need additional help from supportive others to pursue and engage in treatment (Ali et al., 2020).

Research demonstrates that young people often "slip through the cracks" when transitioning from paediatric to adult ED systems – an intentional, planned, and coordinated movement between systems of care (Blum, 2002; Santos et al.,

2025) – often due to drastic differences in how these care models are structured (Dimitropoulos et al., 2023). Paediatric services are designed to recognize the vast developmental needs of young people and integrate families in all aspects of care from assessment to discharge planning (Castillo & Kitsos, 2017); conversely, adult services require individuals to be more independent in the management of their care and family support is not required nor actively pursued (Castillo & Kitsos, 2017). Thus, as young people transition from paediatric to adult care, they may experience a substantial shift in the way care is delivered. In addition, delays in accessing timely and developmentally appropriate care may prolong illness and require more urgent and intensive evidence-based interventions for young people. Taken together, these factors exacerbate discontinuity of care and erode the capacity to address the specific psychosocial needs that are central to AN recovery in young people.

Several barriers to a successful transition from paediatric to adult ED Programs (EDPs) have been identified through qualitative interviews with expert therapists, young people, and their families (Dimitropoulos et al., 2012, 2015a). From the outset, the transfer of care to adult intensive EDPs is often abrupt and uncoordinated leaving older adolescents and young people vulnerable to a discontinuity of care for their illness (Dimitropoulos et al., 2015b). Young people report feeling unprepared for transfers to adult care, due to a lack of discussion with healthcare providers leading up to the transfer. Additionally, young people may experience trepidation about forming new relationships with therapists when entering adult programs. Young people often desire increased autonomy and control over their lives; however, treatment for AN typically involves a high level of external guidance and supervision, which can create tension and resistance to treatment engagement (Dimitropoulos et al., 2015).

On the contrary, there are several systemic facilitators to successfully transitioning young people from paediatric to adult healthcare. First, collaborative treatment approaches that actively include young people as participants in their own care (e.g., through sharing test results and identifying treatment goals) is key to promoting and respecting their autonomy and independence *prior* to the transition (Dimitropoulos et al., 2015). This ensures that young people feel included in discussions and decisions about their own treatment prior to the transfer. Next, providing training to professional to enhance their capacity in better preparing young people, for both adulthood and managing their own adult care. Young people report needing guidance from their paediatric team with their development of self-management skills, which includes preventing the emergence of illness symptoms and taking ownership of their healthcare (Patten et al., 2024). Given the abrupt shift in responsibility from families to the young person as they transition out of paediatric services, research suggests that paediatric services focus on teaching young people with AN about self-advocacy and how to appropriately navigate services in adult care (Dimitropoulos et al., 2025; White & Cooley, 2018). This may include skill acquisition in seeking out specialized adult treatment, identifying treatment-related resources, meal planning, and scheduling their own appointments. Furthermore, young people report needing early, coordinated, and intentional conversations with their paediatric and adult teams – with the presence of their caregiver – about the transition process, the ethos, and expectations of treatment within paediatric versus adult programs, identification of emergency resources during the transition, and maintaining systems of external monitoring after the transfer (Dimitropoulos et al., 2025). Taken together, these facilitators ultimately enable young people with AN to feel supported, learn to navigate varying systems of care, and be active participants in their transition process (Dimitropoulos et al., 2018). Given these significant system-level changes, family-based treatment for transition-aged youth must focus on how best to support the entire family as they experience many life changes alongside the transfer to adult care for the young person with AN.

Why Family Support Matters During Transitions

Family support is vital to the success of AN treatment as adolescents launch into adulthood and transfer to adult care (Dimitropoulos et al., 2016; Mursaleen et al., 2025). Parents and caregivers can provide support by advocating for and with young people, providing structure, emotional support, and practical assistance in preparing for the transfer of care from adolescent to adult treatments (Dimitropoulos et al., 2016; Scanferla et al., 2023). However, parents/caregivers are not always supported to take on this critical role with their child as they enter young adulthood, leaving them feeling uncertain about their caregiving role. The young person's desire for enhanced autonomy as they become an adult can also contribute to conflict at a time when they are needed to offer support (Dimitropoulos et al., 2016).

In a qualitative study conducted by Nadarajah et al. (2021) examining the barriers and facilitators of successful transitions from the perspectives of young people and caregivers, caregivers reported having limited knowledge of the transition process and concerns about the lack of continuity in treatment. Both caregivers and young people reported that an abrupt shift in care and expectations of the young person during the transition process puts them at risk of disengaging in treatment. Conversely, caregivers identified several factors influencing a successful transition between paediatric and adult ED programs. While being knowledgeable about the transition process and initiating contact with adult services was identified as important, caregivers unequivocally reinforced the importance of their involvement in the transition process – from providing their feedback and input to the paediatric team and the adult services where their child has been referred for treatment. They also reinforced that the support and guidance of the paediatric health team – to make recommendations about adult programs, access their networks to identify the right types of programs for their child, and enable joint communication between paediatric and adult ED teams – were essential.

To that end, caregivers discussed a variety of strategies to promote successful transitions including developing a transition passport with their child's medical histories to avoid repeating their symptoms to new providers, hiring a transition coordinator to offer education about the transition process and provide navigational support, as well as gradually "phasing out" paediatric services prior to the transition. Young people in this study also reinforced the importance and need for parental/caregiver support during the transition process, to navigate new expectations associated with greater independence and autonomy in managing their health. They also noted that having caregiver support throughout treatment helped them maintain their recovery and reduced the possibility of relapse with their ED (Nadarajah et al., 2021).

Therapist's Experience with TAY

The therapist perspective is equally critical to identifying areas where young people may need more support during the transition process. Studies that have examined clinical considerations during this unique developmental stage suggest that enhancing autonomy, building resilience and motivation in the young person, and managing longitudinal barriers during the process are essential (Dimitropoulos et al., 2012, 2013; Garland et al., 2019; Lockertsen et al., 2020). In addition, establishing therapeutic rapport and trust within adult care, reconceptualizing the transition for when a young person is ready to leave paediatric care, flexibility in the timing and age criteria for the transition, as well as providing robust transition interventions for patients and families coupled with medical monitoring once a young person is in adult care are all factors identified by therapists as critical for a successful transition (Dimitropoulos et al., 2012, 2013).

During the transition, young people with AN may exhibit a range of behaviours and emotions including difficulty with acceptance of the illness, ambivalence towards change, and reluctance for family involvement in adult care (Garland et al., 2019). While building young peoples' emotional maturity and readiness for change are critical during the transition process, therapists have reported difficulties achieving this in adult care, where the focus shifts abruptly to increased self-sufficiency and responsibility (Lockertsen et al. 2020). This, compounded with the lack of trust between paediatric and adult systems and feelings of insecurity and limited skills in managing AN during the transition, has been reported by therapists to impede successful transitions for young people (Lockertsen et al., 2020).

Nonetheless, therapists in both paediatric and adult ED care play a critical role in guiding young people and families in shifting developmentally appropriate choices for treatment and helping support the young person's engagement in their recovery. Moreover, they are well suited to help establish clear expectations for parental/caregiver involvement during the transition by facilitating productive dialogue between the young person and their caregiver; communicating their competency and therapeutic skills in managing the transition successfully; and aiding in the transfer of alliance, trust, and key information about the young person during the transition process to avoid discontinuity and disengagement in adult services (Dimitropoulos et al., 2012, 2013; Garland et al., 2019; Lockertsen et al., 2020).

Family-Based Treatment (FBT)

FBT is the gold-standard treatment for adolescent AN and their families which emphasizes parental/caregiver empowerment and responsibility in addressing ED symptoms, restoring healthy eating, and includes weight restoration for most young people (Le Grange & Lock, 2007; Lock & Le Grange, 2025). FBT takes a phased approach to care, initially focusing on weight restoration and/or the cessation of other maintaining behaviours (e.g., calorie counting, obsessive weighing, mirror checking, binge eating and compensatory behaviours), gradually shifting age-appropriate eating responsibility back to the adolescents, and finally, considering developmental dilemmas more typical of healthy adolescence (Rienecke & Le Grange, 2022). Family members play a significant role in supporting and empowering the young person with an ED to recover (Dimitropoulos & Freeman, 2016; Singh et al., 2018). Family therapies that focus specifically on ED symptoms are considered the most effective treatment for AN in adolescents (2025). Clinical guidelines recommend the use of FBT with young people diagnosed with AN or BN (Couturier et al., 2020; Crone et al., 2023; National Institute for Health and Care Excellence, 2017; Wilson & Shafran, 2005). These recommendations are supported by a range of randomized controlled trials (RCTs) demonstrating the superiority of FBT in comparison to individual therapy approaches for young people (Le Grange et al., 2007, 2015; Lock et al., 2010).

However, findings from a qualitative study exploring clinical application of the FBT model with TAY showed that therapists make modifications to account for the specific needs of older adolescents (Dimitropoulos et al., 2015). For example, therapists reported utilizing individual therapy with young people alongside the sessions with the family, which is different from how FBT for adolescents is delivered where adolescents are only seen briefly at the beginning of sessions (or not at all in PFT) (Le Grange et al., 2016). These longer individual therapy sessions were used to provide more time for the therapist and young person to build a stronger working relationship and therapeutic alliance during treatment. They were also used to discuss aspects of their meals, symptoms, and/or the disorder that would not otherwise have been shared by younger adolescents (Dimitropoulos et al., 2015). In this study, Dimitropoulos and colleagues (2015) also emphasized the overall role of therapist flexibility, collaboration with parents/caregivers, and addressing developmental issues in treatment planning. One key finding highlighted the importance of actively engaging young people in this therapeutic process, acknowledging their discomfort about losing their independence and conveying to them that parental/caregiver support with eating is temporary (Dimitropoulos et al., 2015). This study among others helped to develop some of the intervention differences employed in FBT-TAY. FBT-TAY was introduced as an adaptation to FBT by Dimitropoulos and colleagues (2015, 2018, 2019) to address the unique needs and developmental challenges of young people with AN. While FBT places full responsibility of renourishment with the parents/caregivers, FBT-TAY takes a balanced approach, respecting the young person's autonomy and incorporating parental/caregiver support in the renourishment process. Throughout the treatment process, FBT-TAY uses a collaborative decision-making approach between the young person, the parent/caregiver, and therapist, acknowledging the agency of the young person while still leveraging parental/caregiver support. FBT-TAY thus shares some characteristics of FBT for BN which also encourages a dialogue between the older adolescent and parents/caregivers in developing strategies to decrease binge eating and purging (Lock & Le Grange, 2005).

Additionally, FBT-TAY addresses concurrent life transitions that may be occurring such as the young person's start of post-secondary education or moving away from home, factoring these life transitions into treatment. Furthermore, FBT-TAY works on building developmentally appropriate skills in the young person and encourages age-appropriate discussions, transition-focused interventions, individual therapy integration, and extended treatment duration. Finally, FBT-TAY can support young people in their recovery journey and successful transition to adulthood.

Structure of the Book

The following chapters describe a detailed evidence-based protocol for the treatment of young people affected by AN and their parents/families. Readers are provided with an introduction to FBT-TAY concepts and strategies with a detailed description of each phase of treatment, a review of the available data and scientific support for this intervention, and discussions of FBT-TAY application with young people in post-secondary education, diverse families, and those without family involvement. This book provides a foundation for therapists who seek a tailored approach of FBT to fit the needs of the young people that are considered "transition-aged youth" with AN, authored by leading experts in FBT-TAY and therapists in the ED field.

Chapters at a Glance:

Chapter 1:

This chapter provides an introduction to the theoretical concepts, intervention style, key intervention strategies, and stages of treatment for FBT-TAY and presents its comparison with FBT.

Chapter 2:

This chapter provides a detailed review of the available data and scientific support for the use of FBT-TAY and other family approaches, particularly in older adolescents and young adult patients with AN.

Chapter 3:

This chapter provides a broad overview of the emotional, cognitive, social, and family developments during young adulthood that must be considered when using FBT-TAY.

Chapter 4:

This chapter describes the pre-treatment evaluation processes needed to be employed to identify and assess individuals for FBT-TAY.

Chapter 5:

This chapter describes key aspects of Session 1 of Phase 1 of FBT-TAY which focuses on understanding the impact of AN on the individual and their family, engaging the young person and the parents/caregivers to work collaboratively and facilitating the application of strategies for renourishment.

Chapter 6:

This chapter describes how to use a Family Meal session to engage the young person and their families to identify patterns of accommodation and disruption to ED behaviours.

Chapter 7:

This chapter describes the remainder of the sessions in Phase 1, with the goal of engaging the young person and their families to relentlessly focus on, and achieve, weight restoration and eating rehabilitation.

Chapter 8:

This chapter describes key aspects of Phase 2 which focuses on strategies for incrementally relinquishing control back to the TAY. It will also include cases that illustrate the four main conceptualizations used in FBT-TAY.

Chapter 9:

This chapter describes the key aspects of Phase 3 which focuses on how in FBT-TAY the therapist and the patient identify future goals and aspirations now that AN is no longer the organizing principle of the patient's life.

Chapter 10:

This chapter describes the challenges that therapists practising FBT-TAY face using this adapted model in different clinical contexts from paediatric to adult programs and in private practice.

Chapter 11:

This chapter explores the challenges and considerations of implementing FBT-TAY with a young adult in post-secondary educational settings.

Chapter 12:

This chapter explores important considerations and factors when applying FBT-TAY for diverse youth and families in clinical practice.

Chapter 13:

This chapter focuses on FBT-TAY considerations for young people without family involvement.

References

Accurso, E. C., Buckelew, S. M., & Snowden, L. R. (2021). Youth insured by medicaid with restrictive EDs – underrecognized and under resourced. *JAMA Pediatrics*, *175*(10), 999–1000. https://doi.org/10.1001/jamapediatrics.2021.2081

Agras, W. S., Lock, J., Brandt, H., Bryson, S. W., Dodge, E., Halmi, K. A., Jo, B., Johnson, C., Kaye, W., Wilfley, D., & Woodside, B. (2014). Comparison of 2 family therapies for adolescent anorexia nervosa: A randomized parallel trial. *JAMA Psychiatry*, *71*(11), 1279–1286. https://doi.org/10.1001/jamapsychiatry.2014.1025

Ali, K., Fassnacht, D. B., Farrer, L., Rieger, E., Feldhege, J., Moessner, M., Griffiths, K. M., & Bauer, S. (2020). What prevents young adults from seeking help? Barriers toward help-seeking for ED symptomatology. *International Journal of Eating Disorders*, *53*(6), 894–906. https://doi.org/10.1002/eat.23266

American Psychiatric Association. (2013). *Diagnostic and statistical manual of mental disorders* (5th ed.). American Psychiatric Publishing.

Andrews, J. L., Ahmed, S. P., & Blakemore, S. J. (2021). Navigating the social environment in adolescence: The role of social brain development. *Biological Psychiatry*, *89*(2), 109–118. https://doi.org/10.1016/j.biopsych.2020.09.012

Arcelus, J., Mitchell, A. J., Wales, J., & Nielsen, S. (2011). Mortality rates in patients with anorexia nervosa and other EDs. A meta-analysis of 36 studies. *Archives of General Psychiatry*, *68*(7), 724–731. https://doi.org/10.1001/archgenpsychiatry.2011.74

Arnett, J. J., Žukauskienė, R., & Sugimura, K. (2014). The new life stage of emerging adulthood at ages 18–29 years: Implications for mental health. *The Lancet Psychiatry*, *1*(7), 569–576. https://doi.org/10.1016/S2215-0366(14)00080-7

Auger, N., Potter, B. J., Ukah, U. V., Low, N., Israël, M., Steiger, H., Healy-Profitós, J., & Paradis, G. (2021). Anorexia nervosa and the long-term risk of mortality in women. *World Psychiatry: Official Journal of the World Psychiatric Association (WPA)*, *20*(3), 448–449. https://doi.org/10.1002/wps.20904

Austin, A., Anderson, A. G., Lee, J., Vander Steen, H., Savard, C., Bergmann, C., Singh, M., Devoe, D., Gorrell, S., Patten, S., Le Grange, D., & Dimitropoulos, G. (2025). Efficacy of ED focused family therapy for adolescents with anorexia nervosa: A systematic review and meta-analysis. *International Journal of Eating Disorders*, *58*(1), 3–36. https://doi.org/10.1002/eat.24252

Barakat, S., McLean, S. A., Bryant, E., Le, A., Marks, P., Touyz, S., & Maguire, S. (2023). Risk factors for EDs: Findings from a rapid review. *Journal of Eating Disorders*, *11*(1), 8–31. https://doi.org/10.1002/erv.2745

Barbosa, A. M. R. (2023). *How the brain can make you starve: The neurobiology of anorexia nervosa* [Master's thesis]. Universidade do Porto (Portugal). Faculdade De Ciencias Da Neutricao E Alimentacao.

Berthoz, S., Maria, A. S., Ringuenet, D., Bourdier, L., Nicolas, I., Blanchet, C., Foulon, C., Lavoisy, G., Godart, N., & Barry, C. (2022). Cognitive flexibility and attention to detail in adolescents and adults with severe forms of anorexia nervosa. *European EDs Review: The Journal of the EDs Association*, *30*(3), 289–297. https://doi.org/10.1002/erv.2883

Blum, R. W. (2002). Improving transition for adolescents with special health care needs from pediatric to adult-centered health care. *Pediatrics*, *110*(6) 1–3. https://pubmed.ncbi.nlm.nih.gov/12456948/

Bohon, C., Weinbach, N., & Lock, J. (2019). A protocol for integrating neuroscience into studies of family-based treatment for anorexia nervosa: An approach to research and potential benefits for clinical care. *Frontiers in Psychiatry*, *10*, 1–9. https://doi.org/10.3389/fpsyt.2019.00919

Broad, K. L., Sandhu, V. K., Sunderji, N., & Charach, A. (2017). Youth experiences of transition from child mental health services to adult mental health services: A qualitative thematic synthesis. *BMC Psychiatry*, *17*(1), 1–11. https://doi.org/10.1186/s12888-017-1538-1

Brockmeyer, T., Febry, H., Leiteritz-Rausch, A., Wünsch-Leiteritz, W., Leiteritz, A., & Friederich, H. C. (2022). Cognitive flexibility, central coherence, and quality of life in anorexia nervosa. *Journal of Eating Disorders*, *10*(1), 1–8. https://doi.org/10.1186/s40337-022-00547-4

Bryant, E., Aouad, P., Hambleton, A., Touyz, S., & Maguire, S. (2022). 'In an otherwise limitless world, I was sure of my limit.' Experiencing anorexia nervosa: A phenomenological metasynthesis. *Frontiers in Psychiatry*, *13*, 1–20. https://doi.org/10.3389/fpsyt.2022.894178

Buhren, K., Schwarte, R., Fluck, F., Timmesfeld, N., Krei, M., Egberts, K., Pfeiffer, E., Fleischhaker, C., Wewetzer, C., & Herpertz-Dahlmann, B. (2014). Comorbid psychiatric disorders in female adolescents with first-onset anorexia nervosa. *European Eating Disorders Review*, *22*(1), 39–44. https://doi.org/10.1002/erv.2254

Cardi, V., Mallorqui-Bague, N., Albano, G., Monteleone, A. M., Fernandez-Aranda, F., & Treasure, J. (2018). Social difficulties as risk and maintaining factors in anorexia nervosa: A mixed-method investigation. *Frontiers in Psychiatry*, *9*, 1–10. https://doi.org/10.3389/fpsyt.2018.00012

Carleton, R. N., Norton, M. A., & Asmundson, G. J. (2007). Fearing the unknown: A short version of the intolerance of uncertainty scale. *Journal of Anxiety Disorders*, *21*(1), 105–117. https://doi.org/10.1016/j.janxdis.2006.03.014

Cass, K., McGuire, C., Bjork, I., Sobotka, N., Walsh, K., & Mehler, P. S. (2020). Medical complications of anorexia nervosa. *Psychosomatics (Washington, D.C.)*, *61*(6), 625–631. https://doi.org/10.1016/j.psym.2020.06.020

Cassin, S. E., & von Ranson, K. M. (2005). Personality and EDs: A decade in review. *Clinical Psychology Review*, *25*(7), 895–916. https://doi.org/10.1016/j.cpr.2005.04.012

Castillo, C., & Kitsos, E. (2017). Transitions from pediatric to adult care. *Global Pediatric Health*, *4*, 1–2. https://doi.org/10.1016/j.cpr.2005.04.012

Chen, E. Y., Weissman, J. A., Zeffiro, T. A., Yiu, A., Eneva, K. T., Arlt, J. M., & Swantek, M. J. (2016). Family-based therapy for young adults with anorexia nervosa restores weight. *International Journal of Eating Disorders*, *49*(7), 701–707. https://doi.org/10.1002/eat.22513

Ciao, A. C., Lebow, J., VandenLangenberg, E., Ohls, O., & Berg, K. C. (2022). A qualitative examination of adolescent and parent perspectives on early identification and early response to EDs. *EDs*, *30*(3), 249–266. https://doi.org/10.1080/10640266.2020.1805960

Couturier, J., Isserlin, L., Norris, M., Spettigue, W., Brouwers, M., Kimber, M., McVey, G., Webb, C., Findlay, S., Bhatnagar, N., Snelgrove, N., Ritsma, A., Preskow, W., Miller, C., Coelho, J., Boachie, A., Steinegger, C., Loewen, R., Loewen, T., Waite, E., Ford, C., Bourret, K., Gusella, J., Geller, J., LaFrance, A., LeClerc, A., Scarborough, J., Grewal, S., Jericho, M., Dimitropoulos, G., & Pilon, D. (2020). Canadian practice guidelines for the treatment of children and adolescents with EDs. *Journal of Eating Disorders*, *8*, 1–80. https://doi.org/10.1186/s40337-020-0277-8

Cripps, S., Pugh, M., & Serpell, L. (2024). Experiences of externalisation in recovery from anorexia nervosa: A reflexive thematic analysis. *Journal of Eating Disorders*, *12*(1), 1–25. https://doi.org/10.1186/s40337-024-01087-9

Crone, C., Fochtmann, L. J., Attia, E., Boland, R., Escobar, J., Fornari, V., Golden, N., Guarda, A., Jackson-Triche, M., Manzo, L., Mascolo, M., Pierce, K., Riddle, M., Seritan, A., Uniacke, B., Zucker, N., Yager, J., Craig, T. J., Hong, S. H., & Medicus, J. (2023). The American Psychiatric Association practice guideline for the treatment of patients with EDs. *The American Journal of Psychiatry*, *180*(2), 167–171. https://doi.org/10.1176/appi.ajp.23180001

Dalle Grave, R. D., Sartirana, M., Sermattei, S., & Calugi, S. (2021). Treatment of EDs in adults versus adolescents: Similarities and differences. *Clinical Therapeutics*, *43*(1), 70–84. https://doi.org/10.1016/j.clinthera.2020.10.015

Danon, M., Duriez, P., & Gorwood, P. (2024). Three clinical indicators of borderline personality disorder in anorexia nervosa: A pilot study. *L'Encephale*, *50*(1), 4–10. https://doi.org/10.1016/j.encep.2022.09.006

Davidson, S., Freeland, A., & Karen, T. (2012). *Improving quality of care and patient safety for transitional youth and young adults: Transitional youth pilot project*. Ontario Provincial Centre of Excellence for Child and Youth Mental Health. https://kmb.camh.ca/eenet/sites/default/files/pdfs/Ottawa-Transitional-Youth-Pilot-Project.pdf

Dennhag, I., Henje, E., & Nilsson, K. (2021). Parental caregiver burden and recovery of adolescent anorexia nervosa after multi-family therapy. *EDs*, *29*(5), 463–479. https://doi.org/10.1080/10640266.2019.1678980

Devoe, D. J., Anderson, A., Bahji, A., Singh, M., Patten, S. B., Soumbasis, A., Ramirez Pineda, A., Flanagan, J., Richardson, C., Lange, T., Dimitropoulos, G., & Paslakis, G. (2022). The prevalence of impulse control disorders and behavioral addictions in EDs: A systematic review and meta-analysis. *Frontiers in Psychiatry*, *12*, 1–17. https://doi.org/10.3389/fpsyt.2021.724034

Devoe, D. J., Dimitropoulos, G., Anderson, A., Bahji, A., Flanagan, J., Soumbasis, A., Patten, S. B., Lange, T., & Paslakis, G. (2021). The prevalence of substance use disorders and substance use in anorexia nervosa: A systematic review and meta-analysis. *Journal of Eating Disorders*, *9*(1), 1–15. https://doi.org/10.1186/s40337-021-00516-3

Dimitropoulos, G., & Freeman, V. E. (2016). The perceptions of individuals with anorexia nervosa regarding their family's understanding of their illness, treatment, and recovery. *EDs*, *24*(4), 375–382. https://doi.org/10.1080/10640266.2015.1090870

Dimitropoulos, G., Freeman, V. E., Allemang, B., Couturier, J., McVey, G., Lock, J., & Le Grange, D. (2015). Family-based treatment with transition age youth with anorexia nervosa: A qualitative summary of application in clinical practice. *Journal of Eating Disorders*, *3*(1), 1–13. https://doi.org/10.1186/s40337-015-0037-3

Dimitropoulos, G., Herschman, J., & Toulany, A. (2016). A qualitative study on the challenges associated with accepting familial support from the perspective of transition-age youth with EDs. In S. Murray, L. Anderson, & L. Cohn (Eds.), *Innovations in family therapy for EDs* (pp. 246–261). Routledge.

Dimitropoulos, G., Landers, A. L., Freeman, V. E., Novick, J., Cullen, O., Engelberg, M., Steinegger, C., & Le Grange, D. (2018). Family-based treatment for transition age youth: Parental self-efficacy and caregiver accommodation. *Journal of Eating Disorders*, *6*(1), 1–11. https://doi.org/10.1186/s40337-018-0196-0

Dimitropoulos, G., Morgan-Maver, E., Allemang, B., Schraeder, K., Scott, S. D., Pinzon, J., Andrew, G., Guilcher, G., Hamiwka, L., Lang, E., McBrien, K., Nettel-Aguirre, A., Pacaud, D., Zwaigenbaum, L., Mackie, A., & Samuel, S. (2019). Health care stakeholder perspectives regarding the role of a patient navigator during transition to adult care. *BMC Health Services Research*, *19*(1), 1–10. https://doi.org/10.1186/s12913-019-4227-6

Dimitropoulos, G., Nicula, M., Krishnapillai, A., Austin, A., Singh, M., Lee, J., Webb, C., Scott, S., de Almeida, A. C. V., Bergmann, C., Vander Steen, H., Kimber, M., Mushquash, C., Norman, L., Sauerwein, J., Keshen, A., Boachie, A., Toulany, A., Levinson, A., . . . Couturier, J. (2025). Transitions for youth and young adults with EDs and/or other mental health conditions: A Canadian guideline. *Journal of Eating Disorders*, *13*(1), 1–27. https://doi.org/10.1186/s40337-025-01343-6

Dimitropoulos, G., Singh, M., Mushquash, C., Kimber, M., Hutt-MacLeod, D., Moore, E. K., Perri, A., Webb, C., Norman, L., Sauerwein, J., Nicula, M., & Couturier, J. (2023). TransitionED: A protocol for Co-designing and implementing Canadian practice guidelines for transitions for youth with EDs. *European EDs Review*, 1–15. https://doi.org/10.1002/erv.3026

Dimitropoulos, G., Toulany, A., Herschman, J., Kovacs, A., Steinegger, C., Bardsley, J., Sandhu, S., Gregory, C., Colton, P., Anderson, J., & Kaufman, M. (2015a). A qualitative study on the experiences of young adults with EDs transferring from pediatric to adult care. *EDs*, *23*(2), 144–162. https://doi.org/10.1080/10640266.2014.976106

Dimitropoulos, G., Toulany, A., Herschman, J., Kovacs, A., Steinegger, C., Bardsley, J., Sandhu, S., Gregory, C., Colton, P., Anderson, J., & Kaufman, M. (2015b). A qualitative study on the experiences of young adults with EDs transferring from pediatric to adult care. *EDs*, *23*(2), 144–162. https://doi.org/10.1080/10640266.2014.976106

Dimitropoulos, G., Tran, A. F., Agarwal, P., Sheffield, B., & Woodside, B. (2012). Navigating the transition from pediatric to adult ED programs: Perspectives of service providers. *International Journal of Eating Disorders*, *45*(6), 759–767. https://doi.org/10.1002/eat.22017

Dimitropoulos, G., Tran, A. F., Agarwal, P., Sheffield, B., & Woodside, B. (2013). Challenges in making the transition between pediatric and adult ED programs: A qualitative study from the perspective of service providers. *EDs*, *21*(1), 1–15. https://doi.org/10.1080/10640266.2013.741964

Downey, A. E., Richards, A., & Tanner, A. B. (2023). Linear growth in young people with restrictive EDs: "Inching" toward consensus. *Frontiers in Psychiatry*, *14*, 1–6. https://doi.org/10.3389/fpsyt.2023.1094222

Dugas, M. J., Gagnon, F., Ladouceur, R., & Freeston, M. H. (1998). Generalized anxiety disorder: A preliminary test of a conceptual model. *Behaviour Research and Therapy*, *36*(2), 215–226. https://doi.org/10.1016/s0005-7967(97)00070-3

Duriez, P., Kaya Lefèvre, H., Di Lodovico, L., Viltart, O., & Gorwood, P. (2021). Increased cognitive flexibility mediates the improvement of EDs symptoms, depressive symptoms and level of daily life functioning in patients with anorexia nervosa treated in specialised centres. *European EDs Review: The Journal of the EDs Association*, *29*(4), 600–610. https://doi.org/10.1002/erv.2829

Eddy, K. T., Tabri, N., Thomas, J. J., Murray, H. B., Keshaviah, A., Hastings, E., Edkins, K., Krishna, M., Herzog, D. B., Keel, P. K., & Franko, D. L. (2017). Recovery from anorexia nervosa and bulimia nervosa at 22-year follow-up. *The Journal of Clinical Psychiatry*, *78*(2), 184–189. https://doi.org/10.4088/JCP.15m10393

Egbert, A. H., Irizarry, B., Lualdi, E., Tortolani, C. C., Donaldson, D. L., & Goldschmidt, A. B. (2024). A qualitative assessment of provider-perceived barriers to implementing family-based treatment for anorexia nervosa in low-income community settings. *Journal of Eating Disorders*, *12*(1), 1–10. https://doi.org/10.1186/s40337-024-01008-w

Elzakkers, I. F., Danner, U. N., Sternheim, L. C., McNeish, D., Hoek, H. W., & Van Elburg, A. A. (2017). Mental capacity to consent to treatment and the association with outcome: A longitudinal study in patients with anorexia nervosa. *BJPsych Open*, *3*(3), 147–153. https://doi.org/10.1192/bjpo.bp.116.003905

Filipponi, C., Visentini, C., Filippini, T., Cutino, A., Ferri, P., Rovesti, S., Latella, E., & Di Lorenzo, R. (2022). The follow-up of EDs from adolescence to early adulthood: A systematic review. *International Journal of Environmental Research and Public Health*, *19*(23), 1–19. https://doi.org/10.3390/ijerph192316237

Friars, D., Walsh, O., & McNicholas, F. (2023). Assessment and management of cardiovascular complications in EDs. *Journal of Eating Disorders*, *11*(1), 1–12. https://doi.org/10.1186/s40337-022-00724-5

Friedman, N. P., & Robbins, T. W. (2022). The role of prefrontal cortex in cognitive control and executive function. *Neuropsychopharmacology: Official Publication of the American College of Neuropsychopharmacology*, *47*(1), 72–89. https://doi.org/10.1038/s41386-021-01132-0

Garland, B. H., Caldwell, K. L., Acosta, A. B., Wiemann, C. M., Gonzales, S. A., & Wolfe, R. S. (2019). Clinical considerations for emerging adults with EDs and transition to adult-based care. *Evidence-Based Practice in Child and Adolescent Mental Health*, *4*(2), 187-201. https://doi.org/10.1111/jora.12687

Gregertsen, E. C., Mandy, W., & Serpell, L. (2017). The egosyntonic nature of anorexia: An impediment to recovery in anorexia nervosa treatment. *Frontiers in Psychology, 8*, 1–9. https://doi.org/10.3389/fpsyg.2017.02273

Gulliver, A., Griffiths, K. M., & Christensen, H. (2010). Perceived barriers and facilitators to mental health help-seeking in young people: A systematic review. *BMC Psychiatry, 10*, 1–9. https://doi.org/10.1186/1471-244X-10-113

Gutierrez-Colina, A. M., Clifford, L., Wade, S. L., & Modi, A. C. (2022). Uncovering key elements of an executive functioning intervention in adolescents: Epilepsy journey. *Clinical Practice in Pediatric Psychology, 10*(2), 150–163. https://doi.org/10.1037/cpp0000410

Hambleton, A., Pepin, G., Le, A., Maloney, D., National ED Research Consortium, Touyz, S., & Maguire, S. (2022). Psychiatric and medical comorbidities of EDs: Findings from a rapid review of the literature. *Journal of Eating Disorders, 10*(1), 1–23. https://doi.org/10.1186/s40337-022-00654-2

Hilbert, A., Hoek, H. W., & Schmidt, R. (2017). Evidence-based clinical guidelines for EDs: International comparison. *Current Opinion in Psychiatry, 30*(6), 423–437. https://doi.org/10.1097/YCO.0000000000000360

Jagielska, G., & Kacperska, I. (2017). Outcome, comorbidity and prognosis in anorexia nervosa. *Psychiatria Polska, 51*(2), 205–218. https://doi.org/10.12740/pp/64580

Jewell, T., Blessitt, E., Stewart, C., Simic, M., & Eisler, I. (2016). Family therapy for child and adolescent EDs: A critical review. *Family Process, 55*(3), 577–594. https://doi.org/10.1111/famp.12242

Kappou, K., Ntougia, M., Kourtesi, A., Panagouli, E., Vlachopapadopoulou, E., Michalacos, S., Gonidakis, F., Mastorakos, G., Psaltopoulou, T., Tsolia, M., Bacopoulou, F., Sergentanis, T. N., & Tsitsika, A. (2021). Neuroimaging findings in adolescents and young adults with anorexia nervosa: A systematic review. *Children, 8*(2), 1–37. https://doi.org/10.3390/children8020137

Kask, J., Ekselius, L., Brandt, L., Kollia, N., Ekbom, A., & Papadopoulos, F. C. (2016). Mortality in women with anorexia nervosa: The role of comorbid psychiatric disorders. *Psychosomatic Medicine, 78*(8), 910–919. https://doi.org/10.1097/PSY.0000000000000342

Keegan, E., Tchanturia, K., & Wade, T. D. (2020). Central coherence and set-shifting between nonunderweight EDs and anorexia nervosa: A systematic review and meta-analysis. *International Journal of Eating Disorders, 54*(3), 229–243. https://doi.org/10.1002/eat.23430

Kelly, A. C., Carter, J. C., & Borairi, S. (2014). Are improvements in shame and self-compassion early in EDs treatment associated with better patient outcomes? *International Journal of Eating Disorders, 47*(1), 54–64. https://doi.org/10.1002/eat.22196

Kenny, T. E., & Lewis, S. P. (2023). More than an outcome: A person-centered, ecological framework for ED recovery. *Journal of Eating Disorders, 11*(1), 1–14. https://doi.org/10.1186/s40337-023-00768-1

Kerr-Gaffney, J., Halls, D., Leppanen, J., & Tchanturia, K. (2021). Exploring neuropsychological and socio-emotional task performance in anorexia nervosa: A cluster analytic approach. *European EDs Review, 29*(5), 802–810. https://doi.org/10.1002/erv.2851

Kerr-Gaffney, J., Harrison, A., & Tchanturia, K. (2018). Social anxiety in the EDs: A systematic review and meta-analysis. *Psychological Medicine, 48*(15), 2477–2491. https://doi.org/10.1017/S0033291718000752

Kimmel, M. C., Ferguson, E. H., Zerwas, S., Bulik, C. M., & Meltzer-Brody, S. (2016). Obstetric and gynecologic problems associated with EDs. *International Journal of Eating Disorders, 49*(3), 260–275. https://doi.org/10.1002/eat.22483

Le Grange, D., Crosby, R. D., Rathouz, P. J., & Leventhal, B. L. (2007). A randomized controlled comparison of family-based treatment and supportive psychotherapy for adolescent bulimia nervosa. *Archives of General Psychiatry*, *64*(9), 1049–1056. https://pubmed.ncbi.nlm.nih.gov/26506579/

Le Grange, D., Hughes, E. K., Court, A., Yeo, M., Crosby, R. D., & Sawyer, S. M. (2016). Randomized clinical trial of parent-focused treatment and family-based treatment for adolescent anorexia nervosa. *Journal of the American Academy of Child and Adolescent Psychiatry*, *55*(8), 683–692. https://doi.org/10.1016/j.jaac.2016.05.007

Le Grange, D., & Lock, J. (2007). *Treating bulimia in adolescents: A family-based approach*. Guilford Press.

Le Grange, D., Lock, J., Agras, W. S., Bryson, S. W., & Jo, B. (2015). Randomized clinical trial of family-based treatment and cognitive-behavioral therapy for adolescent bulimia nervosa. *Journal of the American Academy of Child and Adolescent Psychiatry*, *54*(11), 886–894. https://doi.org/10.1016/j.jaac.2015.08.008

Le Grange, D., Lock, J., Agras, W. S., Moye, A., Bryson, S. W., Jo, B., & Kraemer, H. C. (2012). Moderators and mediators of remission in family-based treatment and adolescent focused therapy for anorexia nervosa. *Behaviour Research and Therapy*, *50*(2), 85–92. https://doi.org/10.1016/j.brat.2011.11.003

Lock, J., Agras, W. S., Bryson, S., & Kraemer, H. C. (2005). A comparison of short- and long- term family therapy for adolescent anorexia nervosa. *Journal of the American Academy of Child and Adolescent Psychiatry*, *44*(7), 632–639. https://doi.org/10.1097/01.chi.0000161647.82775.0a

Lock, J., & Le Grange, D. (2005). Family-based treatment of eating disorders. *The International Journal of Eating Disorders*, *37*(1), S64–S67. https://doi.org/10.1002/eat.20122

Lock, J., & Le Grange, D. (2025). *Treatment manual for anorexia nervosa: A family-based approach* (3rd ed.). Routledge.

Lock, J., Le Grange, D., Agras, W. S., Moye, A., Bryson, S. W., & Jo, B. (2010). Randomized clinical trial comparing family-based treatment with adolescent-focused individual therapy for adolescents with anorexia nervosa. *Archives of General Psychiatry*, *67*(10), 1025–1032. https://doi.org/10.1001/archgenpsychiatry.2010.128

Lock, J., & Nicholls, D. (2020). Toward a greater understanding of the ways family-based treatment addresses the full range of psychopathology of adolescent anorexia nervosa. *Frontiers in Psychiatry*, *10*, 1–8. https://doi.org/10.3389/fpsyt.2019.00968

Lockertsen, V., Nilsen, L., Holm, L. A. W., Rø, Ø., Burger, L. M., & Røssberg, J. I. (2020). Mental health professionals' experiences transitioning patients with anorexia nervosa from child/adolescent to adult mental health services: A qualitative study. *BMC Health Services Research*, *20*(1), 1–9. https://doi.org/10.1186/s12913-020-05740-2

Maunder, K., & McNicholas, F. (2021). Exploring carer burden amongst those caring for a child or adolescent with an ED during COVID–19. *Journal of Eating Disorders*, *9*(1), 1–8. https://doi.org/10.1186/s40337-021-00485-7

Mehler, P. S., & Walsh, K. (2016). Electrolyte and acid-base abnormalities associated with purging behaviors. *International Journal of Eating Disorders*, *49*(3), 311–318. https://doi.org/10.1002/eat.22503

Mehler, P. S., Watters, A., Joiner, T., & Krantz, M. J. (2022). What accounts for the high mortality of anorexia nervosa? *International Journal of Eating Disorders*, *55*(5), 633–636. https://doi.org/10.1002/eat.23664

Mereu, A., Fantoni, T., Caini, S., Monzali, F., Roselli, E., Taddei, S., Lucarelli, S., & Pisano, T. (2022). Suicidality in adolescents with onset of anorexia nervosa. *Eating and Weight Disorders: EWD*, *27*(7), 2447–2457. https://doi.org/10.1007/s40519-022-01384-9

Merz, E. C., Tottenham, N., & Noble, K. G. (2018). Socioeconomic status, amygdala volume, and internalizing symptoms in children and adolescents. *Journal of Clinical Child and Adolescent Psychology: The Official Journal for the Society of Clinical

Child and Adolescent Psychology, American Psychological Association, Division 53, 47(2), 312–323. https://doi.org/10.1080/15374416.2017.1326122

Miles, S., Nedeljkovic, M., & Phillipou, A. (2023). Investigating differences in cognitive flexibility, clinical perfectionism, and ED-specific rumination across anorexia nervosa illness states. *EDs, 31*(6), 610–631. https://doi.org/10.1080/10640266.2023.2206751

Miskovic-Wheatley, J., Bryant, E., Ong, S. H., Vatter, S., Le, A., National ED Research Consortium, Touyz, S., & Maguire, S. (2023). ED outcomes: Findings from a rapid review of over a decade of research. *Journal of Eating Disorders, 11*(1), 1–25. https://doi.org/10.1186/s40337-023-00801-3

Misra, M., & Klibanski, A. (2011). Bone health in anorexia nervosa. *Current Opinion in Endocrinology, Diabetes, and Obesity, 18*(6), 376–382. https://doi.org/10.1097/MED.0b013e32834b4bdc

Momen, N. C., Plana-Ripoll, O., Agerbo, E., Benros, M. E., Børglum, A. D., Christensen, M. K., Dalsgaard, S., Degenhardt, L., de Jonge, P., Debost, J. P. G., Fenger-Grøn, M., Gunn, J. M., Iburg, K. M., Kessing, L. V., Kessler, R. C., Laursen, T. M., Lim, C. C. W., Mors, O., Mortensen, P. B., Musliner, K. L., . . . & McGrath, J. J. (2020). Association between mental disorders and subsequent medical conditions. *The New England Journal of Medicine, 382*(18), 1721–1731. https://doi.org/10.1056/NEJMoa1915784

Mursaleen, M., Shaikh, S. I., & Kamrani, F. (2025). The role of family therapy in treating adolescents with EDs: A systematic review. *International Journal of Social Sciences Bulletin, 3*(3), 308–316. https://doi.org/10.1016/S1056-4993(01)00009-8

Nadarajah, A., Dimitropoulos, G., Grant, C., Webb, C., & Couturier, J. (2021). Impending transition from pediatric to adult health services: A qualitative study of the experiences of adolescents with EDs and their caregivers. *Frontiers in Psychiatry, 12*, 1–14. https://doi.org/10.3389/fpsyt.2021.624942

National Institute for Health and Care Excellence. (2017). *EDs: Recognition and treatment.* https://www.nice.org.uk/guidance/ng69/chapter/Recommendations#identification-and-assessment

Neale, J., Pais, S. M. A., Nicholls, D., Chapman, S., & Hudson, L. D. (2020). What are the effects of restrictive EDs on growth and puberty and are effects permanent? A systematic review and meta-analysis. *The Journal of adolescent health: Official Publication of the Society for Adolescent Medicine, 66*(2), 144–156. https://doi.org/10.1016/j.jadohealth.2019.08.032

Nelson, T. D., Nelson, J. M., Mason, W. A., Tomaso, C. C., Kozikowski, C. B., & Espy, K. A. (2019). Executive control and adolescent health: Toward a conceptual framework. *Adolescent Research Review, 4*(1), 31–43. https://doi.org/10.1007/s40894-018-0094-3

O'Connor, C., McNamara, N., O'Hara, L., McNicholas, M., & McNicholas, F. (2019). How do people with EDs experience the stigma associated with their condition? A mixed-methods systematic review. *Journal of Mental Health, 30*(4), 454–469. https://doi.org/10.1080/09638237.2019.1685081

Obeid, N., Coelho, J. S., Booij, L., Dimitropoulos, G., Silva-Roy, P., Bartram, M., Clement, F., de Oliveira, C., & Katzman, D. K. (2024). Estimating additional health and social costs in ED care for young people during the COVID-19 pandemic: Implications for surveillance and system transformation. *Journal of Eating Disorders, 12*(1), 1–9. https://doi.org/10.1186/s40337-024-01003-1

Olivo, G., Gaudio, S., & Schiöth, H. B. (2019). Brain and cognitive development in adolescents with anorexia nervosa: A systematic review of fMRI studies. *Nutrients, 11*(8), 1–24. https://doi.org/10.3390/nu11081907

Partridge, B. C. (2010). Adolescent psychological development, parenting styles, and pediatric decision making. *The Journal of Medicine and Philosophy, 35*(5), 518–525. https://doi.org/10.3390/nu11081907

Patten, S. B., King, N., Munir, A., Bulloch, A. G. M., Devoe, D., Rivera, D., Byun, J., Cunningham, S., Dimitropoulos, G., Bhattarai, A., & Duffy, A. (2024). Transitions to campus mental health care in university students: Determinants and predictors. *Journal of American College Health*, *72*(8), 2455–2462. https://doi.org/10.1080/07448481.2022.2115303

Peters, K. Z., & Naneix, F. (2022). The role of dopamine and endocannabinoid systems in prefrontal cortex development: Adolescence as a critical period. *Frontiers in Neural Circuits*, *16*, 1–20. https://doi.org/10.3389/fncir.2022.939235

Phillipou, A., Rossell, S. L., Castle, D. J., & Gurvich, C. (2022). Interoceptive awareness in anorexia nervosa. *Journal of Psychiatric Research*, *148*, 84–87. https://doi.org/10.1016/j.jpsychires.2022.01.051

Posner, J., & Steinglass, J. (2024). Neurodevelopmental sequelae of anorexia nervosa. *Journal of the American Academy of Child & Adolescent Psychiatry*, *63*(11), 1069–1071. https://doi.org/10.1016/j.jaac.2023.12.012

Potterton, R., Austin, A., Allen, K., Lawrence, V., & Schmidt, U. (2020). "I'm not a teenager, I'm 22. Why can't I snap out of it?": A qualitative exploration of seeking help for a first-episode ED during emerging adulthood. *Journal of Eating Disorders*, *8*, 1–14. https://doi.org/10.1186/s40337-020-00320-5

Radon, L., Lam, C. B. K., Letranchant, A., Hirot, F., Guillaume, S., & Godart, N. (2022). Bipolar disorders in severe anorexia nervosa: Prevalence and relationships. *Eating and Weight Disorders: EWD*, *27*(3), 1063–1075. https://doi.org/10.1016/j.jaac.2023.12.012

Rienecke, R. D., & Le Grange, D. (2022). The five tenets of family-based treatment for adolescent EDs. *Journal of Eating Disorders*, *10*(1), 1–10. https://doi.org/10.1186/s40337-022-00585-y

Roncero, M., Belloch, A., Perpiñá, C., & Treasure, J. (2013). Ego-syntonicity and ego-dystonicity of eating-related intrusive thoughts in patients with EDs. *Psychiatry Research*, *208*(1), 67–73. https://doi.org/10.1016/j.psychres.2013.01.006

Santos, S., Orkin, J., Abells, D., Allemang, B., Arenas Rodriguez, B., Colapinto, K., Constas, N., Heath, M., Henze, M., John, T., Lippett, R., Miranda, S., Soscia, J., Teicher, J., Thomson, D., Tyrrell, J., Vandepoele, E., Wentzel, K., Yates, D., . . . Toulany, A. (2025). Building bridges: Developing and implementing a new transition to adult care program for youth with complex healthcare needs at a Canadian children's hospital. *Children*, *12*(8), 1–14. https://doi.org/10.3390/children12081043

Sauerwein, J., Austin, A., Singh, M., Pedram, P., Allan, E., Bruett, L., Eckhardt, S., Forsberg, S., Keery, H., Kimber, M., Pradel, M., Accurso, E. C., Le Grange, D., & Dimitropoulos, G. (2025). "FBT is for the rich": A qualitative study examining clinicians' experiences and perceptions of treatment access and engagement for diverse families in family-based treatment *International Journal of Eating Disorders*, *58*(3), 554–563. https://doi.org/10.1002/eat.24351

Scanferla, E., Seryer, S., Pachoud, B., & Gorwood, P. (2023). Transition from an adolescent to an adult ED treatment centre: A qualitative investigation of the experience of inpatients with anorexia nervosa and their carers using interpretative phenomenological analysis. *European EDs Review: The Journal of the EDs Association*, 1–13. https://doi.org/10.1002/erv.3030

Seitz, J., Herpertz-Dahlmann, B., & Konrad, K. (2016). Brain morphological changes in adolescent and adult patients with anorexia nervosa. *Journal of Neural Transmission*, 1–11. https://doi.org/10.1007/s00702-016-1567-9

Singh, S., Accurso, E. C., Hail, L., Goldschmidt, A. B., & Le Grange, D. (2018). Outcome parameters associated with perceived helpfulness of family-based treatment for adolescent EDs. *International Journal of Eating Disorders*, *51*(6), 574–578. https://doi.org/10.1002/eat.22863

Smith, A. R., Zuromski, K. L., & Dodd, D. R. (2018). EDs and suicidality: What we know, what we don't know, and suggestions for future research. *Current Opinion in Psychology*, *22*, 63–67. https://doi.org/10.1016/j.copsyc.2017.08.023

Stefanini, M. C., Troiani, M. R., Caselli, M., Dirindelli, P., Lucarelli, S., Caini, S., & Martinetti, M. G. (2019). Living with someone with an ED: Factors affecting the caregivers' burden. *Eating and Weight Disorders: EWD*, *24*(6), 1209–1214. https://doi.org/10.1007/s40519-018-0480-7

Steinberg, L., Sharp, C., Stanford, M. S., & Tharp, A. T. (2013). New tricks for an old measure: The development of the Barratt Impulsiveness Scale-Brief (BIS-Brief). *Psychological Assessment*, *25*(1), 216–226. https://doi.org/10.1037/a0030550

Sternheim, L. C., Bijsterbosch, J. M., Wever, M. C. M., van Elburg, A. A., & Frank, G. K. W. (2024). Examining anxious temperament in anorexia nervosa: Behavioural inhibition and intolerance of uncertainty and their contribution to trait anxiety in adolescents with anorexia nervosa. *Journal of Affective Disorders*, *348*, 116–123. https://doi.org/10.1016/j.jad.2023.12.035

Streatfeild, J., Hickson, J., Austin, S. B., Hutcheson, R., Kandel, J. S., Lampert, J. G., Myers, E. M., Richmond, T. K., Samnaliev, M., Velasquez, K., Weissman, R. S., & Pezzullo, L. (2021). Social and economic cost of EDs in the United States: Evidence to inform policy action. *International Journal of Eating Disorders*, *54*(5), 851–868. https://doi.org/10.1002/eat.23486

Sy, R., Ponton, K., De Marco, P., Pi, S., & Ishak, W. W. (2013). Quality of life in anorexia nervosa: A review of the literature. *EDs*, *21*(3), 206–222. https://doi.org/10.1080/10640266.2013.779176

Tchanturia, K., Doris, E., & Fleming, C. (2014). Effectiveness of cognitive remediation and emotion skills training (CREST) for anorexia nervosa in group format: A naturalistic pilot study. *European EDs Review*, *22*(3), 200–205. https://doi.org/10.1002/erv.2287

Tchanturia, K., Hambrook, D., Curtis, H., Jones, T., Lounes, N., Fenn, K., Keyes, A., Stevenson, L., & Davies, H. (2013). Work and social adjustment in patients with anorexia nervosa. *Comprehensive Psychiatry*, *54*(1), 41–45. https://doi.org/10.1016/j.comppsych.2012.03.014

Tenconi, E., Collantoni, E., Meregalli, V., Bonello, E., Zanetti, T., Veronese, A., Meneguzzo, P., & Favaro, A. (2021). Clinical and cognitive functioning changes after partial hospitalization in patients with anorexia nervosa. *Frontiers in Psychiatry*, *12*, 1–10. https://doi.org/10.3389/fpsyt.2021.653506

Toulany, A., Willem Gorter, J., & Harrison, M. (2022). A call for action: Recommendations to improve transition to adult care for youth with complex health care needs. *Paediatrics & Child Health*, *27*(5), 297–302. https://doi.org/10.1093/pch/pxac047

Treasure, J., Duarte, T. A., & Schmidt, U. (2020). EDs. *The Lancet*, *395*(10227), 899–911. https://www.thelancet.com/journals/lancet/article/PIIS0140-6736(20)30059-3/abstract

Treasure, J., & Nazar, B. P. (2016). Interventions for the carers of patients with EDs. *Current Psychiatry Reports*, *18*(2), 1–7. https://doi.org/10.1007/s11920-015-0652-3

Treasure, J., & Russell, G. (2011). The case for early intervention in anorexia nervosa: Theoretical exploration of maintaining factors. *The British Journal of Psychiatry: The Journal of Mental Science*, *199*(1), 5–7. https://doi.org/10.1192/bjp.bp.110.087585

Treasure, J., & Schmidt, U. (2013). The cognitive-interpersonal maintenance model of anorexia nervosa revisited: A summary of the evidence for cognitive, socio-emotional and interpersonal predisposing and perpetuating factors. *Journal of Eating Disorders*, *1*(1), 1–10. https://doi.org/10.1186/2050-2974-1-13

Troop, N. A., & Redshaw, C. (2012). General shame and bodily shame in EDs: A 2.5-year longitudinal study. *European EDs Review*, *20*(5), 373–378. https://doi.org/10.1002/erv.2160

United Nations. (2019). *Youth and the 2030 agenda for sustainable development*. United Nations Department of Economic and Social Affairs Youth. https://desapublications.un.org/publications/category/Social%20Development/category/Statistics?_klpuid=GwKq2LGpnkQhX6L36mXkc/con/furuichi/&page=4#:~:text=The%20World%20Youth%20Report%20on,can%20play%20in%20enhancing%20youth%E2%80%A6

van Eeden, A. E., van Hoeken, D., & Hoek, H. W. (2021). Incidence, prevalence and mortality of anorexia nervosa and bulimia nervosa. *Current Opinion in Psychiatry*, *34*(6), 515–524. https://doi.org/10.1097/YCO.0000000000000739

Varela, C., Hoyo, Á., Tapia-Sanz, M. E., Jiménez-González, A. I., Moral, B. J., Rodríguez-Fernández, P., Vargas-Hernández, Y., & Ruiz-Sánchez, L. J. (2023). An update on the underlying risk factors of EDs onset during adolescence: A systematic review. *Frontiers in Psychology*, *14*, 1–22. https://doi.org/10.3389/fpsyg.2023.1221679

Via, E., Calvo, A., de la Serna, E., Blázquez, A., Lázaro, L., Andrés-Perpiñá, S., . . .& Castro-Fornieles, J. (2023). Longitudinal study in adolescent anorexia nervosa: Evaluation of cortico-striatal and default mode network resting-state brain circuits. *European Child & Adolescent Psychiatry*, *32*(3), 513–526. https://doi.org/10.1007/s00787-021-01880-w

Wallis, A., Rhodes, P., Dawson, L., Miskovic-Wheatley, J., Madden, S., & Touyz, S. (2017). Relational containment: Exploring the effect of family-based treatment for anorexia on familial relationships. *Journal of Eating Disorders*, 5(27), 1–10. https://doi-org.ezproxy.lib.ucalgary.ca/10.1016/j.jadohealth.2018.10.115

White, P. H., & Cooley, W. C. (2018). Supporting the health care transition from adolescence to adulthood in the medical home. *Pediatrics*, *142*(5), 1–23. https://doi.org/10.1542/peds.2018-2587

Wilens, T. E., & Rosenbaum, J. F. (2013). Transitional aged youth: A new frontier in child and adolescent psychiatry. *Journal of the American Academy of Child and Adolescent Psychiatry*, *52*(9), 887–890. https://doi.org/10.1016/j.jaac.2013.04.020

Wilson, G. T., & Shafran, R. (2005). EDs guidelines from NICE. *Lancet (London, England)*, *365*(9453), 79–81. https://doi.org/10.1016/S0140-6736(04)17669-1

Wolfe, F., Smythe, H. A., Yunus, M. B., Bennett, R. M., Bombardier, C., Goldenberg, D. L., Tugwell, P., Campbell, S. M., Abeles, M., & Clark, P. (1990). The American College of Rheumatology 1990 criteria for the classification of fibromyalgia. Report of the multicenter criteria committee. *Arthritis and Rheumatism*, *33*(2), 160–172. https://doi.org/10.1002/art.1780330203

Wollast, R., Fossion, P., Kotsou, I., Rebrassé, A., & Leys, C. (2022). Interoceptive awareness and anorexia nervosa: When emotions influence the perception of physiological sensations. *The Journal of Nervous and Mental Disease*, *210*(5), 390–393. https://doi.org/10.1097/NMD.0000000000001458

Chapter 1

What Is FBT-TAY?

This chapter provides a detailed introduction to FBT-TAY, its fundamental principles, and phases of treatment. Additionally, this chapter highlights the similarities and differences between Family-Based Treatment (FBT) and FBT-TAY (see Tables A and B for a comparative breakdown of FBT-TAY and the foundational model of FBT) and other family therapeutic practices.

FBT-TAY Versus FBT

FBT-TAY is an adaptation of FBT, specifically for use with older adolescents and young adults (typically ages 16–25) who are diagnosed with AN (Dimitropoulos et al., 2015). While the central tenet of parental/caregiver empowerment in recovery remains intact for FBT-TAY, it has an additional feature of collaboration and developmental sensitivity towards the young person with AN. These additions recognize the young person's emerging autonomy over their own health, while also acknowledging their parents'/caregivers' role in supporting recovery. In this chapter, we will describe differences between FBT and FBT-TAY. FBT-TAY is a three-phased outpatient treatment, conducted by trained, licensed therapists with a young person and their parents/caregivers over the course of approximately 25 sessions (Dimitropoulos et al., 2018b).

We encourage FBT-TAY therapists to apply this model with flexibility rather than rigidity and to engage in ongoing planning with the family to assess the frequency and cadence of the sessions.

While FBT focuses primarily on empowering parents/caregivers to renourish their child to health, FBT-TAY includes the young person as an active agent of change in their treatment and recovery. Specifically, FBT-TAY places a greater emphasis on empowering the young person to participate in decision-making regarding the procedural aspects of the treatment and non-ED-related issues in their lives, ultimately supporting their self-determination. Enhancing the autonomy of the young person is paramount, as it can promote readiness to transition to adulthood and adult care, support them in beginning to manage their personal

DOI: 10.4324/9781003463351-2

healthcare needs, and build their confidence to advocate for themselves in healthcare settings (Bogossian et al., 2018, 2020) and in their relationships with family and peers and in other contexts of their lives. FBT-TAY differs from traditional FBT by including more individual time between the young person and the therapist before the family meeting (about 10 minutes in FBT and about 30 minutes in FBT-TAY) (Dimitropoulos et al., 2015). These individual sessions are consistent throughout the three phases of treatment. In the first phase of treatment, these sessions are crucial because they help prepare the young person for treatment and aid them in the engagement process. More specifically, individual sessions are used to establish therapeutic alliance, discuss any ambivalence about parent/caregiver involvement in treatment, and empower young people to identify issues that may impede or facilitate their goals for behavioural change. These individual sessions also provide an opportunity for discussions about how and in what ways parental/caregiver support may be needed in the sessions. More specifically, these sessions can allow young people to decide how and when to communicate progress about their weight or eating in the sessions with their parents/caregivers, identify future obstacles to recovery, and/or points of reflection regarding their emerging independence over their eating and physical activities.

Another difference in FBT-TAY in comparison to FBT is how the weight chart is shared in the sessions with caregivers. Like FBT, the target weight range in FBT-TAY is calculated by a medical doctor, such as a family physician or adolescent medicine specialist. Historical growth charts may be reviewed and employed to recommend the target weight range for a young person with AN (Lebow et al., 2017). Developmental stage of the young person, including whether they have achieved full height potential, should be considered while establishing weight targets. While weight restoration is a key component to physical recovery, treatment goals in FBT-TAY include eating a variety of foods, the cessation of compensatory behaviours, and increased ability to eat independently and with new skills to manage anxiety surrounding eating with greater independence. In contrast to FBT, the FBT-TAY therapist works closely with the young person to gradually provide them with the responsibility of sharing their progress of weight changes, eating challenges, and the weight chart (see Phase 1 description below).

In the original FBT as well as FBT-TAY, there are five fundamental tenets that guide the phases, implementation of all the interventions, and interactions with both the young person and their parents/caregivers (Lock & Le Grange, 2025; Reinecke & LeGrange, 2022). First, an agnostic view of the illness is employed to minimize self-blame, shame, and guilt about the development of the illness. As demonstrated below, agnosticism is used to combat the tendency for both parents/caregivers and the young person to unearth underlying and relational "causes" of the illness rather than tackling illness behaviours in the here and now. Second, parental/caregiver empowerment is an integral tenant that views parents/caregivers as the agents of change in facilitating renourishment, weight restoration, and cessation of ED behaviours such as starvation and excessive exercise. Third, externalization – which refers to viewing the AN as separate from the young person – aids in diminishing criticism and re-directing negative and intense emotions towards the disorder rather the young person. Fourth, the FBT therapist utilizes a non-directive, collaborative, and consultative role for the young person and the family. Finally, FBT-TAY therapists relentlessly and persistently focus on addressing ED behaviours and remaining focused on recovery from AN (Lock & Le Grange, 2025; Rienecke & LeGrange, 2022). These principles are utilized throughout each phase of FBT and support the therapist to remain adherent to the model (Lock & Le Grange, 2025). In the next section, we will describe how these principles are slightly modified in FBT-TAY with a greater emphasis of using these tenets to empower the young person and enhance their agency.

Fundamental Principles of FBT-TAY

Agnostic Stance Towards the Illness

Maintaining an agnostic stance on the cause of the AN is a vital aspect of FBT-TAY. EDs are complex and multi-factorial disorders, with numerous contributing factors to their development including genetics, personality, and socio-cultural factors (Bogar et al., 2024; Donato et al., 2022: Levallius et al., 2015; Rieneicke & Le Grange, 2022). There is no research which demonstrates that families are responsible or are to blame for triggering AN (Le Grange et al., 2016; Lock & Le Grange, 2025; Rieneicke et al., 2024; Schaumberg et al., 2017). Moreover, examining why young people have developed their ED is not necessarily beneficial for symptomatic cessation and may even detract them and their family from focusing on the immediate priorities of renourishment and weight restoration (Rienecke & LeGrange, 2022). Consequently, FBT-TAY does not intentionally seek to unearth and process the potential origins of AN but rather aims to support the young person and the family to react differently to the disorder, prioritizing weight restoration and behavioural change (Lock & Le Grange, 2025; Rienecke & LeGrange, 2022; Treasure et al., 2021).

It is commonplace for most parents/caregivers to reflect on the course of the illness and what they and others could have done differently during the emergence of AN. Such reflections and search for understanding may become problematic when parental/caregiver self-blame and guilt contribute to intense and negative emotional experiences and low self-confidence in the ability to rapidly address disordered eating (e.g., Oketah et al., 2023; Williams et al., 2020; Wufong et al., 2019). Unfortunately, such negative feelings can impede caregivers from having the confidence in their capacity to support their child through recovery from AN.

It is critical to address self-blame, guilt, and shame in parents/caregivers about the illness at the beginning and throughout treatment (Lock & Le Grange, 2025; Rienecke & LeGrange, 2022).

Ultimately, therapists must maintain an agnostic view of the illness, regardless of the members (family, friends, partners, etc.) who are present in the treatment sessions (Lock & Le Grange, 2025). Therapists should refrain from gathering historical information or engaging in systemic formulations of the family and, rather, should emphasize providing the family with resources that will help them address the illness based on the knowledge of the young person. Sometimes parents/caregivers (and the young person) have developed a clear link to an event or stressor that may have triggered AN. It is important to validate the lived experiences of the young person and their family when they share difficult events (e.g., an automobile accident, a loss of a loved one, bullying) that may have led to the development and maintenance of the illness. Through validation, the FBT-TAY therapist can invite the young person and the family to defer discussions about these important issues until the eating behaviours have diminished, and health has been restored (Lock & Le Grange, 2025). Opportunities to further discuss such experiences will be briefly addressed in Phase 3 and appropriate referrals for further support may be offered as needed and requested.

Agnosticism and the Young Person

In FBT-TAY, the principle of agnosticism applies to the young person as well as the parents/caregivers and the entire family (e.g., Lock & Le Grange, 2025; Le Grange et al., 2010; Lock & Nicholls, 2020). Many young people may enter this treatment with their own reflections of what may have shaped their relationship with food and weight and the ED behaviours. In the early stages of AN, some young people identify that their symptoms were helpful in managing stressful life events. This contributes to them viewing their illness as having a function (Potterton et al., 2020). Some young people begin to identify experiences, events, and situations that they attribute to the development and maintenance of the AN (Copeland et al., 2015; Longo et al., 2020; Molendijk et al., 2017; Morrison et al., 2022). Rather than invalidate young people's experiences, it is important to recognize their experiences of what may have influenced their illness. During this process, FBT-TAY therapists must reassure young people that opportunities to explore these issues will be deferred until the symptoms of AN have remitted. However, FBT-TAY therapists must also combat any shame, blame, guilt, and stigma that the young person may have about developing the illness (Rienecke & LeGrange, 2022), including low motivation and readiness for change and challenges with recovery (Cripps et al., 2024; Baudinet et al., 2024; Medway et al., 2019). EDs are highly stigmatizing illnesses; erroneous myths that AN is volitional and that recovery is easy to overcome exacerbate the stigma associated with the illness (Brelet et al., 2021; Dimitropoulos et al., 2016; Griffiths et al.,

2015; Mond et al., 2006; Sheens et al., 2016). In addition to remaining agnostic about the illness, the FBT-TAY therapist should provide psychoeducational information about the multi-dimensional nature of AN, the ego-syntonic nature of the illness, and that ambivalence about engaging in behavioural change is commonplace to mitigate self-blame of the young person. Agnosticism towards the young person in the context of this treatment helps set the stage for empowering them to recognize their critical role in recovery alongside their family.

Caregiver Empowerment

Caregiver empowerment is a vital part of FBT and involves building the confidence necessary for parents/caregivers to support their loved ones with AN (Damen et al., 2021; Rienecke, 2017). Given the potentially chronic nature of AN, many parents/caregivers express hopelessness, despair, burden, and guilt, among other distressing emotions (Cripps et al., 2024; Freizinger et al., 2021; Rienecke & LeGrange, 2022). Consequently, it is imperative that parent/caregiver empowerment, one of the five fundamental principles of FBT (Lock & Le Grange, 2025), be addressed throughout FBT-TAY. Ultimately, FBT-TAY works to shore up parental/caregiver empowerment throughout Phase 1, while acknowledging the autonomy and independence of the young person (Dimitropoulos et al., 2018b). Parental/caregiver empowerment is implemented in FBT-TAY by using a strengths-based rather than a pathologizing approach. More specifically, therapists express their belief in parents'/caregivers' abilities and the family, inclusive of the young person to work collaboratively to find recovery-based solutions. Empowering parents/caregivers can help to reduce feelings of fear and self-blame (Dimitropoulos et al., 2018b) and is viewed as vital to build their confidence (Dimitropoulos et al., 2017; Rienecke & LeGrange, 2022). It also provides them with the ability to maintain a strong front against the ED (Rienecke & LeGrange, 2022). Additionally, parental/caregiver empowerment protects parents/caregivers from negotiating and accommodating the ED behaviours and allows them to remain resolute in their efforts to support the young person with various aspects of treatment including meal preparation and mealtimes (Rienecke & LeGrange, 2022).

Empowerment of the Young Person

By the time an adolescent enters early adulthood, the illness may have interfered with the achievement of key milestones associated with this developmental period (see Chapter 7). Consequently, young people with AN may feel a sense of guilt (Burney & Irwin, 2000) and shame (Kelly et al., 2014; Troop & Redshaw, 2012) for not meeting their own and others' expectations. Young people who develop AN in adolescence or relapse back into illness after a period of remission may experience significant impairment psychologically and interpersonally, leading them to feel a greater sense of despair (Heal-Cohen et al., 2025). Many young people may also perceive themselves as a burden to the family (Halvorsen & Heyerdahl, 2007). Intense isolation, profound shame, guilt, and the perception of being a burden to others may hinder young people from sharing their symptoms and acquiescing to their parents'/caregivers' efforts to support them. We believe it is imperative to combat negative feelings harboured by young people towards themselves by elevating the view that they have agency over the illness and can demonstrate this as a first step by temporarily accepting support over difficult aspects of the illness. FBT-TAY therapists must work diligently to empower young people to view themselves as having a critical role to play in therapy and in their own recovery. Special attention should be paid to the experiences young people have had with unsuccessful treatments, or other situations that have elicited hopelessness, as this can have a profound effect on sustaining motivation to challenge the ED and their openness to involving family and other supportive individuals. To counter despair and negativity, parents/caregivers, peers, and extended family members play an important role in instilling and maintaining hope in their young person's capacity to recover from this life-threatening illness, even when the young person may temporarily have no hope for themselves. In fact, research demonstrates that an explicit focus on the part of therapists, parents/caregivers, and other supportive individuals on aligning the young person with their goals and strengths, maintaining hope for recovery, and validating their strengths during treatment (instead of taking a deficit approach) promotes motivation for recovery and enables change with the illness for young people with AN (Dann et al., 2024).

Externalizing the Illness

Externalization, separating the illness from the healthy side of the young person (Lock & Le Grange, 2025; Rienecke & LeGrange, 2022), is a critical intervention to promote a unified team approach – bringing the young person and their caregivers on the same side *against* the illness (Dimitropoulos et al., 2018b; Lonergan et al., 2022). Externalization can be achieved using metaphors and analogies of other illnesses, or by giving the AN a name, and creating a separate identity for illness behaviours (Cripps et al., 2024; Rienecke et al., 2022). Ultimately, using externalization can help decrease expressed emotions, such as criticism and increase parent/caregiver empathy and warmth towards the young person with AN (Rienecke & Le Grange, 2022). While externalization is central to FBT, therapists express the importance of using it alongside other therapeutic techniques like rapport building, the timing of when interventions are introduced, and understanding the perspective of the family (Lonergan et al., 2022).

Team Approach. Externalization is effective for developing a team approach among the family, improving problem-solving, communication, and providing a means to reduce conflict (Lonergan et al., 2022). It conceptualized the AN as outside of the individual who is actively experiencing it, allowing perspectives to shift and encouraging the family to be able to discuss the AN symptoms more openly without fearing alienating the young person (Lonergan et al., 2022).

Externalization facilitates the team in remaining agnostic towards the young person, family, and the disorder and helps shift discussions from the problem to finding practical solutions (Lonergan et al., 2022).

While externalization is important for treatment, it is important to consider the perspectives of young people who have direct experience with the illness. Voswinkel et al. (2021) conducted an exploratory qualitative study to better understand the perspectives of young people regarding externalization. Many young people recognized the importance of externalization as an intervention; however, young people felt that when most of their behaviours were ascribed to the ED, it caused them to feel that their views and feelings were being dismissed and invalidated. While externalization is a useful tool in FBT, providing families and young people with a technique to develop the language to situate the disorder outside of the individual, reducing blame and allowing families to discuss solutions and approaches more freely as a team (Lonergan et al., 2022), considerations must be paid to validating a young person's feelings, thoughts, and actions rather than arguing that everything be viewed singularly through the lens of AN (Voswinkel et al., 2021).

Therapeutic Stance: Consultant to the Young Person and Family in FBT-TAY

Consultation and Collaborative Decision-Making

A consultative and collaborative approach is essential to the FBT-TAY model. In FBT-TAY, the therapist acts as a resource to young people and their caregivers (Dimitropoulos et al., 2015, 2018a). As consultants, therapists share their knowledge about AN, disseminate evidence about the effectiveness of clinical interventions, and share their wisdom gained through experiences of working with young people (Baker et al., 2024; Dimitropoulos et al., 2024; Rienecke et al., 2022). A collaborative approach requires parents/caregivers and the healthy side of the young person to work together to overcome the illness.

It is the responsibility of the therapist to find a middle ground between supporting the young person as an individual, while also valuing their caregiver's role in supporting behavioural changes with the respect to the AN. When using family approaches with TAY, a middle ground can be achieved by acknowledging the strengths of the young person, recognizing the actions of seeking support despite the ambivalence of weight gain, and modifying their eating behaviours (Dodge et al., 2024). In the case that young people are unsure or concerned about the involvement of their parents/caregivers, the therapist may begin by exploring the reasons for and against eliciting caring and hep from supportive adults. If the young person expresses fears about being a burden, it is critical to remind them that supportive adults from parents/caregivers to extended family members are needed, especially in the beginning stages of eating rehabilitation and weight gain. Engaging the young person to delineate how their parents/caregivers may be able to offer valued support with their ED symptoms may be helpful (Dimitropoulos et al., 2018a). It is necessary that therapists continuously acknowledge and celebrate efforts made by the young person and their parents/caregivers to collaborate, like problem-solving how to challenge AN and how to effectively make behavioural changes. Openly discussing ambivalence, while remaining clear with available options, may aid the young person in evaluating the roles parents/caregivers can play in their recovery.

Eating Rehabilitation and Weight Restoration

Similar to the foundational model of FBT, FBT-TAY is an approach that persistently and relentlessly focuses on eating rehabilitation by empowering parents/caregivers to support their young person with eating. Unless the young person is requiring medical admission for medical instability or a mental health crisis, the sessions must be focused on weight restoration and learning how to eat a greater variety and quantity of food, as well as abstaining from compensatory symptoms. Refeeding and symptom disruption must be achieved through youth-parent/caregiver collaboration and by the later conveying compassion and warmth and firmly and assertively stating the need for recovery. A qualitative study on early interventions in AN demonstrated that most young people acquire "mixed feelings" about their parents/caregivers being in charge of their recovery – specifically, by simultaneously sharing frustration about being infantilized during the recovery process, while also feeling relieved that their parents/caregivers cared enough for them to intervene to disrupt the AN behaviours (Chen et al., 2010; Ciao et al., 2022).

Ambivalence about parents/caregivers preparing meals, being present at every meal, and actively prompting the young person to increase their quality and quality of food may feel abnormal, demoralizing, and developmentally inappropriate for young people. Hence, the recognition of how difficult it may be for the young person to feel they are under their caregivers' surveillance must be acknowledged and reframed by FBT-TAY therapists as an act of love and care to combat the illness and should be done in a respectful, direct, and compassionate manner.

Challenges with the Relentless Focus on Renourishment in FBT-TAY

As demonstrated in a recent scoping review, parental/caregiver accommodation and enabling behaviours towards AN are commonplace and happen often in response to the high levels of anxiety, fear, and emotional duress hindering them from disrupting AN behaviours in their loved one. The findings of this review demonstrated that parents/caregivers often accommodate illness behaviours to prevent or de-escalate conflict with their loved one, to reduce their own distress and feelings of self-blame and possible burnout. However, a vicious cycle of reinforcement ensues with parents/caregivers using accommodation to alleviate their child's distress, which leads to them requiring greater reassurance and accommodation of their illness. Another study reported that parent/caregiver burden is associated with higher levels of accommodation and enabling of illness behaviours. Therefore, FBT-TAY therapists must directly discuss the emergence of accommodating responses to the illness and work to identify its sources which may range from parental/caregiver self-blame, fears of reprisal from the young person, and/or the absence of coping or conflict resolution skills to mitigate tensions and arguments during meals.

Additional Considerations When Working with Young People in FBT-TAY

Autonomy and Responsibility in the Young Person

Developing autonomy is an important developmental process for young people, and the desire for enhancing independence increases as they undergo major life transitions such as moving out of their family home, beginning post-secondary education, or joining the workforce. Recognizing the importance of autonomy for young people, the FBT-TAY model integrates this as a core element in the treatment, with autonomous decision-making consistently supported and reinforced within the family and across all phases of treatment. Indeed, the FBT-TAY therapist may consider utilizing externalization to illustrate how AN can interrupt life transitions and experiences that would lay the foundation for the young person to become independent both in the treatment and all aspects of their lives. For example, in the first phase of treatment, it is the role of the therapist to engage the young person in discussions surrounding the procedural features of treatment. The overarching aim of treatment is to empower the young person to have control over their life, engaging them in discussions that are age-appropriate and that respect their independence and self-determination (Dimitropoulos et al., 2018b). However, food-related areas in Phase 1 are primarily relegated to parents/caregivers who guide the renourishment process. When control over eating is limited in the beginning phase of treatment; it is important that parents/caregivers communicate that the young person will reclaim their responsibility for eating related decisions back as treatment progresses. It is important to note this agreement needs to be negotiated and continuously confirmed by both the young person and their parents recognizing that ambivalence in the renourishment process waxes and vanes and must be attended to by the therapist. In early phases of treatment, it is vital to provide opportunities for the young person to have input into aspects of treatment that are non-food related to encourage their engagement in FBT-TAY and enhance their agency to practice taking responsibility for recovery. Examples of choice could include scheduling sessions during preferred times and determining what type of support they may need during and after meals as well as throughout the different phases of FBT (Dimitropoulos et al., 2018a; Gorrell et al., 2019). As the young person progresses through the phases of treatment and enters Phase 2, they must incrementally be given opportunities to trial meal preparation and eat without instrumental or hands-on-support from family members. These opportunities will support young people to develop the skills that are necessary for their recovery, and ultimately, empowering them to have influence over their own treatment.

Flexible Family Involvement

The fundamental principles of FBT-TAY are unchanged regardless of the identified "family of choice" (Dimitropoulos et al., 2014). The young person makes decisions for who will or will not attend therapy and support their recovery (Dimitropoulos et al., 2018a). Young people may choose to involve members of their family, peers, or a partner in their recovery (Dimitropoulos et al., 2014). Geographic proximity to family of origin must be considered by the treatment team and the young person collaboratively to determine who may offer the best support in FBT-TAY (Dimitropoulos et al., 2014). Post-secondary attendance or military service may mean that a young person is a considerable distance from their family of origin. Geographical distance is a common reason that young people choose to involve close friends in their treatment (Dimitropoulos et al., 2014). Software such as FaceTime and Zoom Teleconferencing can be used to overcome this distance and may be particularly useful for meal or emotional support for young people not residing with their family or other supportive individuals (Dimitropoulos et al., 2014).

In comparison to the foundation model of FBT (ages 12–18 years), FBT-TAY allows the young person to have greater input into how the family is conceptualized and understood (Dimitropoulos et al., 2014). Some young people may not have access to family of origin that can support them with meals and the management of symptoms (Dimitropoulos et al., 2014).

This may occur due to (1) significant physical distance between family members making it difficult to be consistently involved in treatment; (2) family suffering from impairing illness, mental or physical, that impedes their ability to support the young person; and (3) a history of abuse that results in a lack of safety (Dimitropoulos et al., 2014). Friends or roommates or other trusted adults can also be included in any phase of FBT-TAY. Randomized controlled trials of parent-focused therapy (PFT; Le Grange et al., 2016) – a family-centred therapeutic approach for adolescent AN adapted from FBT where young people and parents/caregivers are seen in separate sessions, with minimal contact with the young person and no required contact for siblings (Hughes et al., 2014) – demonstrates than FBT is achieving remission in adolescents with AN at the end of treatment but not at follow-up (Le Grange et al., 2016). While an adaptation of FBT, in PFT, attendance of siblings and/or the young person is not feasible nor expected (Le Grange et al., 2016). The young person is also not included in FBT-Guided Self Help where parents/caregivers review materials and receive brief coaching from a guide (see Lock et al., 2021). While sibling involvement is highly encouraged in FBT-TAY, siblings offer an important source of support to the young person (Dimitropoulos et al., 2014). However, young people with AN may chose not to involve their siblings due to confidentiality or privacy concerns, or the sibling themselves may be suffering from an ED or the relationship is strained/distant (Dimitropoulos et al., 2014). Young people may be asked about their preferences of sibling involvement early on in treatment (Dimitropoulos et al., 2014) and have the option to reconsider sibling involvement at any stage of the treatment even if they were not present in earlier phases.

Phases of FBT-TAY

FBT-TAY consists of three phases, similar to the foundation model of FBT for both AN and BN (Lock & Le Grange, 2025; LeGrange & Lock, 2007). However, rather than consisting of approximately 20 family sessions, as the foundational approach to FBT does, FBT-TAY is about 25 sessions (Dimitropoulos et al., 2018a). Throughout all three phases, sessions begin with therapists and the young person meeting for up to 30 minutes (Dimitropoulos et al., 2018a). In contrast to FBT, FBT-TAY does require a greater commitment of the family due to the individual time allotted to meet one-on-one with the young person. These individual sessions aim to establish a therapeutic alliance with the young person, address any uncertainty about parent/caregiver involvement in the treatment process, and empower the young person to identify issues central to the goals of achieving behavioural changes (Dimitropoulos et al., 2015).

Individual sessions with the young person are followed by a 50-minute meeting with the therapist, young person, and their parents/family (Dimitropoulos et al., 2018a). While therapists have the expertise in the treatment of this life-threatening illness, they communicate their trust in the healthy part of the young person – even if a sliver or aspirational – with the support of their parents/caregivers, acknowledging their strengths, resources, and skill to overcome AN.

- **Phase 1:** Sessions 1–10 over a period of 4–8 weeks
  This phase requires the commitment of both the young person and the parents/caregivers in behavioural goals, such as weight restoration and eating rehabilitation. Meetings with the therapist, the young person, and their family members should occur twice a week (if possible) the first week and then

weekly. The overall objective of this first phase of treatment is to engage with the young person to gain weight and develop normal eating as quickly as possible. This should be done with the parent/caregiver taking temporary responsibility for meal preparation and support.

- **Phase 2:** Sessions 11–19 weekly or biweekly meetings
  The focus in Phase 2 is for the young person to gain the skills to eat independently and maintain a healthy target weight. The objective of this phase is to work with the young person to gradually gain greater responsibility for eating independently and practising in different environments (e.g., school, work) with others (e.g., partner, peers) to promote a shared or collaborative management approach to eating rehabilitation. The young person and their family work to identify barriers to the former gaining more responsibility, as well as finding effective strategies, solutions, and developmentally appropriate ways for their parents/caregivers to support their recovery.
- **Phase 3:** Sessions 20–25 weekly or biweekly meetings
  In the third and final phase, meetings take place between the young person and their caregivers with the goal of collaboratively planning ways to prevent relapse as they undergo many life transitions (e.g., starting university, moving out, beginning, or solidifying relationships with a significant other). These family meetings will occur every week or once a month. Additionally, the young person and FBT-TAY therapist may meet to develop a plan to maintain

Table A Comparison of the Key Principles of the FBT-TAY and FBT

Agnostic as to the cause of AN – does not blame the parents/caregiver or child for the disorder.
Empowerment – endeavours to improve self-efficacy in caregivers related to changing maintaining behaviours of AN and return the adolescent to age-appropriate independence.
Non-authoritarian therapeutic stance – therapist joins the family in helping them disrupt maintaining behaviours of AN.
Externalization – AN is seen as an illness that is disrupting adolescent developmental processes.
Focus on symptoms – focus is on the weight gain and compensatory behaviours as well as any other behaviours that maintain AN.
Focus is primarily on the therapeutic relationship with the parents/caregivers with the relationship with the young person taking a secondary role early in treatment.
Young people are not typically asked to track or document their progress or experiences.
Phase 2 – control over some eating elements is slowly and carefully returned to the young person if they are ready.

Table B Summary of the Key Content of FBT and FBT-TAY (in Dimitropoulos et al., 2018a)

FBT-TAY	*FBT*
Agnostic to the cause of AN – does not blame parents/caregivers or young person for the disorder.	Agnostic as to the cause of AN – does not blame the parents/caregiver or child for the disorder.
Empowerment – endeavours to improve self-efficacy in the young person and to manage life without resorting to AN.	Empowerment – endeavours to improve self-efficacy in caregivers related to changing maintaining behaviours of AN and return the adolescent to age-appropriate independence.
Non-authoritarian therapeutic stance – therapist first establishes a therapeutic alliance with the young person and addresses any ambivalence about parent/caregiver involvement in the treatment process. The therapist then joins the young person and parents/caregivers in problem-solving.	Non-authoritarian therapeutic stance – therapist joins the family in helping them disrupt maintaining behaviours of AN.
Externalization – AN is seen as an illness that is disrupting young person's developmental processes.	Externalization – AN is seen as an illness that is disrupting adolescent developmental processes.
Focus on symptoms – therapist works with young people and their parents/caregivers to identify and address factors that may contribute to illness behaviours and might lead to maintenance of AN or relapse in phase 3.	Focus on symptoms – focus is on the weight gain and compensatory behaviours as well as any other behaviours that maintain AN.
Focus on a collaborative, team approach between the therapist, young person, and their parents/caregivers. Therapist engages the young person to identify how their parents/caregivers may be able to best assist them in overcoming symptoms.	Focus is primarily on the therapeutic relationship with the parents/caregivers with the relationship with the young person taking a secondary role early in treatment.
Young people may consider tracking what they eat every day and encouraged to communicate any challenges they experience.	Young people are not typically asked to track or document their progress or experiences.
Phase 2 – control and responsibility with eating may be relinquished over to the young person from the caregivers more quickly due to their greater independence and the fact that they need to practice eating in a variety of eating contexts.	Phase 2 – control over some eating elements are slowly and carefully returned to the young person if they are ready.

Note: The *Journal of the Canadian Academy of Child and Adolescent Psychiatry* has granted permission to reproduce this table contained in Dimitropoulos et al. (2018a).

recovery, identifying potential high-risk environments and situations that may lead to relapse for the individual. This plan, created collaboratively by the young person and FBT-TAY therapist, will be presented to parents/caregivers to elicit their support. Family sessions will serve the purpose of identifying the multiple life transitions that the young person may face as they progress into adulthood. At the final session, the young person and parents/caregivers will collaboratively terminate the treatment.

Conclusions

This chapter provides a detailed introduction of FBT-TAY, describing the principles and the phases of treatment. In addition, a comparative breakdown of key principles of traditional FBT and FBT-TAY was outlined to provide a comprehensive understanding of the uniqueness of this adapted treatment. FBT-TAY is a phased treatment approach for young people aged 16–25. It includes the utilization of many of the same principles and intervention strategies used in FBT. For example, empowerment is used to promote confidence in parents/caregivers, allowing them to take on their crucial role in treatment and withstand negotiation, accommodation, and enabling behaviours of the ED. On the other hand, FBT-TAY therapists support the agency of the young person while gradually supporting them to achieve greater control over recovery as they (re)learn how to eat.

Chapter Summary

Here are the key points of this chapter:

(1) Traditional FBT gives parents/caregivers directive control, while FBT-TAY (ages 16–25) balances caregiver support with the young person's autonomy throughout the course of treatment.
(2) AN is not caused by families or young people; treatment avoids blame and stays focused on renourishment, weight restoration, and behaviour change.
(3) Parents/caregivers are provided with tools and confidence to guide meals without submitting to the illness, while young people are supported to see themselves as capable of change, fostering independence, hope, and ownership of recovery.
(4) The illness is framed as separate from the young person, reducing criticism and conflict, while uniting parents/caregivers, young people, and therapists in a collaborative triad.
(5) The FBT-TAY therapist acts as a consultant, and helps to facilitate joint decision-making, balancing parent/caregiver authority with the young person's autonomy, and guiding collaborative problem-solving.

(6) In Phase 1, there is a relentless focus on renourishment, weight gain, and cessation of AN maintaining behaviours; parent/caregiver supervision is reframed as care, though it can trigger resistance and requires therapist support to reduce enabling and accommodation behaviours towards the young person.
(7) Young people are invited early to make procedural decisions about the process of the treatment and gradually assume responsibility for eating.
(8) FBT-TAY comprises three stages: (1) intensive weight restoration led by parents/caregivers, (2) young person gains independent eating skills with shared responsibility with parents/caregivers, and (3) relapse-prevention and transition planning with collaborative treatment termination.

References

Baker, J. H., Temes, E., Bohon, C., Derenne, J., Duvall, A., & Steinberg, D. (2024). Enhanced family-based treatment for an adolescent with binge-ED: A case report. *Cognitive and Behavioral Practice, 31*(2), 272–282. https://doi.org/10.1016/j.cbpra.2022.12.001

Baudinet, J., Eisler, I., Konstantellou, A., Simic, M., & Schmidt, U. (2024). How young people perceive change to occur in family therapy for anorexia nervosa: A qualitative study. *Journal of Eating Disorders, 12*(1), 1–14. https://doi.org/10.1186/s40337-024-00971-8

Bogár, N., Kővágó, P., & Túry, F. (2024). Increased eating disorder frequency and body image disturbance among fashion models due to intense environmental pressure: A content analysis. *Frontiers in Psychiatry, 15*, 1–11. https://doi.org/10.3389/fpsyt.2024.1360962

Bogossian, A., Gorter, J. W., & Racine, E. (2018). Protocol for a scoping review about ethics in transition programmes for adolescents and young adults with neurodisabilities. *BMJ Open, 8*(8), 1–5. https://doi.org/10.1136/bmjopen-2017-020914

Bogossian, A., Majnemer, A., & Racine, E. (2020). Contextualized autonomy in transitional care for youth with neurologic conditions: The role of the pediatric neurologist. *Journal of Child Neurology, 35*(8), 536–542. https://doi.org/10.1177/0883073820918454

Brelet, L., Flaudias, V., Désert, M., Guillaume, S., Llorca, P.-M., & Boirie, Y. (2021). Stigmatization toward people with anorexia nervosa, bulimia nervosa, and binge ED: A scoping review. *Nutrients, 13*(8), 1–29. https://doi.org/10.3390/nu13082834

Burney, J., & Irwin, H. J. (2000). Shame and guilt in women with eating-disorder symptomatology. *Journal of Clinical Psychology, 56*(1), 51–61. https://doi.org/10.1002/(SICI)1097-4679(200001)56:1<51::AID-JCLP5>3.0.CO;2-W

Chen, E. Y., Le Grange, D., Doyle, A. C., Zaitsoff, S., Doyle, P., Roehrig, J. P., & Washington, B. (2010). A case series of family-based therapy for weight restoration in young adults with anorexia nervosa. *Journal of Contemporary Psychotherapy, 40*(4), 219–224. https://doi.org/10.1007/s10879-010-9146-0

Ciao, A. C., Lebow, J., VandenLangenberg, E., Ohls, O., & Berg, K. C. (2022). A qualitative examination of adolescent and parent perspectives on early identification and early response to EDs. *EDs, 30*(3), 249–266. https://doi.org/10.1080/10640266.2020.1805960

Copeland, W. E., Bulik, C. M., Zucker, N., Wolke, D., Lereya, S. T., & Costello, E. J. (2015). Does childhood bullying predict ED symptoms? A prospective, longitudinal analysis. *International Journal of Eating Disorders*, *48*(8), 1141–1149. https://doi.org/10.1002/eat.22459

Cripps, S., Pugh, M., & Serpell, L. (2024a). Experiences of externalisation in recovery from anorexia nervosa: A reflexive thematic analysis. *Journal of Eating Disorders*, *12*(1), 1–25. https://doi.org/10.1186/s40337-024-01087-9

Cripps, S., Serpell, L., & Pugh, M. (2024b). Processes of change in family therapies for anorexia nervosa: A systematic review and meta-synthesis of qualitative data. *Journal of Eating Disorders*, *12*(1), 1–31. https://doi.org/10.1186/s40337-024-01037-5

Damen, H., Scholte, R. H. J., Vermulst, A. A., van Steensel, P., & Veerman, J. W. (2021). Parental empowerment as a buffer between parental stress and child behavioral problems after family treatment. *Children and Youth Services Review*, *124*, 1–8. https://doi.org/10.1016/j.childyouth.2021.105982

Dann, K. M., Harrison, A., Veldre, A., Hay, P., & Touyz, S. (2024). Embracing a different outlook: Strengths and goals of individuals currently in treatment for anorexia nervosa. *Eating and Weight Disorders*, *29*(1), 1–12. https://doi.org/10.1007/s40519-024-01689-x

Dimitropoulos, G., Freeman, V. E., Allemang, B., Couturier, J., McVey, G., Lock, J., & Le Grange, D. (2015). Family-based treatment with transition age youth with anorexia nervosa: A qualitative summary of application in clinical practice. *Journal of Eating Disorders*, *3*(1), 1–13. https://doi.org/10.1186/s40337-015-0037-3

Dimitropoulos, G., Freeman, V. E., Lock, J., & Le Grange, D. (2017). Clinician perspective on parental empowerment in family-based treatment for adolescent anorexia nervosa. *Journal of Family Therapy*, *39*(4), 537–562. https://doi.org/10.1111/1467-6427.12086

Dimitropoulos, G., Freeman, V. E., Muskat, S., Domingo, A., & McCallum, L. (2016). "You don't have anorexia, you just want to look like a celebrity": Perceived stigma in individuals with anorexia nervosa. *Journal of Mental Health*, *25*(1), 47–54. https://doi.org/10.3109/09638237.2015.1101422

Dimitropoulos, G., Landers, A. L., Freeman, V., Novick, J., Cullen, O., Engelberg, M., Steinegger, C., & Le Grange, D. (2018b). Family-based treatment for transition age youth: Parental self-efficacy and caregiver accommodation. *Journal of Eating Disorders*, *6*(13), 1–11. https://doi.org/10.1186/s40337-018-0196-0

Dimitropoulos, G., Landers, A. L., Freeman, V., Novick, J., Garber, A., & Le Grange, D. (2018a). Open trial of family-based treatment of anorexia nervosa for transition age youth. *Journal of the Canadian Academy of Child and Adolescent Psychiatry*, *27*(1), 50–61. https://pmc.ncbi.nlm.nih.gov/articles/PMC5777691/.

Dimitropoulos, G., Le Grange, D., & Lock, J. (2014). *Research manual: Family-based treatment for transition age youth* [Unpublished manuscript].

Dimitropoulos, G., Singh, M., Sauerwein, J., Pedram, P., Kimber, M., Pradel, M., Eckhardt, S., Forsberg, S., Keery, H., Allan, E., Bruett, L., & Le Grange, D. (2024). Examining clinician's perceptions and experiences working with diverse families in family-based treatment: Common adaptations and considerations for treatment engagement. *International Journal of Eating Disorders*, *57*(3), 635–647. https://doi.org/10.1002/eat.24144

Dodge, E., Baudinet, J., Austin, A., Eisler, I., Le Grange, D., & Dimitropoulos, G. (2024). Family therapy for emerging adults with anorexia nervosa: Expert opinion on evidence, practice considerations, and future directions. *European EDs Review*, 1–11. https://doi.org/10.1002/erv.3129

Donato, K., Ceccarini, M. R., Dhuli, K., Bonetti, G., Medori, M. C., Marceddu, G., Precone, V., Xhufi, S., Bushati, M., Bozo, D., Beccari, T., & Bertelli, M. (2022). Gene variants in EDs. Focus on anorexia nervosa, bulimia nervosa, and binge-ED. *Journal of Preventive Medicine and Hygiene*, *63*(2 Suppl 3), E297–E305. https://doi.org/10.15167/2421-4248/jpmh2022.63.2S3.2772

Freizinger, M., Jhe, G. B., Pluhar, E., & Mancini, L. (2021). Integrating family-based treatment principles in the acute inpatient treatment of adolescents with restrictive EDs. *Psychology Research and Behavior Management, 14*, 449–454. https://doi.org/10.2147/PRBM.S304921

Gorrell, S., Loeb, K. L., & Le Grange, D. (2019). Family-based treatment of EDs: A narrative review. *The Psychiatric Clinics of North America, 42*(2), 193–204. https://doi.org/10.1016/j.psc.2019.01.004

Griffiths, S., Mond, J. M., Murray, S. B., Thornton, C., & Touyz, S. (2015). Stigma resistance in EDs. *Social Psychiatry and Psychiatric Epidemiology, 50*(2), 279–287. https://doi.org/10.1007/s00127-014-0923-z

Halvorsen, I., & Heyerdahl, S. (2007). Treatment perception in adolescent onset anorexia nervosa: Retrospective views of patients and parents. *The International Journal of Eating Disorders, 40*(7), 629–639. https://doi.org/10.1002/eat.20428

Heal-Cohen, N., Allan, S. M., Gauvain, N., Nabirinde, R., & Burgess, A. (2025). Relapse in eating disorders: A systematic review and thematic synthesis of individuals' experiences. *Clinical Psychology and Psychotherapy, 32*(4), 1–19. https://doi.org/10.1002/cpp.70101

Hughes, E. K., Le Grange, D., Court, A., Yeo, M. S., Campbell, S., Allan, E., Crosby, R. D., Loeb, K. L., & Sawyer, S. M. (2014). Parent-focused treatment for adolescent anorexia nervosa: A study protocol of a randomised controlled trial. *BMC Psychiatry, 14*(1), 1–11. https://doi.org/10.1186/1471-244X-14-105

Kelly, A. C., Vimalakanthan, K., & Carter, J. C. (2014). Understanding the roles of self-esteem, self-compassion, and fear of self-compassion in eating disorder pathology: An examination of female students and eating disorder patients. *Eating Behaviors: An International Journal, 15*(3), 388–391. https://doi.org/10.1016/j.eatbeh.2014.04.008

Lebow, J., Sim, L. A., & Accurso, E. C. (2017). Is there clinical consensus in defining weight restoration for adolescents with anorexia nervosa? *EDs, 26*(3), 270–277. https://doi.org/10.1080/10640266.2017.1388664

Le Grange, D., Hughes, E. K., Court, A., Yeo, M., Crosby, R. D., & Sawyer, S. M. (2016). Randomized clinical trial of parent-focused treatment and family-based treatment for adolescent anorexia nervosa. *Journal of the American Academy of Child and Adolescent Psychiatry, 55*(8), 683–692. https://doi.org/10.1016/j.jaac.2016.05.007

Le Grange, D., & Lock, J. (2007). *Treating bulimia in adolescents: A family-based approach*. Guilford Press.

Le Grange, D., Lock, J., Loeb, K., & Nicholls, D. (2010). Academy for EDs position paper: The role of the family in EDs. *International Journal of Eating Disorders, 43*(1), 1–5. https://doi.org/10.1002/eat.20751

Levallius, J., Clinton, D., Bäckström, M., & Norring, C. (2015). Who do you think you are? – Personality in EDed patients. *Journal of Eating Disorders, 3*(3), 1–8. https://doi.org/10.1016/j.jaac.2016.05.007

Lock, J., Couturier, J., Matheson, B. E., Datta, N., Citron, K., Sami, S., Welch, H., Webb, C., Doxtdator, K., & John-Carson, N. (2021). Feasibility of conducting a randomized controlled trial comparing family-based treatment via videoconferencing and online guided self-help family-based treatment for adolescent anorexia nervosa. *International Journal of Eating Disorders, 54*(11), 1998–2008. https://doi.org/10.1002/eat.23611

Lock, J., & Le Grange, D. (2025). *Treatment manual for anorexia nervosa: A family-based approach* (3rd ed.). Routledge.

Lock, J., & Nicholls, D. (2020). Toward a greater understanding of the ways family-based treatment addresses the full range of psychopathology of adolescent anorexia nervosa. *Frontiers in Psychiatry, 10*, 1–8. https://doi.org/10.3389/fpsyt.2019.00968

Lonergan, K., Whyte, A., & Ryan, C. (2022). Externalisation in family-based treatment of anorexia nervosa: The therapist's experience. *Journal of Family Therapy*, *44*(3), 351–369. https://doi.org/10.1111/1467-6427.12380

Longo, P., Marzola, E., De Bacco, C., Demarchi, M., & Abbate-Daga, G. (2020). Young patients with anorexia nervosa: The contribution of post-traumatic stress disorder and traumatic events. *Medicina (Kaunas, Lithuania)*, *57*(1), 1–10. https://doi.org/10.3390/medicina57010002

Medway, M., Rhodes, P., Dawson, L., Miskovic-Wheatley, J., Wallis, A., & Madden, S. (2019). Adolescent development in family-based treatment for anorexia nervosa: Patients' and parents' narratives. *Clinical Child Psychology and Psychiatry*, *24*(1), 129–143. https://doi.org/10.1177/1359104518792293

Molendijk, M. L., Hoek, H. W., Brewerton, T. D., & Elzinga, B. M. (2017). Childhood maltreatment and eating disorder pathology: A systematic review and dose-response meta-analysis. *Psychological Medicine*, *47*(8), 1402–1416. https://doi.org/10.1017/S0033291716003561

Mond, J. M., Robertson-Smith, G., & Vetere, A. (2006). Stigma and EDs: Is there evidence of negative attitudes towards anorexia nervosa among women in the community? *Journal of Mental Health*, *15*(5), 519–532. https://doi.org/10.1080/09638230600902559

Morrison, J., Williams, M. O., & Fox, J. R. E. (2022). Negative childhood events and the development of the anorexic voice: A grounded theory. *Psychology and Psychotherapy*, *95*(4), 1018–1035. https://doi.org/10.1111/papt.12416

Oketah, N. O., Hur, J. O., Talebloo, J., Cheng, C. M., & Nagata, J. M. (2023). Parents' perspectives of anorexia nervosa treatment in adolescents: A systematic review and metasynthesis of qualitative data. *Journal of Eating Disorders*, *11*(1), 1–17. https://doi.org/10.1186/s40337-023–00910-z

Rienecke, R. D. (2017). Family-based treatment of EDs in adolescents: Current insights. *Adolescent Health, Medicine and Therapeutics*, *8*, 69–79. https://doi.org/10.2147/AHMT.S115775

Rienecke, R. D., Johnson, C., Le Grange, D., Manwaring, J., Mehler, P. S., Duffy, A., McClanahan, S., & Blalock, D. V. (2022). Adverse childhood experiences among adults with eating disorders: Comparison to a nationally representative sample and identification of trauma. *Journal of Eating Disorders*, *10*(1), 1–10. https://doi.org/10.1186/s40337-022-00594-x

Rienecke, R. D., & Le Grange, D. (2022). The five tenets of family-based treatment for adolescent EDs. *Journal of Eating Disorders*, *10*(1), 1–10. https://doi.org/10.1186/s40337-022-00585-y

Rienecke, R. D., Trotter, X., & Jenkins, P. E. (2024). A systematic review of EDs and family functioning. *Clinical Psychology Review*, *112*, 1–21. https://doi.org/10.1016/j.cpr.2024.102462

Schaumberg, K., Welch, E., Breithaupt, L., Hübel, C., Baker, J. H., Munn-Chernoff, M. A., Yilmaz, Z., Ehrlich, S., Mustelin, L., Ghaderi, A., Hardaway, A. J., Bulik-Sullivan, E. C., Hedman, A. M., Jangmo, A., Nilsson, I. A. K., Wiklund, C., Yao, S., Seidel, M., & Bulik, C. M. (2017). The science behind the academy for EDs' nine truths about EDs. *European EDs Review*, *25*(6), 432–450. https://doi.org/10.1002/erv.2553

Sheens, E., Rhodes, P., & Dawson, L. (2016). Encountering anorexia: Challenging stigma with recovery stories. *Advances in EDs*, *4*(3), 315–322. https://doi.org/10.1080/21662630.2016.1217495

Treasure, J., Parker, S., Oyeleye, O., & Harrison, A. (2021). The value of including families in the treatment of anorexia nervosa. *European EDs Review*, *29*(3), 393–401. https://doi.org/10.1002/erv.2816

Troop, N. A., & Redshaw, C. (2012). General shame and bodily shame in eating disorders: A 2.5- year longitudinal study. *European Eating Disorders Review*, *20*(5), 373–378. https://doi.org/10.1002/erv.2160

Voswinkel, M. M., Rijkers, C., van Delden, J. J. M., & van Elburg, A. A. (2021). Externalizing your ED: A qualitative interview study. *Journal of Eating Disorders*, *9*(1), 1–12. https://doi.org/10.1186/s40337-021-00486-6

Williams, L. T., Wood, C., & Plath, D. (2020). Parents' experiences of family therapy for adolescent anorexia nervosa. *Australian Social Work*, *73*(4), 408–419. https://doi.org/10.1080/0312407X.2019.1702707

Wufong, E., Rhodes, P., & Conti, J. (2019). "We don't really know what else we can do": Parent experiences when adolescent distress persists after the Maudsley and family-based therapies for anorexia nervosa. *Journal of Eating Disorders*, *7*(1), 1–18. https://doi.org/10.1186/s40337-019-0235-5

Chapter 2

Why Use FBT-TAY? The Scientific and Clinical Rationale

FBT-TAY is a developmental adaptation of the well-established, empirically supported, FBT, designed to address the specific developmental needs of young people with AN. Adolescent FBT is widely used in specialized ED programs to private practice settings across the globe, but its structure and approach do not always align with the greater independence and autonomy sought by young people (ages 16–25). This chapter reviews the scientific evidence supporting FBT-TAY, highlighting studies that demonstrate its acceptability, feasibility, effectiveness, and mechanisms.

Early Insights into FBT-TAY

The origins of this research stem from repeated clinical encounters in FBT implementation at an Ontario, Canada. Preceding the first exploration of FBT and TAY, therapists in Ontario noticed that in their clinical practice, traditionally delivered FBT was not meeting the needs of their emerging adult patients (Dimitropoulos et al., 2012). Specifically, the artificial divide between adolescent and adult treatment made it difficult to use a model of care designed for paediatrics, in an adult system. This initiated conversations on what unique therapeutic challenges may occur when using FBT with young people (older adolescents and emerging adults). In practice, therapists observed that the lack of autonomy, typical of traditional FBT, did not align with the needs of young people and potentially hindered treatment outcomes such as weight gain and eating rehabilitation. Grounded in front-line experience, these observations prompted a more in-depth inquiry into FBT with young people.

The first exploration of FBT adaptations for TAY was conducted by Dimitropoulos et al. (2015), who provided a qualitative summary of its application in clinical settings. This study examined the views of 34 therapists in Ontario, Canada, via individual interview or focus groups. Broadly, therapists emphasized the necessity of adapting traditional FBT principles of parental/caregivers control to meet the developmental needs of young people, who often struggle with the loss

DOI: 10.4324/9781003463351-3

of independence and autonomy during treatment. The authors found that therapists commonly employed a more collaborative approach with young people, involving them more actively in treatment decisions while still maintaining core FBT principles, such as parental/caregiver empowerment and externalization of the ED.

One of the key adaptations reported was extending the amount of individual time spent with young people prior to family sessions (Dimitropoulos et al., 2015). This time allowed therapists to build a therapeutic alliance and address barriers to treatment engagement and motivation. The focus and accompanying strategies for externalization were also modified to engage more directly with young people. For example, rather than the visual metaphors generally used with young people, they were more responsive to insight-based discussions that focused on the ED's impact on areas of their life such as school or relationships. In addition, the delivery of the "urgent message" at the start of treatment was adapted to involve the young person, generally focusing on future-oriented goals (e.g., education, moving out of their parent's/caregiver's home and travel) to highlight the urgency of recovery. This message was also framed in more assertive language to foster engagement.

In terms of the three phases of FBT, therapists reported specific adjustments to each phase (Dimitropoulos et al., 2015). In Phase 1, more psychoeducation was provided on EDs, specifically to justify parental/caregiver involvement. In Phase 2, young people were given more opportunities to eat independently as developmentally appropriate, for example, on university or college campus. Phase 3 involved limited individual work with the young person focused on relapse prevention, body image, and life transitions, which was a greater focus with TAY in comparison to adolescents. Overall, therapists reported that while they adapted the structure and delivery of FBT to meet the developmental needs of TAY, they still adhered to the core tenants of the FBT model: externalization, agnosticism, empowerment, and non-authoritarian stance in treatment. The study ultimately concluded that developmental adaptations are important for the delivery of FBT to TAY.

Translating Early Insights into Practice

Open Trial

Building upon these initial insights, Dimitropoulos et al. (2014) wrote an unpublished treatment manual for FBT-TAY for the use in an open trial of FBT-TAY conducted in Canada (Dimitropoulos et al., 2018a). In an open trial, young people are not randomized to treatment but instead are offered treatment – in this case FBT-TAY – and are allowed to accept or decline. In the open trial, TAY between the ages of 16.5 and 25, with a range of symptom severity and illness duration were included. The trial was conducted across three sites in Toronto, Canada: two paediatric hospitals and one adult hospital. The intention of this open trial was to assess the feasibility, acceptability, and preliminary effectiveness of FBT-TAY for individuals with AN. Of the 60 potential participants approached, about half accepted FBT-TAY, 15% preferred the treatment as usual offered at their ED service, and the remainder declined all treatment for an ED. Of the 27 participants entering FBT-TAY, most were female, Caucasian, and living with their family. On average, young people attended just over 14 sessions of treatment. Some withdrew from the trial for a selection of reasons. Three left the trial because of clinical reasons, such as the need for inpatient treatment because of medical instability or suicidality. Two withdrew for logistical reasons, such as the commuting time or the financial strain of attendance, and one was withdrawn due to a protocol deviation of pursuing another concurrent treatment.

Finally, five withdrew because of patient or family member-initiated reasons, such as difficulty tolerating distressing emotions, and one withdrew due to consecutive missed sessions.

The initial effectiveness of FBT-TAY was evaluated by assessing weight restoration (per cent of median body mass index) and ED thoughts and behaviours. These outcomes were assessed when the young person began treatment, at the end of treatment (up to 25 sessions), and then again at three-month follow-up. Results showed a significant increase in weight restoration and a significant decrease in ED thoughts and behaviours over the trial.

Importantly, this study reinforced that, by engaging young people in the treatment process and emphasizing their role in recovery, the intervention balanced the need for parental/caregiver involvement with the young person's growing autonomy. The findings from this open trial suggest that FBT-TAY is acceptable, feasible, and demonstrates initial effectiveness.

Parental Self-Efficacy and Caregiver Accommodation

A subsequent study by Dimitropoulos et al. (2019a), using the same data from the open trial, examined the impact of FBT-TAY on parental/caregiver self-efficacy and accommodation. Self-efficacy in the context of FBT is defined as the ability of a caregiver to take "charge" of the ED to bring about recovery in their child (Rhodes et al., 2005). Parental/caregiver accommodation refers to inadvertently acquiescing to ED behaviours to try to avoid feeling helpless or angry, or to provide their loved one with reassurance (Sepulveda et al., 2009). Data on these variables were collected during the trial via self-report questionnaires from 39 parents/caregivers (23 mothers and 16 fathers).

Other Family Approaches for TAY

While Dimitropoulos et al. have explored the adaptation of FBT for TAY, alternative approaches have also been explored. To better understand FBT as a tool to promote weight restoration in young people with AN, Chen et al. (2010) conducted a case series of FBT with four patients with AN, aged 18–21. To assess the preliminary acceptability, feasibility, and efficacy, participants were involved in up to 20 sessions of FBT. Only minor changes were made to the original FBT manual, such as utilizing a collaborative approach with the young person and engaging in individual sessions during the final phase of treatment, without family involvement. Three of the four participants were in a "normal" or non-clinical weight and ED behaviour/cognition range at the end of treatment and at follow-up. Additionally, these participants reported not being depressed or only mildly to moderately depressed at this point, in comparison to scores in the "moderate" to "severe depressive" range at pre-treatment. Good psychosocial functioning (i.e., the ability to form and maintain healthy relationships, communicate effectively, and engage in social or school activities) was reported in two of the four participants at the end of treatment, and by three of the four participants at follow-up. Although the results of this study were preliminary, they provided evidence for the acceptability, feasibility, and preliminary efficacy of FBT in young people.

To extend the understanding of the acceptability and efficacy of FBT as a tool for weight restoration in young people with AN, Chen et al. (2016) conducted a larger follow-up study. This study included 22 female participants ranging from age 18 to 26 who were diagnosed with AN or atypical AN. Each participant was required to designate a support adult, and together, they were enrolled in this trial of FBT for six months. The primary outcome of this study was the BMI of participants and whether it fell in normal weight ranges. Secondary outcomes included the nature of the ED, ED obsessions and compulsions, other primary psychiatric disorders (Axis I), and the global assessment of functioning.

Adaptations were made to FBT to accommodate young people resulting in FBT-Y and included:

> 1) participants were empowered to choose who their support adult was, 2) a collaborative approach was utilized between the participant and their therapist, 3) developmental issues specific to the participant were addressed, and 4) in the final phase of treatment, participants had the option to increase the duration of their individual therapy sessions, without their supportive adult.

At the end of FBT-TAY, participants rated the treatment as "more than moderately but less than completely suitable," demonstrating a high acceptability although room for improvement.

Further, 15 participants fell within the normal-weight BMI range. This was maintained at the 6-month follow-up, and by the 12-month follow-up, 13 were still in this range (however, it is important to note that four participants in the group were already minimally normal weight at baseline). The effect sizes of BMI changes were large from baseline to the end of treatment, as well as from baseline to the follow-up visits, with results comparable to those for FBT for adolescents with AN. At the end of FBT-Y, ED psychopathology scores as measured by ED cognitions and behaviours were deemed non-clinical for 13 participants. Additionally, at 6- and 12-month follow-up visits, 11 and 10 participants were still below the clinical BMI cut-off, respectively. All other secondary outcomes, ED obsessions and compulsions, other Axis I disorders, and global functioning improved after treatment. These two studies by Chen et al. (2010, 2016) support the use of FBT approaches for young people with AN, especially when a supportive adult is willing to participate.

In 2020, Nyman-Carlsson et al. conducted an RCT comparing a model of individual Cognitive Behavioural Therapy (CBT) and adapted for young adults (CBT-YA) to an FBT related approach adapted for young adults (FT-YA). The study recruited and randomized 74 participants (ages 17–24) with an AN diagnosis. The rationale for this study was that specific treatment considerations needed to be put in place for emerging adults; however available treatments did not bridge the gap between adolescent and adult care. The study aimed to explore whether the treatments (CBT-YA and FT-YA) would result in an increase of BMI and reduction of ED symptoms, with a secondary aim of exploring potential differences between the CBT and FT groups. FT-YA was adapted from the Lock et al. (2001) model, with a particular emphasis on adding individual sessions and removing the family meal component. Additionally, the number and order of separated and family sessions in phases three and four were not fixed but adapted based on the needs of the participant and the family.

FBT-TAY Versus Other Family Therapeutic Practices

FBT-TAY is distinct from other family therapeutic practices, the most common being systemic family therapy (SyFT). SyFT is based on systems theory, which views the family as an interconnected system, with any problems understood within the context of relationships and interactions (Pote et al., 2000). SyFT is a broad approach that can be used for a range of mental health disorders or relational issues, whereas FBT-TAY was developed specifically for AN. These two treatments also have different therapeutic goals; while FBT-TAY is pragmatically focused on the ED by restoring weight and normalizing eating, SyFT aims to improve family dynamics by strengthening communication and resolving conflicts. A randomized controlled trial by Agras et al. (2014) including 164 patients with AN and their families compared the adolescent form of FBT to SyFT. Both treatments were delivered in 16 one-hour sessions across nine months. Clinical outcomes were similar for young people in both treatments, with 40.7% of those in FBT and 39.0% of those in SyFT achieving weight restoration by one-year follow-up.

However, young people in FBT gained weight significantly faster over the first eight weeks of treatment. There was also a cost savings associated with FBT, largely due to the greater number of hospital days adolescents in SyFT needed (Agras et al., 2014).

Findings showed BMI increased significantly from baseline to post-treatment in both groups. The study also highlighted that FT-YA, unlike CBT-YA, continued to show improvements to BMI (although not statistically significant) after treatment, which may point to the importance of family support for young people with AN. The study also found that while parental/caregiver support is important, living physically with the family did not show to be a critical treatment element; despite 60% of FBT-YA participants moving away from home while undergoing treatment, authors found it did not show impact on treatment outcomes (Nyman-Carlsson et al., 2020).

Current Limitations of FBT-TAY

There are several limitations to the existing research in the area which should be noted. First, the seminal studies in FBT-TAY (e.g., Dimitropoulos et al., 2015, 2018a, 2018b, 2019b) did not measure the long-term impact of the adapted model on treatment or clinical outcomes in young people and their parents/caregivers. Within the open trial (Dimitropoulos et al., 2018a), the follow-up period for treatment outcome variables as defined within the study (weight restoration, cessation of ED symptoms and behaviours) was three months, which did not allow insight into whether young people sustained improvements in outcome variables long-term (at 6–12-months or longer). In addition, the dropout rate for treatment was moderate (46.15%), making generalizations of the efficacy of this adapted model to a majority of TAY in ED treatment more challenging (Dimitropoulos et al., 2018a). There is also generally a lack of documented evidence on applications of FBT-TAY within community settings (e.g., community organizations delivering evidence-based ED treatments), as most participants in existing studies were recruited within hospital-based inpatient or tertiary care; however, applications of the model within primary care and private practice are emerging (see Chapter 10) and should be further explored. Finally, despite the evidence base for FBT TAY, there are no RCTs comparing FBT-TAY to treatment as usual (Dimitropoulos et al., 2019b); future research efforts should focus on publishing high-quality RCTs in FBT-TAY examining long-term treatment outcomes in a variety of care settings (e.g., primary and tertiary care, private practice, community settings).

Conclusion

In summary, there are compelling clinical and scientific findings that support the rationale for use of an adapted FBT with emerging adults with AN. The FBT-TAY studies by Dimitropoulos et al. (2015, 2018a, 2018b, 2019a, 2019b) demonstrate the acceptability, feasibility, and initial effectiveness of FBT-TAY. More specifically, they provide preliminary evidence that FBT-TAY improves weight, reduces ED thoughts and behaviours, and improves family functioning and parental/caregiver self-efficacy. They also explore the potential mechanisms of change underlying the improvement of clinical outcomes in comparison to an adolescent population. Other variations of FBT or FBT-related approaches have also been developed and piloted with TAY experiencing AN, all demonstrating preliminary effectiveness or efficacy. Overall, the evidence suggests that the inclusion of individual time, a slightly extended treatment duration, and an autonomy-supportive approach are important for this age group and that FBT-TAY is acceptable and feasible in delivering these approaches. FBT-TAY represents a pivotal advancement in the treatment of AN, offering a structured yet adaptable approach that supports both ED recovery and the transition to adulthood (Dimitropoulos et al., 2015, 2018a, 2018b, 2019b).

Chapter Summary

Here are the key points of this chapter:

(1) Traditional FBT does not adequately meet the needs of many older adolescents and emerging adults, who require more independence and collaboration in the treatment process.
(2) Early qualitative research showed therapists emphasized developmental adaptations while keeping core principles of FBT such as externalization, agnosticism, and parental/caregiver empowerment.
(3) An open Canadian trial (Dimitopoulos et al., 2018a) found FBT-TAY to be feasible, acceptable, and effective, with improvements in weight restoration and reductions in ED symptoms.
(4) Parents/caregivers reported feeling more confident and less likely to accommodate the illness, even if these changes did not necessarily directly account for recovery outcomes among young people.
(5) International adaptations of FBT for young people also demonstrated promising results, often involving "supportive adults" in treatment.
(6) Overall, early evidence suggests that FBT-TAY is acceptable, feasible, and effective, as it offers both a structured and flexible model that helps to balances renourishment with autonomy and developmental needs.

References

Agras, W. S., Lock, J., Brandt, H., Bryson, S. W., Dodge, E., Halmi, K. A., Jo, B., Johnson, C., Kaye, W., Wilfley, D., & Woodside, B. (2014). Comparison of 2 family therapies for adolescent anorexia nervosa: A randomized parallel trial. *JAMA Psychiatry (Chicago, Ill.)*, *71*(11), 1279–1286. https://doi.org/10.1001/jamapsychiatry.2014.1025
Chen, E. Y., Le Grange, D., Doyle, A. C., Zaitsoff, S., Doyle, P., Roehrig, J. P., & Washington, B. (2010). A case series of family-based therapy for weight restoration in young adults with anorexia nervosa. *Journal of Contemporary Psychotherapy*, *40*(4), 219–224. https://doi.org/10.1007/s10879-010-9146-0

Chen, E. Y., Weissman, J. A., Zeffiro, T. A., Yiu, A., Eneva, K. T., Arlt, J. M., & Swantek, M. J. (2016). Family-based therapy for young adults with anorexia nervosa restores weight. *International Journal of Eating Disorders*, *49*(7), 701–707. https://doi.org/10.1002/eat.22513

Dimitropoulos, G., Freeman, V. E., Allemang, B., Couturier, J., McVey, G., Lock, J., & Le Grange, D. (2015). Family-based treatment with transition age youth with anorexia nervosa: A qualitative summary of application in clinical practice. *Journal of Eating Disorders*, *3*, 1–13. https://doi.org/10.1186/s40337-015-0037-3

Dimitropoulos, G., Tran, A. F., Agarwal, P., Sheffield, B., & Woodside, B. (2012). Navigating the transition from pediatric to adult eating disorder programs: Perspectives of service providers. *The International Journal of Eating Disorders*, *45*(6), 759–767. https://doi.org/10.1002/eat.22017

Dimitropoulos, G., Landers, A. L., Freeman, V. E., Novick, J., Cullen, O., Engelberg, M.,. . .& Le Grange, D. (2019a). Family-based treatment for transition age youth: Parental self-efficacy and caregiver accommodation. *Journal of Eating Disorders*, *6*, 1–11. https://doi.org/10.1186/s40337-018-0196-0

Dimitropoulos, G., Landers, A. L., Freeman, V., Novick, J., Cullen, O., & Le Grange, D. (2019b). Family-based treatment for transition age youth: The role of expressed emotion and general family functioning. *EDs*, *27*(5), 419–435. https://doi.org/10.1080/10640266.2018.1529472

Dimitropoulos, G., Landers, A. L., Freeman, V., Novick, J., Garber, A., & Le Grange, D. (2018a). Open trial of family-based treatment of anorexia nervosa for transition age youth. *Journal of the Canadian Academy of Child and Adolescent Psychiatry*, *27*(1), 50–61. https://pmc.ncbi.nlm.nih.gov/articles/PMC5777691/

Dimitropoulos, G., Landers, A. L., Freeman, V. E., Novick, J., Cullen, O., Engelberg, M., Steinegger, C., & Le Grange, D. (2018b). Family-based treatment for transition age youth: Parental self-efficacy and caregiver accommodation. *Journal of Eating Disorders*, *6*(1), 1–11. https://doi.org/10.1186/s40337-018-0196-0

Dimitropoulos, G., Le Grange, D., & Lock, J. (2014). *Research manual: Family-based treatment for transition age youth* [Unpublished manuscript].

Lock, J., Le Grange, R., Agras, W. S., & Dare, C. (2001). *Treatment manual for anorexia nervosa: A family-based approach*. New York: Guilford Press.

Nyman-Carlsson, E., Norring, C., Engström, I., Gustafsson, S. A., Lindberg, K., Paulson-Karlsson, G., & Nevonen, L. (2020). Individual cognitive behavioral therapy and combined family/individual therapy for young adults with anorexia nervosa: A randomized controlled trial. *Psychotherapy Research*, *30*(8), 1011–1025. https://doi.org/10.1080/10503307.2019.1686190

Pote, H., Stratton, P., Cottrell, D., Boston, P., Shapiro, D., & Hanks, H. (2000). Leeds systemic family therapy manual. *Journal of Family Therapy*, *25*, 236–262. https://www.researchgate.net/publication/338389429_Leeds_Systemic_Family_Therapy_Manual

Rhodes, P., Baillie, A., Brown, J., & Madden, S. (2005). Parental efficacy in the family-based treatment of anorexia: Preliminary development of the Parents Versus Anorexia Scale (PVA). *European EDs Review: The Professional Journal of the EDs Association*, *13*(6), 399–405. https://doi.org/10.1002/erv.661

Sepulveda, A. R., Kyriacou, O., & Treasure, J. (2009). Development and validation of the accommodation and enabling scale for EDs (AESED) for caregivers in EDs. *BMC Health Services Research*, *9*, 1–13. https://doi.org/10.1186/1472-6963-9-171

Chapter 3

Overview of Late Adolescent and Young Development in FBT-TAY

This chapter provides a general overview of late adolescence and young adult development. However, it does not attempt to provide a comprehensive discussion on this expansive subject but will share an overview of how developmental factors impact the delivery of FBT-TAY. To augment the materials discussed, we hope the references at the end of the chapter will be utilized by therapists to increase their knowledge in areas where additional detail may be needed.

After this introduction, the chapter is divided into three main sections: Brief overview of early and middle adolescence, as it is not uncommon for unfinished developmental tasks from this earlier period to young adolescence (ages 11–18 years); late adolescent developmental tasks and developmental issues of young adulthood (ages 19–26 years); and a summary with key learning points. In the first two sections, we discuss cognitive, emotional, and social development capacities and their role in delivering FBT-TAY for young people. For example, cognitive skills typically increase over the course of adolescence and young adulthood potentially allowing for greater understanding of how AN is affecting thinking and behaviours (Anderson, 2001; Blakemore & Chowdhury, 2006; Boyer, 2006; Holmbeck et al., 2000; Lee et al., 2013) and may potentially interfere with academic and employment opportunities. Similarly, abilities to express and regulate emotions also typically improve during this period. And, in conjunction with improved cognitive and emotional abilities, the social skills needed to explore changes in relationships with parents/caregivers, friends, and more intimate relationships are a crucial aspect of this developmental period. Of course, there is tremendous individual variation and non-linear progress along these developmental trajectories in young people generally, but the impact of a serious disorder like AN adds to the challenges of moving through them with mastery. In addition, there are potentially different challenges by gender even though most follow a similar trajectory; however, some male identified adolescents sometimes lag or express some developmental issues differently from adolescents who are female identified.

DOI: 10.4324/9781003463351-4

Developmental Factors in Implementing FBT-TAY

In general, the therapist should appreciate the developmental capacities and challenges of each young person they treat to best engage and involve them appropriately. Unlike much younger adolescents, FBT-TAY necessarily involves more input from older adolescents and emerging adults (Dimitropoulos et al., 2018) and to do so means appreciating their level of mastery of cognitive, emotional, and social developmental abilities during treatment (Prinstein et al., 2019). The onset of AN is typically during adolescence; subsequently, the disorder has a significant impact on the expected developmental processes of this period (Smink et al., 2014).

Approximately 90% of cases of AN begin during adolescence. Exactly why adolescence and young adulthood are a high risk period is unknown; during this period, the adolescent brain is undergoing a major remodelling process, including pruning and re-shaping white matter tracts in the brain to increase efficiency of information processing (Meyer & Lee, 2019; Stevens et al., 2009). White matter (myelin sheath) development helps to improve the efficiency of communication among different parts of the brain, but it is possible that this extensive remodelling may lead to impairments. The goal of this period is to create a more efficient adult brain as these anatomical changes underlie those improved abilities to think, manage feelings, and plan (Casey et al., 2010). In contrast to adults, young people use different part of their brains – specifically the amygdala – to preferentially process information. The amygdala focuses on emotional response rather than analytic processing (Casey & Caudie, 2013) (Ackerman, 2012); as a result, thinking in adolescence is often "coloured" by emotions which accounts for the sometimes-dramatic nature of arguments and beliefs in this age group.

Alongside structural changes, the neurotransmitter profile of the brain changes affecting mood and emotion regulation. Serotonin systems are rapidly developing and these neurochemical changes may sometimes lead to biologically based emotional and behavioural problems including those associated with mood, anxiety, and EDs (Duvvuri et al., 2009). One complication that is associated with AN-induced starvation is diminished production of serotonin arising in part due to the required pre-cursor nutrients (particularly tryptophan) that are not sufficiently consumed (Ferguson et al., 1999; Kaye et al., 2005).

A related starvation induced problem is related to hormone production (Rubinow et al., 1998). During starvation, the body minimizes expenditures that are non-essential including oestrogen. These hormones have effects on brain development as well as other aspects of physical health (e.g., bone deposition) (Golden et al., 2002). In addition to these impacts, changes in gene expression appear to respond to the presence of these hormone increasing the post-pubertal risk of AN (Klump et al., 2007, 2010).

In healthy young people, these structural and neurotransmitter changes during adolescence lead to more mature skills such as planning, advanced language use, improved set-shifting, improved emotion regulation, and enhanced global processing (Arnsten & Rubia, 2012). Thus, limitations related to these abilities in adolescents and young people with AN may contribute to how they engage and contribute to FBT-TAY.

Changes in the brain and the body do not take place in a vacuum but evolve in the context of family and social milieu (Nelson et al., 2005; Welch & Fairburn, 1996). These environments convey risk and resilience as well as opportunities for testing and exploring how cognitive, emotional, and physical changes affect relationships. Increased stress, trauma, and impoverishment lead to greater likelihood of mental health problems. However, supportive familial and social contexts are protective against these problems and may instead allow for an appropriate environment for practising these new abilities and skills. Younger adolescents are often dependent on their families and local social opportunities, but during later adolescence and young adulthood, in many cultures, it is normative to develop their social lives outside the family and local environments. This often means leaving home, finding employment, attending and residing on college or university campus, as well as developing intimate relationships outside the family. Some have conceptualized this period of social development outside the family as "separation and individuation" where older adolescents and young people must learn to relinquish their dependence on parents and families and embark on a life of increasing social and emotional autonomy (Erikson, 1950, 1968). While there is also considerable cultural variability in how young people navigate the process of a more independent identity, it nonetheless appears to be central to generational change and contributes to ED expression (Wildes et al., 2001).

Brief Overview of Early and Middle Adolescence

While the overall focus of this chapter is on developmental factors in FBT-TAY aimed at the later stages of adolescence and the start of young adulthood, in some cases of AN, there are adolescent developmental issues that typically arise during an earlier life stage that still affect the abilities and challenges of this older person when in FBT-TAY. For this reason, we are providing a very brief review of some of the key developments of younger adolescents that may be useful for therapists to assess when embarking on FBT-TAY.

Because AN sometimes coincides with the onset of physical changes associated with puberty, delays may be experienced due too poor nutrition and pubertal impacts of the body may still be problematic in TAY (Culbert et al., 2009). Adolescence through young adulthood is a time of physical growth and sexual maturation (Shirtcliff et al., 2009). Increases in sex and growth hormone production begin at about age 8 in girls and 10 in boys (Montemayor, 2018). Increases in height and weight typically continue through about age 17 years in girls and age

19 years in boys. Practically, this means that there is an average 25% increase in height and 50% increase in weight during this period. At the same time, sex hormones lead to menarche and breast development in young women. Boys' penis and testes increase to adult size, and their voices deepen. It is common for adolescents to struggle with some of these changes as they interact with social and familial processes (Golden et al., 2003; McCabe et al., 2001). This may lead to attempts to change or stop these processes through restrictive eating and exercise leading to development of AN (Ackard & Peterson, 2001). Not only does AN impede physical sexual and physical development, but due to these changes, the drive to engage in age-appropriate sexual exploration also diminishes. The failure to develop or accept post-pubertal body habitus may continue to be a problem in young people, and an FBT-TAY therapist should evaluate how this might affect the course of treatment.

Another area of development that AN may disrupt is emotional expression and regulation. Improved emotion awareness and self-management comes hand in hand with improved abstract cognitive skills (Barrett et al., 2018). However, with starvation, there is often a blunting or flattening of emotions and for the young person with AN, this may contribute to an initial feeling of emotional control (Harrison et al., 2010). However, blunting emotions is not emotion regulation and in time, the habit of suppressing and avoiding feelings may lead to serious challenges in building and growing connections with others (Tchanturia et al., 2014).

This interplay between starvation and emotions may lead to failure to take on the important adolescent developmental challenge of exploring peer relationships (Bukowski et al., 2019). While in younger years, the family is the main source of social connection, with adolescence, there is a need to find a social role outside the family and to engage emotionally with those unrelated peers. This is a period of evaluating and participating in the development of social identities and hierarchies. Initially this role may be based on physical appearance and perceived sexual maturity; thus, those with AN may be at a disadvantage resulting from their disorder. The consequences of social failures during earlier adolescence may contribute to the maintenance of AN symptoms (Horesh et al., 1996; Russell et al., 2009) and be part of the challenges in FBT-TAY as the young person may need to start or re-start the social engagement processes missed or not mastered earlier in their development.

Late Adolescence and Young Adulthood

As noted, the brief review of common issues in adolescents is provided because it may help therapists understand the abilities of the young person in FBT-TAY to participate in treatment. Some adolescents with AN are chronologically at the age such that one would expect them to be in late adolescence, but their illness could have left them unresolved earlier adolescent issues. If the FBT-TAY therapist identifies this as a likely issue, then, the therapist should try to ensure that treatment accounts for the developmental age and abilities rather than chronological age alone to match their interventions to the real capacities of the young person.

For the majority of young people, the key issues they are facing are squarely in the domain of later adolescence and adulthood. Young people in this period are typically far clearer about what they are trying to accomplish and better able to regulate their emotions. They are less impulsive and have a more coherent sense of who they are and what they want even as they remain far from fully settled in their identity (Erikson, 1968). These increased capacities enhance a need for and interest in increased autonomy and ability and wish for self-determination. As a result, this is a period of increased independence and separation from parents and family. The term "individuation" has been used to describe this overall process typically characterized by increased time away from the family/home in work or social pursuits and often intensifying romantic and sexual relationships (Koepe & Denissen, 2012). Some adolescents struggle during this period if they are ambivalent or unsure of their abilities to separate from their parents/caregivers and families and conversely if parents/caregivers are not supportive of these developmental needs. In FBT-AN in contrast to FBT-TAY, this is often a focus of Phase 3 of treatment in young people who are 16–18 years old. In FBT-TAY, this is instead often part of the initial treatment negation even when a young person with AN continues with severe distortions related to eating, weight, and food (Blakemore & Chowdhury, 2006; Cachelin et al., 1999; Keel et al., 2000; Tchanturia et al., 2012).

The FBT-TAY therapist should expect that young people will have cognitive abilities that are near adult levels at this stage, including the ability to fully utilize abstract concepts and symbolic thinking consistently. For typically developing young people without AN, this means they are better able to use global processing, use experience to learn, draw associations, and integrate knowledge; further, they are usually less self-centred and begin to live more in the "real world" and see themselves as part of a larger social and cultural context. However, some studies document specific cognitive "inefficiencies" in young people with AN (e.g., Lang et al., 2015). It is unclear if these result from heritable differences in cognitive styles (Fonville et al., 2013; Tchanturia et al., 2012) or from AN. Specifically these reports suggest that there are two cognitive challenges related to cognitive flexibility (ability to set shift) (Roberts et al., 2007) and a cognitive bias toward focusing on details rather than the big picture (i.e., difficulties in global processing (Roberts et al., 2007). In the context of FBT-TAY, these cognitive processing styles could interfere with working as effectively in treatment, especially when the young person is asked to entertain the idea of trying new behaviours (flexibility) or to take on the seriousness of AN to their body, mind, social, and vocational life (big picture thinking). As suggested above, because these kinds of cognitive inefficiencies are seen in adults more than adolescents

(Lock et al., 2018), it is unclear whether they result from ongoing AN or a risk factor for more enduring AN. In any event, the FBT-TAY therapist should consider them in evaluating how best to work with each young person.

In addition to overall cognitive abilities, emotional awareness and self-management skills improve during late adolescence leading to an overall increased capacity to engage meaningfully in the therapeutic processes without being as overwhelmed by unfamiliar or strong emotions.

This means that when involving this age group in FBT-TAY, the therapist should expect less emotional intensity or withdrawal, allowing for more meaningful engagement. This reduced lability can mean that emotional outbursts that disrupt therapy should be fewer and, when they do occur, should be more easily managed with an increased capacity to learn from them (Barber et al., 2008). Of course, as with cognitive capacities, the development of AN and its maintenance over time can inhibit emotional development and some young people will not have reached the level of emotional maturity expected (Davies et al., 2012; Harrison et al., 2010; Oldershaw, et al., 2010). In these cases, the FBT-TAY therapist should consider the emotional capacities that are present and help the young person with continued awareness and regulation of them as they participate in therapy.

As a result of ongoing cognitive capacities and emotional awareness, a sense of an increasingly coherent sense of self or identity is emerging. There is an evolving sense of having a social identity but also a more attenuated private self that is increasingly informed by self-reflection and learning rather than simply parroting of socially condoned expectations related to gender, social class, or peer values. With this independence of thought and action, self-worth and validation are less dependent on peers or group values. In the case of AN, however, this sense of identity can sometimes be stalled or foreclosed as the sense of self-worth and even identity is thought to consist primarily of the behaviours, thoughts, and concerns related to the disorder (Lock, 2020). Over time, it may seem that AN is all that is left of the promising young person before the disorder began. The loss of a strong sense of an identity apart from AN is a target of FBT-TAY through externalization of the disorder strategies but can be harder for both the young person and parents/caregivers, partners, and friends to hold onto if the illness has been enduring because so much of the other aspects of the young person's interests and abilities have been sacrificed to AN. The strategies needed to effectively externalize AN in the context of FBT-TAY are key therapist skills and are described elsewhere in this manual.

Perhaps the biggest changes in late adolescence and young adulthood are related to the changing social milieu, especially as it relates to exploring relationships outside the family and home.

While younger adolescents mostly keep their social sphere local and home based, older adolescents begin to explore a broader social environment, especially as they begin working or attending activities in the broader community. In the age of social media, these kinds of explorations are sometimes being undertaken earlier in adolescence – at least online – but by late adolescence, meeting, making friends, and socializing based on social media contacts increase. The topic of social media and its impact of socialization processes in adolescence and young adulthood is a broad one and details about the pros and cons of its use are still being debated (Plaisme et al., 2020). However, it is increasingly common for young people to have both friends and romantic partners that originate through social media contacts and may remain fully virtual relationships. The use of social media to support ED behaviours through communities of others that have AN may complicate socialization with peers without EDs resulting in a limited and potentially hazardous support for continuing with the disorder (Plaisme et al., 2020). On the other hand, some suggest that peers who have recovered are a potential resource for support for making necessary changes that will help recovery efforts. For the FBT-TAY therapist, the role of online friends and supports may arise in either of these incarnations and should be remembered as a possible influential factor in treatment.

With the development of greater social support outside the family, late adolescents and young people are able to separate more appropriately and successfully from their families of origin in concert with their social/cultural milieu. However, adolescents with AN can get "stuck" in their families because of their illness and its impact on their health, school, and broader socialization (Lock, 2020). AN is an illness that at its worst leads to increased isolation from others and the maintaining behaviours of self-starvation, excessive exercise, and obsessional worry over body size and weight are most effective when others are not around to provide "corrective" comments about the dangers of these behaviours and worries. So, the young person tries to keep a distance from others as the disorder advances. Over time this distance leads to the habit of social isolation and fear and anxiety about being with others and especially eating with others – a common social activity – is reinforced. As a result of this social isolation, some young people with AN will be participating in FBT-TAY with very little social support that would be developmentally in line with their chronological age. This may in turn lead to a conflicted dependence on parents/caregivers for social and emotional needs that most would have outgrown at this stage.

The conflicted nature of this dependence arises from a recognition that the young person still needs their parents/caregivers because they cannot support themselves physically, emotionally, or financially, but they have at the same time the legal and expected developmental agency to be more independent. Parents/caregivers may also feel trapped in the unhealthy dependence pattern and have their own frustrations about needing to take care of a young person who they expected to be more independent of them at this point. As the FBT-TAY therapist is beginning this work, these frustrations may contribute to challenges the family must overcome as they embark in treatment.

However, sometimes the young person has negotiated more independence and has a partner or is living outside the home (e.g., attending college or university away from home). In these cases, who and how family members participate in FBT-TAY is an important consideration. If the partner is going to play the key role in helping the young person with weight restoration rather than the parents/caregivers, this will require careful consideration and support. It can be challenging for therapists to help partners navigate monitoring, encouraging, and setting limits on AN behaviours when they are couple. So, while it is more developmentally expected that young people have partners, these types of partnerships are usually new to them and many are learning how to be with another person intimately for the first time – which is challenging in itself without the added burden of one partner needing to take active care of their partner with AN (Bulik et al., 2011). The FBT-TAY therapist will need to discuss these issues with the partners before embarking in treatment and help them make the best decision about if and how a partner can be involved.

If parents/caregivers are continuing to help the young person with renourishment or the recovery process but will be doing so while their adult child is away from home for many or all meals, then strategies to facilitate distanced monitoring and support will be key to successful implementation of FBT-TAY. Again, additional details about ways therapists can help families with these dilemmas are found elsewhere in this manual (Chapter 11). For this current chapter, the importance of the development of increasingly appropriate independence from parents/caregivers while still gaining the support they need will help to allay the frustrations and conflicts that sometimes characterize the relationship between young people and their parents/caregivers with over dependency persisting because of AN (Stierlin, 1974; Woodside et al., 2002).

Conclusions

Late adolescence and young adulthood constitute a period of substantial transformation, during which young people consolidate their cognitive capacities, refine emotional regulation, form more stable identities, and expand their social networks beyond the family. When AN is present, these normative developmental processes are frequently disrupted or delayed by the combined effects of starvation, neurobiological change, emotional constriction, and social withdrawal. Attending to the distinction between chronological age and developmental functioning is critical for FBT-TAY therapists in understanding the young person's needs, capacities, and readiness for treatment. By integrating developmental understanding into treatment planning and delivery, FBT-TAY can support not only medical stabilization and symptom reduction but also the restoration of disrupted developmental trajectories, fostering connectedness, self-direction, and engagement in a young person's life beyond the illness.

Chapter Summary

Here are the key points of this chapter:

(1) Development of cognitive, emotional, and social capacities continues for young people and will affect the delivery of FBT-TAY.
(2) Therapists conducting FBT-TAY should have a sound understanding of typical developmental issues in late adolescence and young adulthood, an understanding of the likely impact of AN on these developmental processes, and an appreciation of these developmental factors on conducting FBT-TAY.
(3) Addressing expectations of the young person of FBT-TAY requires that therapists assess the developmental abilities, skills, and readiness as part of the initial treatment process.
(4) Unfinished developmental milestones from earlier adolescence related to body acceptance, ability to think flexibly and globally, emotional awareness and regulation, social skills and management of independence/dependency needs are all possible challenges for therapists conducting FBT-TAY.
(5) Many late adolescents and young people with AN, progressed well through earlier stages of adolescence, have increased cognitive abilities, emotional awareness and regulation skills, and social abilities that will enhance their meaningful contributions to FBT-TAY.
(6) Neurobiological changes in adolescence – including brain remodelling, neurotransmitter shifts, and hormone suppression from starvation – affect mood, cognition, and emotion regulation, influencing engagement in therapy.
(7) Social development during late adolescence involves individuation and building relationships outside the family, but AN often drives isolation; therapists should help youth rebuild supportive, safe connections.
(8) Involvement of family, partners, or peers must be tailored to the young person's living context, with strategies for both in-home and distance support to balance autonomy and renourishment.

References

Ackard, D. M., & Peterson, C. B. (2001). Association between puberty and disordered eating, body image, and other psychological variables. *International Journal of Eating Disorders*, *29*(2), 187–194. https://doi.org/10.1002/1098-108X(200103)29:2<187::AID- EAT1008>3.0.CO;2-R

Ackerman, D. (2012). *An alchemy of mind*. Scribner.

Anderson, V. (2001). Development of executive functions through late childhood and adolescence in an Australian sample. *Developmental Psychology*, *20*(1), 385–406. https://doi.org/10.1207/S15326942DN2001_5

Arnsten, A. F. T., & Rubia, K. (2012). Neurobiological circuits regulating attention, cognitive control, motivation, and emotion: Disruptions in neurodevelopmental psychiatric disorders. *Journal of the American Academy of Child and Adolescent Psychiatry*, *51*(4), 356–367. https://doi.org/10.1016/j.jaac.2012.01.008

Barber, J., Gallop, R., Crits-Christoph, P., Barrett, M., Klostermann, S., McCarthy, K., & Sharpless, B. (2008). The role of the alliance and techniques in predicting outcome of supportive-expressive dynamic therapy for cocaine dependence. *Psychoanalytic Psychology*, *25*(3), 461–482. https://doi.org/10.1037/0736-9735.25.3.461

Barrett, L., Lewis, M., & Haviland-Jones, J. (2018). *Handbook of emotions* (4th ed.). Guilford.

Blakemore, S., & Chowdhury, S. (2006). Development of the adolescent brain: Implications for executive function and social cognition. *Journal of Child Psychology and Psychiatry*, *47*(3-4), 296–312. https://doi.org/10.1111/j.1469-7610.2006.01611.x

Boyer, T. W. (2006). The development of risk-taking: A multi-perspective review. *Developmental Review*, *26*(3), 291–345. https://doi.org/10.1016/j.dr.2006.05.002

Bukowski, W., Lauren, B., & Rubin, K. (Eds.). (2019). *Handbook of peer interactions, relationships, and groups* (2nd ed.). Guilford Press.

Bulik, C. M., Baucom, D. H., Kirby, J. S., & Pisetsky, E. (2011). Uniting couples (in the treatment of) anorexia nervosa (UCAN). *International Journal of Eating Disorders*, *44*(1), 19–28. https://doi.org/10.1002/eat.20790

Cachelin, F. M., Striegel-Moore, R. H., Elder, K. A., Pike, K. M., Wilfley, D. E., & Fairburn, C. G. (1999). Natural course of a community sample of women with binge ED. *International Journal of Eating Disorders*, *25*(1), 45–54. https://doi.org/10.1002/(SICI)1098-108X(199901)25:1<45::AID-EAT6>3.0.CO;2-3

Casey, B. J., & Caudle, K. (2013). The teenage brain: Self control. *Current directions in psychological science. A Journal of the American Psychological Society*, *22*(2), 82–87. https://doi.org/10.1177/0963721413480170

Casey, B. J., Jones, R. M., Levita, L., Libby, V., Pattwell, S. S., Ruberry, E. J., Soliman, F., & Somerville, L. H. (2010). The storm and stress of adolescence: Insights from human imaging and mouse genetics. *Developmental Psychobiology*, *52*(3), 225–235. https://doi.org/10.1002/dev.20447

Culbert, K. M., Burt, S. A., McGue, M., Iacono, W. G., & Klump, K. L. (2009). Puberty and the genetic diathesis of disordered eating attitudes and behaviors. *Journal of Abnormal Psychology (1965)*, *118*(4), 788–796. https://doi.org/10.1037/a0017207

Davies, H., Swan, N., Schmidt, U., & Tchanturia, K. (2012). An experimental investigation of verbal expression of emotion in anorexia and bulimia nervosa. *European EDs Review*, *20*(6), 476–483. https://doi.org/10.1002/erv.1157

Dimitropoulos, G., Landers, A. L., Freeman, V., Novick, J., Garber, A., & Le Grange, D. (2018). Open trial of family-based treatment of anorexia nervosa for transition age youth. *Journal of the Canadian Academy of Child and Adolescent Psychiatry*, *27*(1), 50–61. https://pmc-ncbi-nlm-nih-gov.ezproxy.lib.ucalgary.ca/articles/PMC5777691/

Duvvuri, V., Bailer, U., & Kaye, W. (2009). *Altered serotonin function in anorexia and bulimia nervosa*. Elsevier Academic Press.

Erikson, E. (1950). *Childhood and society*. WW Norton and Company.

Erikson, E. (1968). *Identity: Youth and crisis*. Norton.

Ferguson, C. P., La Via, M. C., Crossan, P. J., & Kaye, W. H. (1999). Are serotonin selective reuptake inhibitors effective in underweight anorexia nervosa? *International Journal of Eating Disorders*, *25*(1), 11–17. https://doi.org/10.1002/(SICI)1098-108X(199901)25:1<11::AID-EAT2>3.0.CO;2-U

Fonville, L., Lao-Kaim, N. P., Giampietro, V., Van den Eynde, F., Davies, H., Lounes, N., Andrew, C., Dalton, J., Simmons, A., Williams, S. C. R., Baron-Cohen, S., & Tchanturia, K. (2013). Evaluation of enhanced attention to local detail in anorexia nervosa using the embedded figures test; an fMRI Study. *PloS One*, *8*(5), 1–7. https://doi.org/10.1371/journal.pone.0063964

Golden, N. H., Katzman, D. K., Kreipe, R. E., Stevens, S. L., Sawyer, S. M., Rees, J., Nicholls, D., & Rome, E. S. (2003). EDs in adolescents: Position paper of the Society for adolescent medicine. *Journal of Adolescent Health*, *33*(6), 1–8 https://doi.org/10.1016/s1054-139x(03)00326-4

Golden, N. H., Lanzkowsky, L., Schebendach, J., Palestro, C. J., Jacobson, M. S., & Shenker, I. R. (2002). The effect of estrogen-progestin treatment on bone mineral density in anorexia nervosa. *Journal of Pediatric & Adolescent Gynecology*, *15*(3), 135–143. https://doi.org/10.1016/S1083-3188(02)00145-6

Harrison, A., Sullivan, S., Tchanturia, K., & Treasure, J. (2010). Emotional functioning in EDs: Attentional bias, emotion recognition and emotion regulation. *Psychological Medicine*, *40*(11), 1887–1897. https://doi.org/10.1017/S0033291710000036

Holmbeck, G., Colder, C., Shapera, W., Westhoven, V., Keneally, L., & Updegrove, A. (2000). Working with adolescents: Guides from developmental psychology. In P. Kendall (Ed.), *Child and Adolescent Therapy*. Guilford.

Horesh, N., Apter, A., J, I., Danziger, Y., Miculincer, M., Stein, D., Lepkifker, E., & Minouni, M. (1996). Abnormal psychosocial situations and EDs in adolescence. *Journal of the American Academy of Child and Adolescent Psychiatry*, *35*(7), 921–927. https://doi.org/10.1097/00004583-199607000-00019

Kaye, W. H., Frank, G. K., Bailer, U. F., Henry, S. E., Meltzer, C. C., Price, J. C., Mathis, C. A., & Wagner, A. (2005). Serotonin alterations in anorexia and bulimia nervosa: New insights from imaging studies. *Physiology & Behavior*, *85*(1), 73–81. https://doi.org/10.1016/j.physbeh.2005.04.013

Keel, P. K., Mitchell, J. E., Miller, K. B., Davis, T. L., & Crow, S. J. (2000). Social adjustment over 10 years following diagnosis with bulimia nervosa. *International Journal of Eating Disorders*, *27*(1), 21–28. https://doi.org/10.1002/(SICI)1098-108X(200001)27:1<21::AID-EAT2>3.0.CO;2-F

Klump, K. L., Keel, P. K., Sisk, C., & Burt, S. A. (2010). Preliminary evidence that estradiol moderates genetic influences on disordered eating attitudes and behaviors during puberty. *Psychological Medicine*, *40*(10), 1745–1753. https://doi.org/10.1017/S0033291709992236

Klump, K. L., Perkins, P., Burt, S. A., McGue, M., & Iacona, W. (2007). Puberty moderates genetic influences on disordered eating. *Psychological Medicine*, *37*(5), 627–634. https://doi.org/10.1017/S0033291707000189

Koepke, S., & Denissen, J. J. A. (2012). Dynamics of identity development and separation–individuation in parent–child relationships during adolescence and emerging adulthood – A conceptual integration. *Developmental Review*, *32*(1), 67–88. https://doi.org/10.1016/j.dr.2012.01.001

Lang, K., Lloyd, S., Khondoker, M., Simic, M., Treasure, J., & Tchanturia, K. (2015). Do children and adolescents with anorexia nervosa display an inefficient cognitive processing style? *PloS One*, *10*(7), 1–13. https://doi.org/10.1371/journal.pone.0131724

Lee, K., Bull, R., & Ho, R. M. H. (2013). Developmental changes in executive functioning. *Child Development*, *84*(6), 1933–1953. https://doi.org/10.1111/cdev.12096

Lock, J. (2020). *Adolescent-focused therapy for anorexia nervosa: A developmental approach*. Guilford.

Lock, J., Fitzpatrick, K. K., Agras, W. S., Weinbach, N., & Jo, B. (2018). Feasibility study combining art therapy or cognitive remediation therapy with family-based treatment for adolescent anorexia nervosa. *European EDs Review*, *26*(1), 62–68. https://doi.org/10.1002/erv.2571

McCabe, M., Ricciardelli, L., & Finemore, J. (2001). The role of puberty, media and popularity with peers on strategies to increase weight, decrease weight and increase muscle tone among adolescent boys and girls: Special eating science. *Journal of*

Psychosomatic Research, 52(3), 145–153. https://doi-org.ezproxy.lib.ucalgary.ca/10.1016/S0022-3999(01)00272–0

Meyer, H. C., & Lee, F. S. (2019). Translating developmental neuroscience to understand risk for psychiatric disorders. *American Journal of Psychiatry, 176*(3), 179–185. https://doi.org/10.1176/appi.ajp.2019.19010091

Montemayor, R. (2018). *Sexuality in adolescence and emerging adulthood.* Gilford Press.

Nelson, E., Leibenluft, E., McClure, E., & Pine, D. (2005). The social re-orientation of adolescence: A neuroscience perspective on the process and its relation to psychopathology. *Psychological Medicine, 35*, 163–174. https://doi.org/10.1017/s0033291704003915

Oldershaw, A., Hambrook, D., Tchanturia, K., Treasure, J., & Schmidt, U. (2010). Emotional theory of mind and emotional awareness in recovered anorexia nervosa patients. *Psychosomatic Medicine, 72*(1), 73–79. https://doi.org/10.1097/PSY.0b013e3181c6c7ca

Plaisme, M., Robertson-James, C., Mejia, L., Nunez, A., Wolf, J., & Reels, S. (2020). Social media and teens: A needs assessment exploring the potential role of socila media in promoting health. *Social Media + Society, Jan-March, 6*(1), 1–11. https://doi.org/10.1177/2056305119886025.

Prinstein, M., Youngstrom, E., Mash, E., & Barkley, R. (2019). *Treatment of disorders in childhood and adolescence.* New York: Guilford Press.

Roberts, M., Tchanturia, K., Stahl, D., Southgate, L., & Treasure, J. (2007). A systematic review and meta-analysis of set-shifting ability in EDs. *Psychological Medicine, 37*(8), 1075–1084. https://doi.org/10.1017/S0033291707009877

Rubinow, D. R., Schmidt, P. J., & Roca, C. A. (1998). Estrogen–serotonin interactions: Implications for affective regulation. *Biological Psychiatry (1969), 44*(9), 839–850. https://doi.org/10.1016/S0006-3223(98)00162-0

Russell, T. A., Schmidt, U., Doherty, L., Young, V., & Tchanturia, K. (2009). Aspects of social cognition in anorexia nervosa: Affective and cognitive theory of mind. *Psychiatry Research, 168*(3), 181–185. https://doi.org/10.1016/j.psychres.2008.10.028

Shirtcliff, E. A., Dahl, R. E., & Pollak, S. D. (2009). Pubertal development: Correspondence between hormonal and physical development. *Child Development, 80*(2), 327–337. https://doi.org/10.1111/j.1467-8624.2009.01263.x

Smink, F. R. E., van Hoeken, D., Oldehinkel, A. J., & Hoek, H. W. (2014). Prevalence and severity of DSM-5 EDs in a community cohort of adolescents. *International Journal of Eating Disorders, 47*(6), 610–619. https://doi.org/10.1002/eat.22316

Stevens, M. C., Skudlarski, P., Pearlson, G. D., & Calhoun, V. D. (2009). Age-related cognitive gains are mediated by the effects of white matter development on brain network integration. *NeuroImage (Orlando, Fla.), 48*(4), 738–746. https://doi.org/10.1016/j.neuroimage.2009.06.065

Stierlin, H. (1974). *Separating parents and adolescents.* The New York Times Book Company.

Tchanturia, K., Davies, H., Roberts, M., Harrison, A., Nakazato, M., Schmidt, U., Treasure, J., & Morris, R. (2012). Poor cognitive flexibility in EDs: Examining the evidence using the wisconsin card sorting task. *PloS One, 7*(1), 1–5. https://doi.org/10.1371/journal.pone.0028331

Tchanturia, K., Doris, E., & Fleming, C. (2014). Effectiveness of cognitive remediation and emotion skills training (crest) for anorexia nervosa in group format: A naturalistic pilot study. *European EDs Review, 22*(3), 200–205. https://doi.org/10.1002/erv.2287

Welch, S. L., & Fairburn, C. G. (1996). Childhood sexual and physical abuse as risk factors for the development of bulimia nervosa: A community-based case control study. *Child Abuse & Neglect, 20*(7), 633–642. https://doi.org/10.1016/0145-2134(96)00051-8

Wildes, J. E., Emery, R. E., & Simons, A. D. (2001). The roles of ethnicity and culture in the development of eating disturbance and body dissatisfaction: A meta-analytic review. *Clinical Psychology Review*, *21*(4), 521–551. https://doi.org/10.1016/S0272-7358(99)00071–9

Woodside, D. B., Bulik, C. M., Halmi, K. A., Fichter, M. M., Kaplan, A., Berrettini, W. H., Strober, M., Treasure, J., Lilenfeld, L., Klump, K., & Kaye, W. H. (2002). Personality, perfectionism, and attitudes toward eating in parents of individuals with EDs. *International Journal of Eating Disorders*, *31*(3), 290–299. https://doi.org/10.1002/eat.10032

Chapter 4

Setting Up Treatment for FBT-TAY

In this chapter, we describe the pre-treatment evaluation processes utilized by FBT therapists to assess individuals and their family members prior to initiating (FBT-TAY). Although FBT-TAY therapists are not required to provide a comprehensive pre-evaluation to begin this treatment, this chapter suggests an approach that may be employed to facilitate an assessment with older adolescents, young people, and their family members considering outpatient FBT-TAY over a higher level of care such as day treatment or partial hospitalization. In the first part of the chapter, we describe what assessment measures may be employed and the types of areas targeted by those with nutritional, medical, and psychological/psychiatric expertise during the evaluation process. An interdisciplinary approach is highly recommended to ensure that the complex psychological and physical challenges that accompany AN are assessed and treated not only at the pre-evaluation stage but also throughout the phases of FBT-TAY which will be described in Chapters 5–9.

The evaluation process described in this chapter consists of various components that may occur in a single session or over several meetings during a short period of time (e.g., 2–3 weeks).

This decision may depend on whether the interdisciplinary team is co-located in the same service setting or distributed across different agencies and organizations. It is necessary for the young person (and their parents/caregivers if appropriate) to provide consent for sharing medical, nutritional, and psychological reports with the FBT-TAY therapists. The young person's confidentiality about issues outside of the ED must be kept in strict confidence and only shared with others with their written and informed consent. FBT-TAY therapists like all other professionals must be aware and adhered to confidentiality policies and work within their scope of practice as outlined by their professional college and association.

DOI: 10.4324/9781003463351-5

Key Considerations for the Initial Intake Session with the Young Person with AN

There are varying pathways that a young person may undertake before they come to the attention of a physician, an ED specialist, or mental health professional. During the initial intake or evaluation session with the FBT-TAY therapist, a number of areas should be explored to establish a relationship with the young person and to also understand their personal journey with AN. FBT-TAY therapists may consider exploring with whom the young person has shared their AN with, what pivotal points led to the young person disclosing that they have an ED, and their previous treatment history (if any at all). As described in previous chapters, many young people may have been receiving or received care from a specialized adolescent ED or mental health clinic. Some of these young people may have been brought to care by their family members and therefore did not explicitly or independently ask for assistance from professionals and/or supportive adults for their AN. Hence, special attention must be paid to building a therapeutic alliance through transparency and trust building especially with young people who now have agency to seek or decline support for their ED. It is important that FBT-TAY therapists focus on process and procedural issues related to FBT-TAY with the young person which will help reduce ambiguity and uncertainty about treatment (this will be illustrated in Chapters 5–8). When working with young people with AN, the evaluation process and FBT-TAY phases in general should be delivered flexibly and compassionately with attention to the relationship. Every interaction with the young person is an opportunity to contemplate how AN jeopardizes and diminishes their agency and autonomy and the importance of supportive adults such as their parents/caregivers to help them with recovery.

Age of Entry into ED Treatment and for FBT-TAY

As it is often the case that a young person is brought to a paediatric ED program by their parents/caregivers, FBT-TAY therapists should keep in mind that age at entry point is an important indication of when to use the FBT-TAY model. Depending on the age guidelines of the clinical setting, a young person will likely experience a transition from paediatric care to adult care at some point in their developmental trajectory. This age range for transitioning to adult care settings differs across countries, regions, and service areas. When considering engagement, it is important to consider how families are supported in the adult model or adult systems of care. In programs where there are both paediatric and adult treatment streams available, it is necessary that the work that begins in a paediatric ED program (EDP) continues in an adult program to avoid treatment delays and provide continuous and seamless care.

Supporting the Transition to the Adult System

Alongside utilizing FBT-TAY, other steps are needed to support such a transition to the adult system. This includes proactively developing a transition plan early on in treatment and beginning preparations for ongoing sessions after the move to adult services. For example, an evidence-based framework for ED treatment transition from paediatric mental health services to adult mental health services, TRIPS (Ragnhildstveit et al., 2024), has outlined that early discussion about transitions, assessing transition readiness of both patients and families, and planned preparations for transfer of care are essential for young people with EDs to ensure continuity of treatment and facilitation of understanding, trust, and synergy among all parties. Building these transition strategies into practice with young people is essential to ensuring treatment and recovery continuity as they emerge into adulthood and adult health services.

Similarly, there are current guidelines for therapists and other providers working with young people with EDs transitioning from paediatric to the continuum of adult services. Most recently, Dimitropoulos and colleagues (2025) published evidence-informed clinical practice guidelines for young people with EDs and other mental health conditions transitioning from paediatric to adult care using a scoping review and consensus-building methodology with a panel of researchers, service providers, individuals with lived experience, and health system decision-makers. Specific recommendations from the published guidelines include integrated and collaborative care in transition interventions and/or initiatives (i.e., integrating management of concurrent medical and mental health concerns, including young people in the development and implementation of transition interventions); using validated measurement tools during the transition such as the Transition Readiness Assessment Questionnaire (TRAQ) to assess for transition readiness; understanding the long-term outcomes of young people with EDs and other mental health conditions after the transition process; and measuring factors impacting the transition process (e.g., acceptance, transfer, discharge rates) to better understand how to improve transitions for young people with EDs and other mental health conditions to adult care. These guidelines underscore the need for valid, effective, and sustainable transition measurements, interventions, and outcomes, ultimately to bolster continuity of care during the transition process for all young people with EDs.

Conversely, there are many young people who have never pursued any interventions for their AN prior to meeting with FBT-TAY therapists. Many young people seek treatment for a comorbid psychiatric diagnosis rather than AN symptoms, in non-specialized mental health clinics. In such cases, young people may express reluctance to disclose to anyone that they have AN but experience less stigma seeking mental health support for other mental health disorders or physical ailments or unexplained and often ambiguous physical symptoms. Due to the ego-syntonic nature of AN (Gregersten et al., 2017), many young people may deny or minimize their symptoms and/or fear they are not "sick enough" to need assistance for AN. In such instances, these young people may have seen many professionals and received a range of assessments for other mental health conditions and medical procedures to rule out other physical ailments. Of course, it is also possible that young people may have physical or psychiatric co-morbidities alongside their AN, which must be considered when evaluating the application of FBT-TAY. Finally, some young people may have never pursued any previous professional support for physical and mental health issues. The disclosure of AN may be recent and shared with a trusted adult in an educational system, like a guidance counsellor or sports coach, or with a family member or a close peer. For young people, coming forward to family or other trusted individuals for assistance for AN may be more difficult due to several factors. In Western societies, there is significant pressure placed on most young people to be self-reliant and solely responsible for their mental wellness and recovery from ill health. Young people who developed AN as an adolescent may not want to disclose this to their families and other adults, peers, and professionals. They may be afraid that others will be disappointed in them that they did not recover on their own or sustain recovery if they relapsed. Others fear that they will be a burden to the people in their lives, especially if others previously participated in receiving treatment with them in paediatric ED programs. For young people sharing this illness for the first time, there may be concerns that others will be upset with them for not saying something sooner or for allowing the illness to become more entrenched. Potterton et al.'s (2020) qualitative study found that young adult participants described feeling embarrassed to be suffering with a perceived "adolescent or child" issue, and this often deterred them from reaching out for help due to shame and embarrassment. Young people are often fearful that if they say they have AN, others will not perceive them as "sick enough" and in need of treatment. These negative perceptions of help-seeking frequently hinder young people from disclosing their illness leading them to rely solely on themselves to disrupt problematic eating behaviours (Potterton et al., 2020). The evaluation process with the young person is a first step to understanding the development of AN in the context of a professional relationship. The evaluation offers an initial opportunity for the young person to share their struggles and unresolved issues that arose for them as they decided to ask for assistance.

Weight Stigma

Internalized and externalized weight stigma has also been shown to be a major contributing factor to the development of EDs in young people and may significantly influence their subsequent health-seeking behaviours. Weight stigma refers to the prejudice, discrimination, or stereotypes related to an individual's body weight or size (Salvia et al., 2023) and includes prevalent societal attitudes and beliefs about weight and individuals who exist in larger bodies (Alberga et al., 2016; Pearl, 2018; Rubino et al., 2020; Salvia et al., 2022). Evidence suggests that internalized weight stigma may lead to increased ED psychopathology, negative self-evaluation of one's body, and diminished quality of life (Ralph et al., 2022; Wagner et al., 2020). In addition, experiences of weight stigma and/or other traumatic events related to weight (e.g., weight-based teasing, bullying, and exclusion on the basis of weight) may contribute to the development of EDs and/or increase disordered eating in individuals with pre-existing EDs (Almeida et al., 2011; Durso et al., 2012; Schvey et al., 2013). Weight stigma is largely misunderstood and not always acknowledged by the broader health and medical community, which can lead to the mis/underdiagnosis and treatment of EDs, especially for those who live in larger bodies (Ralph et al., 2022).

Weight stigma has also been shown to influence the health seeking behaviours and quality of care for young people. Research consistently demonstrates that when healthcare providers hold negative beliefs and attitudes towards higher-weight individuals, the quality of care they receive is subsequently diminished, leading to avoidance in help-seeking, reduced collaboration and communication with their providers, and, at times, disengagement from services (Puhl & Suh, 2015; Puhl et al., 2020). In addition, young people may fear discussing concerns related to their weight or eating with their treatment team if they have previously experienced weight-based stigmatization or discrimination (e.g., Ralph et al., 2022); this, compounded with research which suggests that negative familial beliefs and attitudes surrounding weight also contribute to body dissatisfaction and subsequent disordered eating in young people (e.g., White et al., 2023), makes it imperative for therapists to consider the influence of internalized and externalized weight stigma and societal beliefs towards weight and eating on the onset of EDs for young people in treatment. Weight stigma adds to the treatment-seeking ambivalence many young people with AN struggle to overcome. While those with AN are generally underweight, they perceive themselves as overweight and fat and thus are anxious about weight stigma in much the same way as a young person who is at a higher weight.

Relatedly, therapists also experience barriers to FBT implementation relating to weight stigma (Gioia et al., 2025). In the context of FBT, weight stigma may influence weight restoration as a treatment target for higher-weight individuals with AN or those who have experienced weight-based discrimination in past (Ralph et al., 2022). FBT therapists also report feeling anxious disclosing their patient's weight during regular weigh-ins if they feel it may cause their patient distress or heightened dysregulation due to weight stigma (Gioia et al., 2025; Waller & Turner, 2016). As such, therapists must be uniquely attuned to the influence of weight stigma on treatment engagement and subsequent treatment targets for young people in FBT-TAY. It is generally recommended that FBT-TAY therapists assess for past experiences of trauma related to weight, weight-based discrimination, and weight stigma and approach these conversations with young people with a great deal of respect and care. Therapists must also examine their own internalized weight stigma (Ralph et al., 2022) and reflect whether this may impact their delivery of FBT-TAY.

Evaluation and Assessment Process: Interview with the Young Person

An FBT-TAY therapist must approach the young person with compassion, kindness, and curiosity in this initial meeting and begin with broad, open-ended questions that are not leading, presumptuous, or directive of the young person. The interview should begin in a non-threatening manner by asking the young person to share a bit about themselves, their social activities and engagement in employment or education, as well as their involvement with peers and family.

The interviewer can then probe what brought the young person to seek support "right now." The exploration of the onset of the illness and the timeline for disclosing, seeking, and receiving care are critical discussions that help further build trust and rapport with the young person.

While taking a history of the emergence of disordered eating, explore what the young person believes may have contributed to AN and what factors continue to maintain the problematic eating behaviours. The FBT-TAY therapist may explore how the young person feels about attending an assessment/evaluation session that will also involve their parents/caregivers. For many young people, they may be approaching the session with trepidation and shame. Young people report that they fear disappointing others in their lives, including their parents/caregivers, with whom they do not want to create unnecessary worry or problems. It is helpful to reassure the young person that they are not to blame, nor responsible for the illness and that ED behaviours, and that recovery is difficult without assistance from others in their environment, including parents/caregivers, siblings, and peers. It is also important to acknowledge that the young person may continue to hold ambivalent feelings about engaging others in their lives in their treatment and that this is a natural and common response. If internalized or externalized weight stigma prevails within the young person or the family system, the FBT-TAY therapist should provide psychoeducation information on the importance of weight-neutral conversations related to bodies and eating, as well as promoting body image acceptance and focusing on health in recovery (e.g., see Ralph et al., 2022).

Questions to Consider During the Evaluation and Assessment Process

During the pre-evaluation session, the FBT-TAY therapist may consider asking the following broad questions: What does the young person believe contributed to the AN? What did they first notice about themselves that made them think their relationship with food was problematic?

What worried them the most/least about their relationship to their bodies and how they assessed their value as a human being? What type of feedback did they receive from others about their weight, shape, and size? How did this make them feel about themselves? Then, using the assessment to probe specific questions about eating patterns such the quantity, quality, and variety of food eaten, the therapist may ask the following questions. How often do they eat during the day? When do they eat? What do they eat? When are they less likely to eat? Explore which professionals know about the AN or other mental health and physical health conditions. What was their experience seeking and accessing care for their ED? Were any assessments conducted? What type of feedback did they receive about their illness from others, including family doctors, paediatricians, school personnel (e.g., guidance counsellors and school psychologist and social workers), and dietitians or nutritionists? Explore historical and current changes in eating, weight, and whether any triggers or life circumstances or emotional experiences make eating better or worse for them. Examine the methods used to restrict eating or rid themselves of food consumed. Have they involved others in their care? How did they involve others in their care? What was that like for them? Ask about restrictive eating, level of physical activity, and purging behaviours from laxative use to diuretics. What foods do they exclude?

FBT-TAY therapists should communicate genuine concern while also relaying their confidence that the young person has the capacity to make change to their AN with the help of their parents/caregivers. The FBT-TAY therapist needs to strike a balance between providing psychoeducational information and eliciting input from the young person on how to find their voice through the fog of the illness to make non-AN-based decisions about how to regain their life, dignity, and integrity (Zaitsoff et al., 2015). Developmental sensitivity, treatment framing, and establishing shared goals are each important considerations when engaging with the young person at the start of treatment and developing a therapeutic alliance (McCormick et al., 2023). Acknowledging the young person's autonomy and identity and positioning them as collaborators in their treatment are important to remain sensitive to their developmental stage. Furthermore, emphasizing and framing the parent/caregiver renourishment role as a temporary supportive role can serve as a motivator to engage the young person in treatment. Lastly, aligning with the young person and the caregiver on shared treatment goals (e.g., attending university or returning to sports) and what recovery means for them are important reflections to promote agency early in treatment. Given that young people with AN may have received care in community-based organizations and/or adult treatment settings, it may be even more important to develop and solidify the therapeutic alliance with the young person whose sense of agency and self-determination are experienced as salient and under threat for involving their families and other supportive adults. In addition to therapeutic alliance, it is important to evaluate how the young person's current living situation, level of functioning, and independence will contribute to decisions about whether caregiver involvement is likely feasible and acceptable in FBT-TAY.

Introducing the Involvement of Family and Other Supports

The FBT-TAY therapist directly asks the young person who they would like to invite for a family interview. To facilitate this discussion, the therapist asks questions about who the young person identifies as being in their immediate supportive network. The interviewer may explore broadly about parents/caregivers, siblings, friends, and/or partners. They may further explore with the young person if they would like to invite their siblings (if they have any). Given the age of the young person, it is important that they decide whether they want to include their siblings. Parent-focused family therapy (PFT) is a form of delivery of FBT that includes only parents and has been shown to be as effective as whole family therapy delivered FBT in several trials and potentially more helpful for families with high levels of criticism (Eisler et al., 2000; Le Grange et al., 1992, 2016). Although research suggests that sibling involvement may not be associated with improved outcomes (e.g., weight or eating outcomes), their supportive role should not be underestimated and if desired by the young person, siblings should be encouraged to attend FBT-TAY. If the young person has a close friend and/or partner, it is also appropriate to involve them in the assessment if the young person believes these supportive individuals may have insights into their illness while also playing a role in supporting their recovery. Young people often have close relationships with others in their lives who may know more about them and their struggles with AN than their family of origin. It is important to recognize that the young person has the right to include people in their sphere of support in FBT-TAY. The FBT-TAY therapist must balance whether the supportive members in the young person's life will play a primary or secondary role in supporting with renourishment especially in Phase 1.

In collaboration with the young person, the FBT-TAY therapist will determine whom to invite to a family/caregiver evaluation. To help with this decision-making process about who should attend the pre-assessment meeting, it is important to prioritize the involvement of adults like parents/caregivers, grandparents, or extended family members who have had a long-standing relationship with the young person and the moral, legal, and ethical responsibility to provide care. Once a decision is made about who will be attending the family evaluation session, explore if the young person would like to be present during the interview with their parents/caregivers/supportive people. If they prefer not to be present, ask them if they want to join at the end of the family interview to receive a summary of what was discussed from their parents/caregivers. The therapist should encourage the young person to identify the pros and cons of a meeting with or without their family while emphasizing that this decision is entirely for them to make. Regardless of whether the young person elects to attend the session with or without their parents/caregivers or other important members of their support group, explore what the young person imagines their loved ones might say about them and the presenting concerns about the AN. Here are a few questions to facilitate this discussion: What do they think their parents/others know or do not know about the AN? Might they share the same concerns or different views about the AN and the need for treatment? Are they closer to one parent/caregiver or the other? Does one parent/caregiver have more information than the other about the AN? By probing about the young person's perceptions of what others think of the AN, the FBT-TAY therapist may learn about any major concerns and fears regarding the involvement of family members in a meaningful way in their treatment.

Evaluation Session with the Family Members and/or Young Person

In the session with the family members, the FBT-TAY therapist introduces the purpose of the evaluation, which is to better understand everyone's level of knowledge and awareness of AN and their potential role in supporting the young person with recovery. The FBT therapist begins the evaluation with an openness to understand the unique perspective of each parent/caregiver regarding their child's difficulties with food and weight. The FBT-TAY therapist employs some of the following questions to facilitate this discussion: What supports/treatments have they accessed for themselves, the young person, and the family as a whole? What worked well or not well in supporting their adult child with the ED? What do they believe will be the best way to support the young person with treatment and recovery? What do they view as their strengths as parents/caregivers that convince them that they can support their adult child with recovery? As noted above, depending on the young person's preference, they may be invited to join at the end of the session with the parents/caregivers to receive an update directly from their family about what was discussed. Alternatively, the young person and the family may be invited for another session to share their learnings from the evaluations and shared efforts to work collaboratively in addressing the AN.

In the next section of this chapter, we introduce the diagnostic criteria for AN, the measures that may employ with youth people, and the nutritional and medical areas that may be investigated by experts with the necessary knowledge and training in the psychological, medical, and nutritional impact of this illness on individuals.

Overview of AN Diagnosis Criteria

According to the Diagnostic Statistical Manual (5th Edition) (American Psychiatric Association, 2013), a determination of AN is achieved if the following criteria are met:

- Obtaining a body weight that is low because of restrictive eating and the absence of any eating.
- Persistent drive to achieve a weight that is lower than their actual weight.
- Major concerns with one's body and physical appearance.
- Inaccurately viewing one's body and fearing weight gain.

AN Weight Criteria

Whenever possible, therapists are encouraged to define low weight based on growth charts, z-scores, and per cent median Body Mass Index. In addition to these metrics, therapists are encouraged to use their expertise and clinical judgement when considering what is deemed low weight for a young person. It is critical that therapists interpret weight criteria through the lens of an age-appropriate framework (APA, 2013; Gray et al., 2015) and individualized weight targets. Utilizing historical growth records, even for individuals that have reached adult height/weight, is highly recommended.

Self-Report and Therapist Rated Instruments

Self-report and therapist-rated instruments are useful tools for practice and research, providing a toolbox to assess a range of physical and psychological symptoms and behaviours (Schaefer et al., 2021). These tools are especially useful in areas where healthcare professionals may lack experience with EDs and are not prepared to diagnose and manage them (Ivancic et al., 2021). The most common standardized ED measurements by therapists in primary care are the ED Examination Questionnaire (EDE-Q), the Eating Attitudes Test (EAT-26), and the SCOFF (CORC, n.d.; Eating Attitudes Test (EAT-26). All of these measures are self-report tools that aim to assess the severity of one's behaviours associated with eating (CORC, n.d.; Eating Attitudes Test (EAT-26). There are also several standardized tools used to assess key family variables in the context of FBT, including (but not limited to) parental self-efficacy with the Parents Versus Anorexia Scale (PVA) and accommodation and enabling behaviours in Accommodation and Enabling Scale for EDs – Revised (AESED-R).

Common Self-Report Questionnaires

The EDE-Q was adapted from the EDE semi-structured interview and can now be used as a self-report questionnaire ranking 28 items on a 7-point scale

(CORC, n.d.; Nagata et al., 2020). It contains four subscales: restraint, eating concern, shape concern, and weight concern. These subscales are combined to assess the frequency, range, and severity of behaviours that can be associated with the diagnosis of an ED in the last 28 days (CORC, n.d.; Nagata et al., 2020).

While there are adaptations of this tool, such as the Youth EDE-Q (Y-EDE-Q) and the EDE-Adolescent (EDE-Q), the original EDE-Q is the best suited for transitional aged youth and emerging adults (CORC, n.d.). The EAT-26 is a shortened screening tool that allows for early identification of an ED ultimately leading to earlier treatment (Eating Attitudes Test (EAT-26), n.d.; Papini et al., 2022). Using a Likert-like scale, ranging from one (often) to three (always), it records the self-reported symptoms and concern characteristics of an ED using a three-factor structure: dieting, bulimia and food preoccupation, and oral control (Eating Attitudes Test (EAT-26), n.d.; Mincey & Michelle Hunnicutt Hollenbaugh, 2022; Papini et al., 2022). It has been used widely with emerging adults (Okamoto et al., 2018; Sanlier et al., 2017; Wider et al., 2023).

Lastly, the SCOFF is a 5-item, yes-or-no questionnaire designed to raise awareness that an ED may be present (Bazzazian et al., 2022; Coop et al., 2024). Although the SCOFF was created to target adult populations, it has been validated widely in various other age groups including children, adolescents, and young adults (Bean, 2020; Gellere & Beitane, 2024; Shaikh & Kayani, 2014). While none of these measurements result in a proper diagnosis, they may assist with further clinical assessments (CORC, n.d.; Eating Attitudes Test (EAT-26).

Common Family Questionnaires

The PVA (Rhodes et al., 2005) is a 7-item self-report questionnaire which assesses parental/caregiver self-efficacy in FBT overtime. This measure specifically assesses parents' and caregivers' perceived ability to promote recovery in their child throughout the course of treatment. Each question is rated on a four-point Likert-type scale ("Strongly Disagree" to "Strongly Agree"), with higher scores indicating greater parental/caregiver self-efficacy to bring about recovery in their child. The questionnaire has been validated in both paediatric and adult populations (Gorrell et al., 2024; Rhodes et al., 2005). More recently, baseline parental PVA scores were important moderators of adaptive treatment of FBT for those who did not respond early and therefore had a significantly poorer chance of recovery (Lock et al., 2024).

The AESED-R is a 33-item self-report questionnaire assessing the degree of accommodation and enabling behaviours that parents/caregivers of a young person with an ED engage in. This questionnaire has been adapted from the AESED (Sepulveda et al., 2009), assessing the frequency of engagement in accommodation and enabling behaviours in the past one month. The measure has been validated primarily in parents/caregivers but has also included other relatives including siblings, spouses, and peers (Sepulveda et al., 2009).

Nutrition and Medical Team Evaluation

It is important to note that the evaluations described in this section are not typically conducted by the FBT-TAY therapists. Instead, the FBT-TAY therapists should carefully work with others with expertise to assess the young person's medical and nutritional status. The FBT-TAY therapist and interdisciplinary team should provide the young person with psychoeducation material about AN while they are conducting nutritional and medical assessments which may enhance motivation for recovery, such as discussing risk of bone fractures which may impact sports previously enjoyed.

- Both can also help determine % of expected body weight, % weight loss, and rapidity of weight loss.
- Must have medical treatment and monitoring to ensure medical stability and safety to participate in outpatient treatment like FBT-TAY
- Check for malnutrition and rule out other reasons for weight loss and malnutrition.

As young people often straddle paediatric and adult healthcare systems, assessments should be respectful of their autonomy and identity development, while still involving appropriate support (e.g., caregivers, partners). Additionally, young people may be experiencing delays in their growth, puberty, or neurocognitive development which must be factored into their nutritional assessment and treatment goals. Possible changes to their metabolic and hormonal balances must be assessed through history, physical exam, bloodwork, etc., as these are highly impacted by chronic malnutrition (e.g., hypothalamic amenorrhea, bradycardia, and acute kidney injury) (Tanir et al., 2020; Mattar et al., 2011). Cardiac instability is often a major reason for young people with AN being admitted to higher-level care such as an inpatient setting or acute care. Furthermore, many young people with AN may appear to be in a higher weight but have severe malnutrition and coinciding health complications (Potterton et al., 2020). If secondary amenorrhea is present in females for more than six months, it is recommended to prioritize tools such as DXA (dual x-ray absorptiometry) scans, which assess fat-free mass, bone mineral density, and fat mass distribution, and BIA (bioelectrical impedance analysis), which monitors hydration and lean mass, that may be helpful in providing a comprehensive view of young person's physical health (Tanir et al., 2020; Mattar et al., 2011). Lastly, refeeding syndrome is a known complication of treating AN (Skowrońska et al., 2019) which is the result of drastic shifts in renourishment and can be fatal. An excerpt from the Understanding and Assessing for Refeeding Syndrome in Severe EDs by Phillip Maehler, MD, reports that

> when the body is starved or severely malnourished, the heart muscle may atrophy causing diminished cardiac output, and the body begins to break

> down its own tissues – including fats and muscle – in an attempt to create the energy needed to maintain basic bodily functions. These changes can affect the body's major electrolytes, including phosphorus, potassium and magnesium. During refeeding, the body secretes insulin, and the kidneys retain salt and water. This weight gain and visible changes in body size associated with severe water retention can be particularly distressing for patients that fear weight gain or suffer from body image concerns and/or body dysmorphia. Edema will generally resolve with continued management of refeeding.
>
> (Acute Center for EDs and Sever Malnutrition, 2021, p. 1)

It is important for initial assessments to include lab work to identify electrolyte imbalances (e.g., phosphate, potassium, magnesium) and to monitor for other possible medical complications (Tanir et al., 2020; Mattar et al., 2011).

In addition to the nutrition evaluation scope, initial nutrition assessment should focus on the most pertinent factors to commence refeeding and establish current eating patterns (Royal College of Psychiatrists, 2005), including:

- recent changes in eating habits
- rate of weight loss
- binge eating behaviours
- vomiting or laxative misuse
- gastrointestinal function (including gastroesophageal reflux, constipation, early satiety, and post-prandial fullness)
- hydration habits
- restrictions on the variety of acceptable foods
- other conditions that may require dietary management (such as diabetes)
- presence of conditions that may affect nutritional requirements (such as infection or growth)
- use of appetite suppressants

The multi-disciplinary team should obtain consent from the young person for the medical and nutritional assessments prior to them being shared with the other team members including the FBT-TAY.

An important caveat when working with emerging adults with AN is that they are likely to present with persistent or emerging comorbid mental health issues. In contrast to adolescents with a short duration of illness, a wholly narrow focus on eating in Phase 1 (and 2) may not be appropriate if the young person and the parents/caregivers raise concerns about serious co-morbid diagnosis such as depression, mood disorders, OCD, and anxiety. If the family is concerned about co-morbid diagnoses, the therapist should respond to this concern by referring to an appropriate therapist who can further assess and treat when needed. It is not the responsibility of the therapist conducting FBT for young people to investigate the presence of other mental health issues. An appropriate referral and assistance with mental health issues may also help validate the feelings and experiences of a young person who has perceived others as overlooking other sources of pain and stress in their lives.

Once all the preliminary psychological, nutritional, and medical assessments have been completed, the FBT-TAY reviews the various treatment available to the young person and their caregivers. Options should be outlined based on their availability and suitability for the young person. Open discussion of the pros and cons of available options (e.g., Residential vs. FBTTAY vs. CBT-E) should be considered in this important clinical discussion. This is an opportunity to obtain concerns from the young person, the family, and the care team while ensuring there is time to consider available options and determine the best course of action that aligns with individual needs, finances, and treatment availability.

Setting up FBT-TAY Treatment

The FBT-TAY therapist typically contacts both the young person and their family by phone or the use of a virtual meeting either one week or a few days before the first FBT-TAY session. The purpose of this call is to communicate how urgent it is for all of them to attend the first meeting. The FBT-TAY therapist checks in with the young person and each parent/caregiver (if possible), reviewing the purpose of FBT-TAY, the seriousness of the ED, and the importance of involving family members to support the young person with this life-threatening and psychologically impairing mental illness. It is critical that the therapist acknowledges how hard it might be for the young person to involve their parents/caregivers because of fear of losing control and their autonomy being diminished. Conversely, the therapist should remind the parents/caregivers that they can play an important role in supporting their adult child because they deeply love them and have insider knowledge of what strategies have been previously helpful when they are under duress.

The FBT-TAY therapist firmly states everyone must be present at the first meeting so that the parents/caregivers and the young person can discuss how to work together to address the AN. The therapist provides psychoeducational information about AN highlighting the urgency of intervening to change the course of the illness and the dire consequences of inaction. The therapist conveys that all of this will be done using a strengths-based, compassionate, supportive, and non-judgmental therapeutic approach. The therapist further uses this telephone conversation to review the need for medical monitoring. This is also an opportunity to engage the young person in a conversation of who, in their supportive network, they would like to include in FBT-TAY and at what stages. The young person is directly asked about whether they would like to invite their sibling(s) to attend the first session or the family meal for instance. They are encouraged to think about the benefits and potential disadvantages of not involving others like their siblings in FBT-TAY if they reside (or not) with them. The therapist communicates that this is an exploratory discussion and that they will periodically be asked about who should be included in the different phases of the treatment.

In this final section, we provide some examples of what to discuss during the pre-session with the young person and/or the parents/caregivers.

Put Forward a Convincing Request to the Young Person

At the forefront of the therapist's conversations with the young person, consider different approaches or analogies that may be employed to persuade them to accept support and care from those who love them the most because recovering from an ED can be lonely and very overwhelming.

To alleviate some of the reluctance of the young person, the FBT-TAY therapists may share the following:

(1) The main purpose of this meeting is to discuss with the people who love them the most what they are experiencing with their mental health and AN.
(2) In this meeting, they will have the opportunity to have their voice heard about their fears and concerns about involving their family in treatment.
(3) Together, they will identify what the healthy side of them wants (or does not want) from other people in their life while pursuing treatment for the AN.

Put Forward a Convincing Request to the Parents/Caregivers

When speaking with supportive adults, it is paramount that the FBT-TAY therapist state that young people with AN require hope, encouragement, and a high level of hands-on support from meal to meal especially during the early stages of treatment. Regardless of the young person's age, parents/caregivers must be reminded that they attend all of the FBT-TAY sessions because they are part of the solution rather than bystanders of the recovery process or a source of the problem.

To prepare the parents/caregivers, the FBT-TAY therapist may consider relaying the following:

(1) Parents/caregivers will have the opportunity to learn how best to support a young person with a life-threating illness like AN in ways that feel empowering and non-stigmatizing to your child.
(2) In this session, they will collaboratively share their journey with the illness and what skills, knowledge, and experiences they bring that will help them work towards recovery from AN.
(3) As the most important people in the young person's life, they can remind them of their strengths, healthy side, and supportive network that will be elicited to facilitate recovery when the illness feels all-encompassing.

Conclusions

In this chapter, we summarize the pre-treatment evaluation processes utilized by therapists prior to starting FBT for young people who have developed AN in early or late adolescence or when AN has recurred. We have reviewed measures to use and sample questions to aid during assessment and discussed the role of the inter-disciplinary team. A multi-disciplinary evaluation is recommended that involves specialized professionals from paediatricians/adolescent medicine specialists to child or adult psychiatrist and others (e.g., psychologists, nurses, social workers) to facilitate the FBT-TAY therapist to start this developmentally tailored treatment that will be explained in the next few chapters.

Chapter Summary

Here are the key points of this chapter:

(1) The pre-treatment evaluation involves medical, nutritional, and psychological input to ensure safety and readiness for outpatient FBT-TAY, with therapists working together as an interdisciplinary team.
(2) The initial intake session focuses on hearing the young person's story, treatment history, and disclosure of AN, which helps to build a foundation for mutual trust and a generative therapeutic relationship.
(3) Therapists must validate the young person's ambivalence about involving family, while reframing parents/caregivers as supportive allies rather than sources of blame.
(4) FBT-TAY helps bridge the gap between paediatric and adult care by balancing collaboration with youth independence and ensuring continuity of treatment.
(5) Shame, weight stigma, and fears of not being "sick enough" often delay help-seeking, so therapists should use empathy and curiosity to reduce isolation and self-blame for the young person.
(6) Family members, siblings, partners, or other chosen support should be involved in FBT-TAY, with the young person guiding decisions about who participates in their recovery journey.
(7) Structured questionnaires (e.g., EDE-Q, EAT-26, SCOFF, PVA, and AESED-R) and medical/nutritional evaluations (labs, bone scans, and cardiac monitoring) are used to create a comprehensive clinical picture of the young person and their family.
(8) Prior to the first session, therapists emphasize urgency and compassion, encouraging full family participation while reassuring young people and parents/caregivers that recovery is possible when support is united.

References

Acute Center for EDs and Sever Malnutrition. (2021). *Understanding and assessing for refeeding syndrome in severe EDs*. https://www.acute.org/sites/default/files/file/2021-04/Refeeding_Syndrome_Severe_Eating_Disorders.pdf

Alberga, A. S., Russell-Mayhew, S., von Ranson, K. M., & McLaren, L. (2016). Weight bias: A call to action. *Journal of Eating Disorders*, *4*(1), 1–6. https://doi.org/10.1186/s40337-016-0112-4

Almeida, L., Savoy, S., & Boxer, P. (2011). The role of weight stigmatization in cumulative risk for binge eating. *Journal of Clinical Psychology*, *67*(3), 278–292. https://doi.org/10.1002/jclp.20749

American Psychiatric Association, DSM-5 Task Force. (2013). *Diagnostic and statistical manual of mental disorders: DSM-5™* (5th ed.). American Psychiatric Publishing, Inc.

Bazzazian, S., Ozgoli, G., Kariman, N., Nasiri, M., Mokhtaryan-Gilani, T., & Hajiesmaello, M. (2022). The translation and psychometric assessment of the SCOFF ED screening questionnaire: The Persian version. *Journal of Eating Disorders*, *10*(1), 1–9. https://doi.org/10.1186/s40337-022-00564-3

Bean, G. J. (2020). An item response theory analysis of the SCOFF Questionnaire in a seventh grade population. *International Journal of Social Work*, *5*(2), 1–20. https://doi.org/10.4148/2161-4148.1056

Coop, A., Clark, A., Morgan, J., Reid, F., & Lacey, J. H. (2024). The use and misuse of the SCOFF screening measure over two decades: A systematic literature review. *Eating and Weight Disorders: EWD*, *29*(1), 1–12. https://doi.org/10.1007/s40519-024-01656-6

CORC. (n.d.). *ED examination questionnaire (EDE-Q)*. Child Outcome Research Consortium. https://www.corc.uk.net/outcome-measures-guidance/directory-of-outcome-measures/eating-disorder-examination-questionnaire-ede-q/

Dimitropoulos, G., Nicula, M., Krishnapillai, A., Austin, A., Singh, M., Lee, J., Webb, C., Scott, S., Vieira de Almeida, A. C., Bergmann, C., Vander Steen, H., Kimber, M., Mushquash, C., Norman, L., Sauerwein, J., Keshen, A., Boachie, A., Toulany, A., Levinson, A., . . . Couturier, J. (2025). Transitions for youth and young adults with eating disorders and/or other mental health conditions: A Canadian guideline. *Journal of Eating Disorders*, *13*, 1–27. https://doi.org/10.1186/s40337-025-01343-6

Durso, L. E., Latner, J. D., White, M. A., Masheb, R. M., Blomquist, K. K., Morgan, P. T., & Grilo, C. M. (2012). Internalized weight bias in obese patients with binge ED: Associations with eating disturbances and psychological functioning. *International Journal of Eating Disorders*, *45*(3), 423–427. https://doi.org/10.1002/eat.20933

(EAT-26) Eating Attitudes Test. (n.d.). *The eating attitudes test (EAT-26)*. Retrieved July 7, 2025, from https://www.eat-26.com/

Gellere, I., & Beitane, I. (2024). Association of dietary habits with EDs among Latvian youth aged 18–24. *Behavioral Sciences (Basel, Switzerland)*, *14*(9), 1–10. https://doi.org/10.3390/bs14090766

Gioia, A. N., Morales, C., Laboe, A. A., Dolan, S. C., & Reilly, E. E. (2025). Clinical experiences using family based treatment for EDs. *International Journal of Eating Disorders*, *58*(4), 735–747. https://doi.org/10.1002/eat.24373

Gorrell, S., Sanzari, C. M., Ziegenhardt, P. S., Spell, J., Johnson, M. G., Whitlow, B., & Saigal, M. (2024). Preventing eating pathology among elite adolescent ballet dancers: A pilot trial of the Athlete Body Project. *Eating Disorders*, *32*(6), 666–685. https://doi.org/10.1080/10640266.2024.2337525

Gray, E. K., Murray, H. B., Eddy, K. T., Levine, M. P., & Smolak, L. (2015). Diagnosing anorexia nervosa. In *The WILEY handbook of EDs* (pp. 93–104). John Wiley & Sons, Ltd. https://doi.org/10.1002/9781118574089.ch8

Gregertsen, E. C., Mandy, W., & Serpell, L. (2017). The egosyntonic nature of anorexia: An impediment to recovery in anorexia nervosa treatment. *Frontiers in Psychology*, *8*, 1–9. https://doi.org/10.3389/fpsyg.2017.02273

Ivancic, L., Maguire, S., Miskovic-Wheatley, J., Harrison, C., & Nassar, N. (2021). Prevalence and management of people with EDs presenting to primary care: A national study. *The Australian and New Zealand Journal of Psychiatry*, *55*(11), 1089–1100. https://doi.org/10.1177/0004867421998752

Le Grange, D., Eisler, I., Dare, C., & Russell, G. F. M. (1992). Evaluation of family treatments in adolescent anorexia nervosa: A pilot study. *The International Journal of Eating Disorders*, *12*(4), 347–357. https://doi.org/10.1002/1098-108X(199212)12:4<347::AID-EAT2260120402>3.0.CO;2-W

Le Grange, D., Hughes, E. K., Court, A., Yeo, M., Crosby, R. D., & Sawyer, S. M. (2016). Randomized clinical trial of parent-focused treatment and family-based treatment for adolescent anorexia nervosa. *Journal of the American Academy of Child and Adolescent Psychiatry*, *55*(8), 683–692. https://doi.org/10.1016/j.jaac.2016.05.007

Lock, J. D., Le Grange, D., Bohon, C., Matheson, B., & Jo, B. (2024). Who responds to an adaptive intervention for adolescents with anorexia nervosa being treated with family-based treatment? Outcomes from a randomized clinical trial. *Journal of the American Academy of Child and Adolescent Psychiatry*, *63*(6), 605–614. https://doi.org/10.1016/j.jaac.2023.10.012

Mattar, L., Godart, N., Melchior, J. C., & Pichard, C. (2011). Anorexia nervosa and nutritional assessment: Contribution of body composition measurements. *Nutrition Research Reviews*, *24*(1), 39–45. https://doi.org/10.1017/S0954422410000284

McCormick, K. A., Chatham, A., Klodnick, V. V., Schoenfeld, E. A., & Cohen, D. A. (2023). Mental health service experiences among transition-age youth: Interpersonal continuums that influence engagement in care. *Child & Adolescent Social Work Journal*, *40*(4), 525–536. https://doi.org/10.1007/s10560-022-00890-0

Mincey, K. A., & Michelle Hunnicutt Hollenbaugh, K. (2022). Exploring the experiences of people who engage with pro-ED online media: A qualitative inquiry. *International Journal for the Advancement of Counseling*, *44*(4), 660–679. https://doi.org/10.1007/s10447-022-09483-z

Nagata, J. M., Ganson, K. T., & Austin, S. B. (2020). Emerging trends in eating disorders among sexual and gender minorities. *Current Opinion in Psychiatry*, *33*(6), 562–567. https://doi.org/10.1097/YCO.0000000000000645

Okamoto, Y., Miyake, Y., Nagasawa, I., & Yoshihara, M. (2018). Cohort survey of college students' eating attitudes: Interventions for depressive symptoms and stress coping were key factors for preventing bulimia in a subthreshold group. *BioPsychoSocial Medicine*, *12*(1), 1–8. https://doi.org/10.1186/s13030-018-0127-y

Papini, N. M., Jung, M., Cook, A., Lopez, N. V., Ptomey, L. T., Herrmann, S. D., & Kang, M. (2022). Psychometric properties of the 26-item eating attitudes test (EAT-26): An application of Rasch analysis. *Journal of Eating Disorders*, *10*(1), 1–13. https://doi.org/10.1186/s40337-022-00580-3

Pearl, R. L. (2018). Weight bias and stigma: Public health implications and structural solutions. *Social Issues and Policy Review*, *12*(1), 146–182. https://doi.org/10.1111/sipr.12043

Potterton, R., Richards, K., Allen, K., & Schmidt, U. (2020). EDs during emerging adulthood: A systematic scoping review. *Frontiers in Psychology*, *10*, 1–16. https://doi-org.ezproxy.lib.ucalgary.ca/10.3389/fpsyg.2019.03062

Puhl, R., & Suh, Y. (2015). Stigma and eating and weight disorders. *Current Psychiatry Reports*, *17*(3), 1–10. https://doi.org/10.1007/s11920-015-0552-6

Puhl, R. M., Himmelstein, M. S., Hateley-Browne, J. L., & Speight, J. (2020). Weight stigma and diabetes stigma in US adults with type 2 diabetes: Associations with diabetes self-care behaviors and perceptions of health care. *Diabetes Research and Clinical Practice*, *168*, 1–9. https://doi.org/10.1016/j.diabres.2020.108387

Ragnhildstveit, A., Tuteja, N., Seli, P., Smart, L., Uzun, N., Bass, L. C., Miranda, A. C., Ford, T. J., & Neufeld, S. A. S. (2024). Transitions from child and adolescent to adult mental health services for EDs: An in-depth systematic review and development of a transition framework. *Journal of Eating Disorders*, *12*(1), 1–17. https://doi.org/10.1186/s40337-024-00984-3

Ralph, A. F., Brennan, L., Byrne, S., Caldwell, B., Farmer, J., Hart, L. M., Heruc, G. A., Maguire, S., Piya, M. K., Quin, J., Trobe, S. K., Wallis, A., Williams-Tchen, A., & Hay, P. (2022). Management of eating disorders for people with higher weight: Clinical practice guideline. *Journal of Eating Disorders*, *10*(1), 1–42. https://doi.org/10.1186/s40337-022-00622-w

Rhodes, P., Baillie, A., Brown, J., & Madden, S. (2005). Parental efficacy in the family-based treatment of anorexia: Preliminary development of the Parents Versus Anorexia Scale (PVA). *European Eating Disorders Review*, *13*(6), 399–405. https://doi.org/10.1002/erv.661

Royal College of Psychiatrists. (2005). *Guidelines for the nutritional management of anorexia nervosa.* Royal College of Psychiatrists.

Rubino, F., Puhl, R. M., Cummings, D. E., Eckel, R. H., Ryan, D. H., Mechanick, J. I., Nadglowski, J., Ramos Salas, X., Schauer, P.R., Twenefour, D., & Dixon, J. B. (2020). Joint international consensus statement for ending stigma of obesity. *Nature Medicine*, *26*(4), 485–497. https://doi.org/10.1038/s41591-020-0803-x

Salvia, M. G., Ritholz, M. D., Craigen, K. L., & Quatromoni, P. A. (2023). Women's perceptions of weight stigma and experiences of weight-neutral treatment for binge ED: A qualitative study. *EClinicalMedicine*, *56*, 1–12. https://doi.org/10.1016/j.eclinm.2022.101811

Sanlier, N., Navruz Varli, S., Macit, M. S., Mortas, H., & Tatar, T. (2017). Evaluation of disordered eating tendencies in young adults. *Eating and Weight Disorders: EWD*, *22*(4), 623–631. https://doi.org/10.1007/s40519-017-0430-9

Schaefer, L. M., Crosby, R. D., & Machado, P. P. (2021). A systematic review of instruments for the assessment of EDs among adults. *Current Opinion in Psychiatry*, *34*(6), 543–562. https://doi.org/10.1097/YCO.0000000000000746

Schvey, N. A., Roberto, C. A., & White, M. A. (2013). Clinical correlates of the Weight Bias Internalization Scale in overweight adults with binge and purge behaviours. *Advances in EDs: Theory, Research and Practice*, *1*(3), 213–223. https://doi.org/10.1080/21662630.2013.794523

Sepulveda, A. R., Kyriacou, O., & Treasure, J. (2009). Development and validation of the Accommodation and Enabling Scale for Eating Disorders (AESED) for caregivers in eating disorders. *BMC Health Services Research*, *9*(1), 1–13. https://doi.org/10.1186/1472-6963-9-171

Shaikh, M. A., & Kayani, A. (2014). Detection of EDs in 16–20 year old female students–perspective from Islamabad, Pakistan. *JPMA. The Journal of the Pakistan Medical Association*, *64*(3), 334–336. https://doaj.org/toc/0030-9982

Skowrońska, A., Sójta, K., & Strzelecki, D. (2019). Refeeding syndrome as treatment complication of anorexia nervosa. *Psychiatria Polska*, *53*(5), 1–11. https://doi.org/10.12740/pp/onlinefirst/90275

Tannir, H., Itani, L., Kreidieh, D., El Masri, D., Traboulsi, S., & El Ghoch, M. (2020). Body composition in adolescents and young adults with anorexia nervosa: A clinical review. *Current Rheumatology Reviews*, *16*(2), 92–98. https://doi.org/10.1093/jpepsy/jsae012

Wagner, A. F., Butt, M., & Rigby, A. (2020). Internalized weight bias in patients presenting for bariatric surgery. *Eating Behaviors*, *39*, 1–6. https://doi.org/10.1016/j.eatbeh.2020.101429

Waller, G., & Turner, H. (2016). Therapist drift redux: Why well-meaning clinicians fail to deliver evidence-based therapy, and how to get back on track. *Behaviour Research and Therapy*, *77*, 129–137. https://doi.org/10.1016/j.brat.2015.12.005
White, H. J., Sharpe, H., & Plateau, C. R. (2023). Family body culture, disordered eating and mental health among young adult females during COVID−19. *Eating Behaviors*, *51*, 1–6. https://doi.org/10.1016/j.eatbeh.2023.101792
Wider, W., Mutang, J. A., Chua, B. S., Lin, J., Kamu, A., & Pang, N. T. P. (2023). Assessing the factor structure of the Eating Attitude Test-26 among undergraduate students in Malaysia. *Frontiers in Nutrition*, *10*, 1–8. https://doi.org/10.3389/fnut.2023.1212919
Zaitsoff, S., Yiu, A., Pullmer, R., Geller, J., & Menna, R. (2015). Therapeutic engagement: Perspectives from adolescents with EDs. *Psychiatry Research*, *230*(2), 597–603. https://doi.org/10.1016/j.psychres.2015.10.010

Chapter 5

Phase 1 – Session 1

Three goals for Session 1:

(1) To engage the young person and parents/caregivers in FBT-TAY.
(2) To obtain detailed information about how AN developed and interrupted the growth and physiological, psychological, and interpersonal development of the young person. Specific information is gathered about how AN has restricted independence, self-determination, and autonomy of the young person and the opportunity to launch into adulthood.
(3) To obtain preliminary information about the family structure, communication patterns, and natural supports (i.e., degree of autonomy and independence in the young person, parenting style(s), conflicts, and warmth) and how the family may promote or impede weight restoration and eating rehabilitation.

To achieve these main goals, FBT-TAY therapists undertake the following interventions:

(1) Weighing the young person (and assessing the presence of compensatory behaviours).
(2) Greeting and engaging the young person and their family in a sincere but caring manner.
(3) Obtaining history of the development of AN behaviours and their impact on the family.
(4) Externalizing AN by separating the cognitions and behaviours associated with AN from the young person and thereby reduce guilt and self-blame in the young person and parents/caregivers/supporters. This also aims to increase parental/supportive adults' empathy for the struggles of the young person with AN and leads to increased self-compassion in the young person themselves.

DOI: 10.4324/9781003463351-6

(5) Emphasizing the seriousness of AN and the difficulty in recovering (gaining weight, eating normally, and minimizing the thoughts and fears related to weight and eating) by orchestrating an intense scene for both the young person and their parents/caregivers.
(6) Charging the young person and the parents/caregivers with the task of working collaboratively on the goals of weight restoration and AN symptom reduction.
(7) Preparing the young person and their parents/caregivers for the family meal in the next session.

(Please note that we will use parents/caregivers and family interchangeably in Chapters 5– 8. Young people can invite people from their support network including extended family, peers, or a partner to any part of the treatment. For ease of reading, we will use either parent/caregivers or families.)

Weighing Patient (and Assessing the Presence of Compensatory Behaviours)

As was the case in the foundational approach of FBT for AN and BN, at the beginning of each session of FBT-TAY, the young person is weighed, and a compensatory log is used to document binge eating and purging behaviours if these are present. It is usually helpful to plot the weight change on a chart in the presence of the young person in the individual session and then share the chart with the family. Compensatory behaviours when present can be plotted on the symptom log prior to the family session, and this log is then shared with the parents/caregivers. Both the weight chart and the compensatory log will be used as information for the young person and their family related to achieving Phase 1 goals (see Figures 5.1 and 5.2). The rationale for plotting the weight and the symptoms with the young person first is that there is a concerted effort to move from the therapist sharing these logs to the young person doing this in Phase 2. The FBT-TAY therapist incrementally gives over the responsibility to the young person to speak about their progress, weight changes, and the presence of symptoms and requests for support in the later stages of treatment (or whenever the TAY is ready to take on these tasks).

Greeting the Family and the Young Person in a Sincere and Caring Manner

The FBT-TAY therapist should use a therapeutic style that communicates warmth, compassion, and firmness towards both the young person and their family. When working with young people and their parents/caregivers, the FBT-TAY therapist should strive to strike a balance between empowering the parents/caregivers but acknowledging the autonomy and independence of the young person.

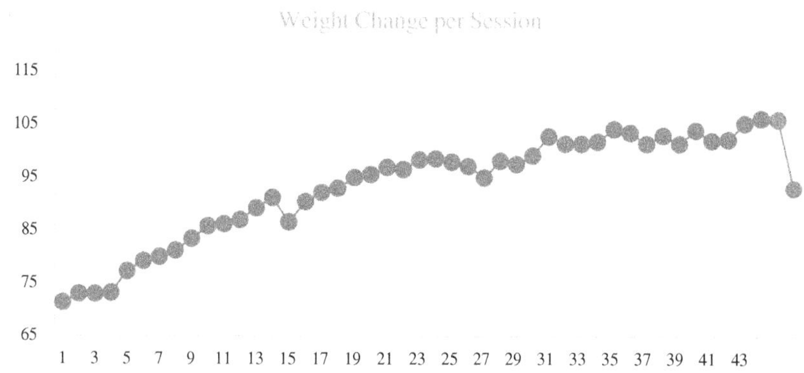

Figure 5.1 Weight Log

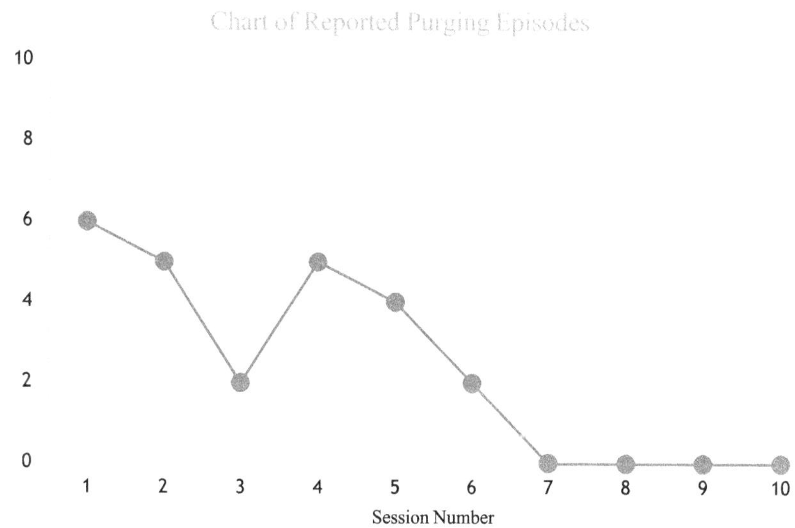

Figure 5.2 Compensatory Log

To achieve this goal, the therapist should make eye contact with both parents/caregivers and the young person and pose questions of each of them individually. The therapist then directly acknowledges the considerable courage taken by the young person to initiate the FBT-TAY treatment with their parents/caregivers. In turn, the FBT-TAY therapist also recognizes the unrelenting love and support of the parents/caregivers for their child and their willingness to walk beside them during the journey of recovery. This sets the stage for the therapist to engage the family in a discussion where they mutually share their experiences of the illness.

The FBT-TAY therapist endeavours to set a tone that communicates the seriousness of the illness and how important it is that the parents/caregivers and the young person work together against the AN. This collaborative stance is a clear departure from FBT for adolescent AN where parents/caregivers are asked to take charge and defer involvement of the adolescent in decision-making about food and eating until they are steadily gaining weight and eating without significant protest (e.g., Phase 2). This first meeting also serves to highlight the importance of immediately beginning the work of achieving rapid and early weight gain, since early weight gain (1.5–2 kg in the first month of treatment) is associated with improved outcomes for AN (Doyle et al., 2010; Le Grange et al., 2014). Along the same lines as FBT for AN and BN, FBT-TAY therapists gather information about how AN has interrupted the growth and physiological and psychological development of the young person. Specific information is gathered about how AN has restricted the freedom and autonomy of the young person and stifled their efforts to achieve interdependence from their parents/caregivers.

Obtaining Historical and Current Information about AN

During the first family session, the FBT-TAY therapist takes a history of what young people and their parents/caregivers have previously attempted to address AN symptoms (what has worked, has not worked or effectively works some of the time). This provides the FBT-TAY therapist with an opportunity to highlight how difficult it is to recover from AN despite significant consequences associated with this illness. The FBT-TAY therapist also focuses on elevating the strengths, skills, and personal power of the young person and the family and adult support system. The FBT-TAY therapist may ask the following questions: "What does the family think about the illness?" "How has it interfered with the developmental tasks associated with emerging adulthood (medical, psychological, social, academic, and relational)?" "What steps has the young person taken to address the eating symptoms/weight loss?" "How has the young person changed since developing the ED?" "What have they lost (gained)?" "How has the family attempted to assist the young person with the ED?" "What strengths does the family have to help support their young person?" Young people are likely to describe intense feelings and negative thoughts about their weight (and any changes to their weight) if they increase their eating. The FBT-TAY therapist provides emotional support but firmly states that weight gain is imperative.

History of Family Functioning

In the first family session, the FBT-TAY therapist begins to gather information about the family (i.e., degree of autonomy and independence in the young person, parenting style(s), conflicts, and warmth) and how this may promote or make it difficult to gain weight. Based on the history obtained regarding AN and family functioning, the FBT-TAY therapist will obtain comprehensive information encompassing the individual, parental/caregiver, and familial factors which will help them determine where greater therapeutic focus is needed to help foster behaviour change. Table C highlights important areas that therapists should pay particular attention to throughout the phases of treatment. Adhering to the fundamental principle of agnosticism of FBT, FBT-TAY therapists are not gathering information to create psychodynamic or systemic formulations about the family and individual pathology. Instead, they are seeking to amplify the strengths and resources of the family and the young person that will help them combat the influence of the illness while also recognizing potential impediments to parents/caregivers effectively addressing ED behaviours. In many ways, this too is a departure from how FBT is utilized for adolescents with AN and BN where the assumption is that changes in family functioning are a result of AN or BN and not general family processing or systemic issues that may have been present before the development of the ED. While the assumption is that parents/caregivers are not the cause or maintaining factor of AN, the nuanced role of their support requires an understanding of family functioning to help build a collaborative approach between the young person and their family. This is especially the case when AN has been present for some time or when it has recurred.

Externalization

Michael White, the founder of Narrative Family Therapy, developed the intervention of externalization which is a way of separating AN from the young person's greater self (Heywood et al., 2022). Separating the disorder from the young person helps to demote AN from a source of identity and instead establishes it as a medical/psychological/behavioural problem that hinders this greater self from developing holistically (Pereira Santos et al., 2023). Use of externalization invites the young person to explore the dominant themes about how AN has an impact on their identity and other salient areas of their lives. Similarly, externalization allows caregivers to consider how AN has shaped their family and their relationships with the young person with AN. Externalization is much more effective if FBT-TAY therapists utilize the information provided by young people and their parents/caregivers during their discussion about their concerns, examples and experiences of the illness over time. FBT-TAY therapists can use metaphors and analogies of other illnesses (e.g., diabetes, cancer) to provide examples of names given to AN. The purpose of externalization is to help reduce the young person's and parents'/caregivers' blame, guilt, and shame about the illness. This is important because guilt and self-blame reduce motivation, confidence, and the willingness to collaboratively address AN directly. FBT-TAY therapists may creatively develop names of the problem or metaphors that the young person and family believe has resonance for them. This intervention can

Table C Taking a History

Young person and illness	*Parents/caregivers*	*Family*
• Degree of independence and autonomy prior to the illness	• Type of parenting style (authoritative versus authoritarian)	• Family structure: intact versus blended and separated family
• Degree to which the individual has launched into adulthood	• The context of the parents'/caregivers' lives (work and other personal life commitments)	• Life stage of the family: degree to which the structure of the family has changed to accommodate the transition of the young person from adolescence to adulthood
• Degree of intrinsic and extrinsic motivation to engage in treatment	• Willingness of parents/caregivers to support and refeed the young person	• Family culture: religious, ethnic, racial background, etc.
• Ability to externalize the illness	• Ability to externalize the illness	• Ability of other family members (siblings, grandparents and other key caregivers) to externalize the illness
• Ability to trust others especially parents/caregivers and FBT therapist	• Recognize the seriousness of the illness	

also be used throughout therapy to help increase empathy and warmth towards the young person and challenge pathologizing and negative narratives that are disempowering. To achieve this, therapists may use externalization to model how to simultaneously acknowledge the influence of the illness on the young person while also emphasizing their strength in being able to identify the adverse effect of AN on their lives.

Lock and Le Grange (2012) advocate that for some families using a Venn diagram may help to differentiate the healthy side of the young person and the unhealthy side accounted for by the ED, but other metaphors or analogies are often useful as well (see Figure 5.3).

Following the naming of the problem, the young person and the family are invited to map the effects of the problem since the onset of the AN on both. To facilitate externalization of the problem, the FBT-TAY therapist may ask the following questions to assist the young person and the family to deconstruct the problem: In what ways does AN affect your relationships with important people in your life?" "How has the AN interfered with you achieving your personal,

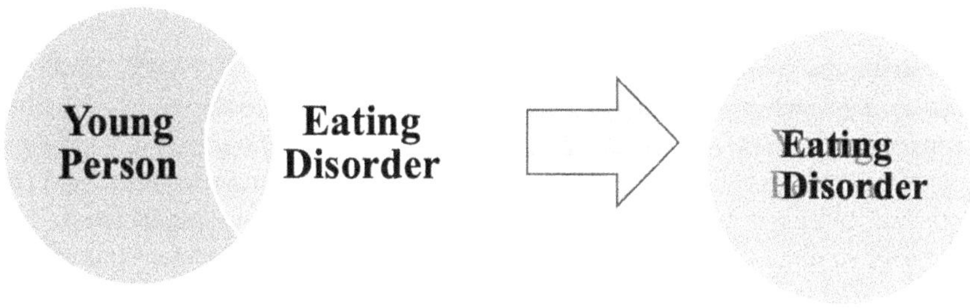

Figure 5.3 Externalization Using a Venn Diagram

relational, academic, and social goals? When does the problem occur more or less in your life?" Which aspects of your life has the AN interrupted or sidelined? The young person is then invited to critically evaluate the effects of the illness on their life. The goal of these questions is to facilitate a conversation that allows the young person to determine the effects of AN on them.

Externalization of the illness also allows the young person and their family to think about how they can work as a team to undermine the illness when it is powerful. The young person can think about when the illness is more present in their day-to-day lives and/or interactions with their family members. Conversely, FBT-TAY therapist can also ask the parents/caregivers to describe what behaviours/attitudes they attribute to the illness and when they observe glimpses of the healthier side of the young person.

We strongly advocate that FBT-TAY therapists seek collaboration of the young person. However, ambivalence associated with the illness may not always make it possible for the young person to consistently eat without the persistent and unrelenting support of their parents/caregivers and others from their supportive network. To persuade the parents/caregivers to take on the role of supporting eating and managing symptoms, it may help to remind them that parents/caregivers or other supportive adults often take on roles that may feel developmentally awkward or tasks that are unusual when someone is sick (e.g., donating an organ or unusual care such as when the young person has major medical complications). One example may include a young person who has broken their leg and needs a parent/caregiver to live with them to help with feeding and support them to attend medical appointments until they can resume their regular activities again. It is also important to emphasize that the parents/caregivers are providing care that is typically undertaken by an interdisciplinary team on an inpatient/day-treatment setting or residential care. By encouraging the young person to work with their parents/caregivers, we may also be supporting them to remain autonomous in their lives (outside of eating/weight gain) by staying out of intensive treatments such as inpatient or day hospital care.

Orchestrating an Intense Scene

For both the young person and their parents/caregivers, FBT-TAY therapists use their expertise about the life-threatening illness and the short and long-time consequences of AN to simultaneously emphasize: (a) young people need their parents/supportive family members to support them through recovery and (b) parental/caregiver support is required to facilitate the weight gain process. The message is directed at increasing a sense of urgency about treatment in *both* the young person and their parents/caregivers. FBT-TAY therapists are also attuned to the level of anxiety in the young person and the family. The use of the intense scene permits FBT-TAY therapist to increase (or mobilize) the anxiety enough to propel parents/caregivers and the young person to work together to reduce eating symptoms and promote weight restoration.

However, the FBT-TAY therapist also modulates the anxiety if it hinders the parents/caregivers from working effectively together and collaboratively with the young person against the illness. To modulate the anxiety in the parents/caregivers and young person, the therapist communicates that they have the strengths and resources needed to mitigate the adverse effects of the illness on the TAY. Excessive anxiety and fears in the parents/caregivers may contribute to parents/caregivers expressing anger, criticism, and frustration that serve only to create conflict and tensions rather than a supportive family environment.

The urgency of parental/caregiver involvement in supporting their child to make behavioural changes must be communicated repeatedly, especially when it appears that there is a lack of appreciation of the severity of this illness. FBT-TAY therapists may need to pay careful attention and greater time orchestrating the intense scene if they observe that parents/caregivers are demoralized by the illness and exhausted by ongoing efforts to convince the TAY to eat and gain weight over time. To orchestrate an intense scene, FBT-TAY therapists may consider conveying the following information – the high mortality and morbidity rates associated with AN; the increased medical, psychological, academic, and social consequences associated with this illness; and the lack of empirically based treatments for adults with AN – and illustrate the short- and long-term effects of AN on the lives of clients with whom you have worked. In the context of persistent AN, FBT-TAY therapists must emphasize that parental/caregiver support of the ED is imperative to help mitigate against chronicity, increase medical and psychiatric morbidity, and a decrease in social and academic achievements. This intervention is not psychoeducational, but intended to be highly motivational, aiming to break through any avoidance, minimization, or denial that has kept the young person and their adult caregivers from taking action to help them. FBT-TAY therapists must acknowledge parental/caregiver burnout and apathy while also emphasizing that they have the skills, resources, and knowledge to help the young person with AN recover. To elicit hope, therapists may further describe that they will utilize their expertise and skills to support parents/caregivers in working together to help their child overcome AN.

Expectations About the Treatment Process

It is imperative that the message about the seriousness of illness and the need for a collaborative approach between parents/caregivers and young person be provided in the context of expectations about the treatment process. The intense scene and the message about the illness must be delivered in the context of the potential challenges that the young person and the parents/caregivers will face as they engage throughout this treatment. FBT-TAY therapists should emphasize that the illness will become increasingly "loud" as parents/caregivers and the healthy side of the young person become united in their efforts to address ED behaviours. The FBT-TAY therapist may also describe to the young person that the illness will attempt to undermine their efforts towards recovery by becoming disparaging and critical. It is important for the parents/caregivers and the young person to know that it is common for families to become frustrated and irritated with the relentless focus on eating and meal planning in the treatment process. There will be times in the treatment that they will feel that the FBT-TAY therapist is overlooking other issues that may seem as significant (or more pressing) as the eating and weight change or stabilize. FBT-TAY therapist may further highlight that conflict may intensify between the parents/caregivers and between the young person over the next few months. The FBT-TAY therapist should express to the parents/caregivers that young people may not always vocalize their appreciation for parental/caregiver support and recovery, especially during Phase 1. At the same time, some young people may feel that they are a burden to their parents/caregivers for them participating in such an intensive and time-consuming treatment.

Charging the Parents/Caregivers and the Young Person with the Task of Collaborating on Eating and Weight Restoration or Avoidance of Weight Suppression

The parents/caregivers and young person are charged with the task of actively agreeing to work collaboratively to address the illness. The content of the urgent call to action is similar to the message that therapists would communicate if they were working with children and adolescents. However, the emphasis of the message needs to consider the developmental stage of the young person. For this to work, the young person will need to "allow" or "give permission" to their parents/caregivers to support them with eating and meals. In contrast to working with children and young adolescents in FBT, young people must accept the support of their parents/caregivers in their treatment. It would be inappropriate to ask a 12-year-old if their parents/caregivers can help them to recover from a serious illness such as AN. However, young people have the legal right to pursue treatment (or not) without any parental/caregiver involvement. When working with individuals over the age of 18, FBT-TAY therapists must acknowledge that the young person is in a difficult predicament, and it will not be easy to involve their parents/caregivers in meal support. It is important to emphasize to the young person that this level of parental/caregiver involvement is temporary and necessary for recovery. The parents/caregivers are the best people to address restrictive eating and other ED symptoms because they know the young person and they are invested in their health, well-being, and future.

Once the FBT-TAY therapist has described the seriousness of the illness, the need for urgent action, and the work that must be undertaken to support recovery, the therapist must directly ask for the parents/caregivers to make a commitment alongside the TAY. The FBT-TAY therapist may ask: "What are your thoughts about taking on parental/caregiver control of the illness? Is this something that you are willing to do? What would you like to communicate to your child about the illness? What do you think they need to know about the lengths that you will take to control the illness and support their recovery?" FBT-TAY therapists cannot assume that parents/caregivers have accepted the charge to engage in this intensive behavioural treatment if they have not explicitly made a commitment to themselves and the young person with AN. It is at this point in the session that the parents/caregivers will share their thoughts about whether they think AN is a serious enough illness to warrant their involvement. FBT-TAY therapists must directly address parental/caregiver ambivalence about taking control over the illness and support with eating and weight gain in their child. Similarly, the FBT-TAY therapist turns to the young person to acquiesce to their parents/caregivers taking the responsibility to temporarily support them with meal preparation, shopping, meals, and addressing symptoms. The following questions may serve as helpful tools in engaging the young person in this discussion: What are your thoughts about your parents/caregivers working with your healthy side to help you take control of this life-threating illness? What does giving this control over to your parents/caregivers say about you? Your commitment to yourself? Your future? What you value? Reinforcement of the temporary nature of this request should be highlighted in this discussion as well.

Preparation for the Family Meal

Building on the young person's agreement that their parents/caregivers can temporarily "take charge or responsibility" for supporting them with eating/meals, the FBT-TAY therapist asks the parents/caregivers to bring a meal for them to eat during the session that they believe will help the young person gain weight and begin to normalize eating. The FBT-TAY therapist looks directly at the parents/caregivers and asks that they bring a meal that they think their young person needs to eat to overcome the AN. It will be imperative that the FBT-TAY therapist communicates that the parents/caregivers must make this decision without involvement of the young person with AN because it will be difficult to discern how much the AN is dictating what foods the family can prepare and bring to the session. The

FBT-TAY therapist reminds the young person that they actively defer making any decisions about what their parents/caregivers will bring to the family meal. This will provide the young person with an opportunity to take the first step to putting the parents/caregivers in charge of supporting their recovery by starting with making decisions about the first meal. The young person will be invited to observe and share what it is like to relinquish the control over eating to others even when it is their choice. It is critical to remind them that ambivalence is normal, intense fears are to be expected, and their family will be available to provide emotional support. FBT-TAY therapists may want to emphasize that the young person can continue to have influence and control over areas of their lives that are not related to food and weight. The FBT-TAY therapist will want to reiterate the importance of both parents/caregivers attending and the siblings (if any and the young person has agreed). Although the FBT-TAY therapists may respond to logistical questions (i.e., where the meal will be held), therapists may want to steer away from responding to any specific questions about what food the family should bring to the session.

Common Challenges, Opportunities, and Potential Mitigating Strategies

We highlight three typical situations that may arise during or immediately after Session 1 from the young person not wanting to be a burden to their family, parents/family members experiencing disempowerment, and the young person exercising their agency to pursue a different treatment.

Challenge 1: The Young Person Perceives Themselves as a Burden

The young person communicates significant scepticism about their parents/caregivers willingness to participate in FBT-TAY because the treatment is too time consuming and intense.

As a consultant to both the young person and their parents/caregivers, the FBT-TAY therapist encourages the young person to explore what may underpin these reservations in a respectful and collaborative way. The following questions may be posed:

> I can see that this is a dilemma for you X – you care deeply for your family and don't want them to feel obligated to invest in a treatment that relies heavily on them to support you. [Therapist turns to the parents/caregivers], What would you like to say to X when you hear them say that you are unable to participate due to competing demands? What are the reasons you believe your involvement in X's recovery is critical? You know X better than anyone else, what does X need to hear or see that will convince them that you are committed to working with them against the ED?

The opportunity for the young person and their family to communicate their wish to work together will need to be reinforced throughout the phases of FBT-TAY as fears and doubts about parents/caregivers wanting to support recovery may persist especially when conflict and tensions over meals escalate.

Challenge 2: The Young Person Declines FBT-TAY

As demonstrated in the literature, young people with EDs often do not want their families involved in their treatment. Either during or after Session 1, the young person emphatically states that they would prefer an individualized intervention or intensive treatment where they can work with other "patients" closer to their age. The FBT-TAY therapist supports the young person to communicate this decision to their parents/caregivers and what level of emotional, instrumental, and financial support to pursue an alternate treatment. Conversely, parents/families are invited to reflect on their emotional reaction to their child's decision and what level of communication they require with the adult treatment providers to provide them with reassurance that the care is progressing well and that they are supporting them in a way that is optimal. The FBT-TAY provides other treatment options including cognitive behavioural therapy and dialectical behaviour therapy to intensive specialized services in day to residential care. The FBT-TAY therapist may provide national or international ED information where reliable sources of evidence-based interventions are described. In addition to the dissemination of resources, referral sources, the FBT-TAY therapist may invite the young person to work either individually or with their family to identify the pros and cons of different treatment options and consider next steps.

Challenge 3: Parental/Caregiver Burnout

It is not uncommon for parents/families to express exhaustion and burnout due to a combination of factors from the illness itself and other life circumstances (e.g., caring for ailing parents/caregivers or economic hardships). In addition to adhering closely to the principles of FBT (e.g., externalization, agnosticism to counter parental/caregiver blame, shame and guilt), the FBT-TAY therapist may work with the parents/caregivers to ascertain if others in their extended network can support them with household tasks and family responsibilities such as caring for other children, stepping in to offer an occasional reprieve from supporting with meals. It is also the responsibility of the FBT-TAY therapists to provide a comprehensive list of informal and formal support resources that are available for caregivers from online or in-person peer support or support groups, psychoeducational webinars, individual or couple therapy.

Key Global and National Caregiver Resources for EDs

The following organizations offer high-quality, evidence-informed resources and supports for parents/caregivers of young people experiencing EDs. These supports include educational guides, skills-based tools, helplines, peer-support networks, and family-focused information designed to enhance caregiver capacity and improve treatment engagement.

National ED Information Centre (NEDIC) – Canada

NEDIC is a national education and advocacy organization dedicated to providing ED education, information, resources, and connections to treatment for individuals with EDs and their families. NEDIC provides a comprehensive suite of caregiver-focused supports, including a live helpline, evidence-based fact sheets, and accessible written guides addressing family support strategies, communication, coping, and navigating care systems. Their resource library contains material tailored specifically for parents, caregivers, partners, and siblings.

National Initiative for EDs (NIED) – Canada

The National Initiative for EDs (NIED) is a national education and advocacy organization focused on improving outcomes for individuals with EDs and their families who support them. NIED positions caregivers at the centre of its mission, offering educational resources, family- oriented information packages, service-navigation tools, and public awareness materials. Their caregiver-focused publications, including safety planning tools, treatment-navigation guidance, and recovery support information, are widely referenced across Canadian health systems. NIED also provides webinars, presentations, and an expanding library of caregiver training resources designed to reduce isolation, improve caregiver knowledge, and strengthen family capacity to support recovery.

Kelty Mental Health Resource Centre – Canada (British Columbia Based)

The Kelty Mental Health Resource Centre connects individuals with EDs and their families with resources and information during their treatment journey. Kelty provides caregiver-oriented educational resources on topics such as understanding EDs, relapse prevention, body image, media literacy, and supportive communication. Their digital library includes videos, fact sheets, and guides that are widely used by families and therapists.

F.E.A.S.T. (Families Empowered and Supporting Treatment for EDs) – International

F.E.A.S.T. is a global, non-profit organization that offers structured support for families of individuals with EDs, aiming to provide programs and resources to caregivers and families centred around providing support, information, skills, resources, and tools as they navigate recovery for their child. F.E.A.S.T includes skill-building toolkits, moderated online forums, training videos, webinars, and peer-support groups for caregivers and siblings. Their materials emphasize practical strategies for supporting recovery and fostering caregiver confidence.

Beat Eating Disorders – United Kingdom

Beat Eating Disorders is a national UK-based charity that provides information, resources, and a national helpline for individuals with EDs and their families. Beat provides a wide range of services for caregivers, including dedicated helplines, online support groups, educational materials, and structured guidance for those supporting children, adolescents, and adults. Their SOLACE program offers regular online support sessions specifically designed for carers navigating the complexities of ED recovery.

The Eating Disorder Foundation (Colorado, USA)

Based in Denver, this foundation functions as a community resource centre offering free, confidential, non-clinical supports and services for individuals with EDs and families. Services include caregiver support groups, recovery-focused family sessions, and educational programs aimed at reducing stigma and increasing caregiver understanding of ED recovery. Many supports are offered in hybrid or virtual formats, allowing accessibility beyond the local region.

InsideOut Institute for Eating Disorders – Australia

InsideOut is Australia's national institute for research, knowledge translation, and clinical excellence in EDs. With a team that includes leading researchers, clinicians, and policy-makers,

> InsideOut maintains an extensive evidence-based resource library tailored for families and caregivers. Materials include treatment information, practical strategies for supporting recovery, guidance on meal support, and tools for understanding eating-disorder symptoms and their impact on family systems.

National EDs Collaboration (NEDC) – Australia

The National EDs Collaboration (NEDC) is a federally supported initiative that provides a coordinated, evidence-based framework for improving ED prevention, early identification, and treatment across Australia. NEDC offers a comprehensive suite of caregiver resources, including a dedicated *Families and Supports* portal with accessible and practical guidance on recognizing early warning signs and practical strategies for supporting a loved one throughout treatment and recovery. For example, their caregiver guide, *Caring for a Young Person with an ED*, provides structured advice on communication, distress management, system navigation, and caregiver wellbeing. NEDC also hosts fact sheets, professional guidelines, and e-learning modules aligned with best-practice, family-inclusive care, making their materials valuable for caregivers and therapists internationally.

Conclusions

The first session of FBT-TAY for young people uses the same interventions as in FBT for adolescents with AN (Lock & Le Grange, 2007, 2012, 2025), but there are important differences in the way these interventions are conducted with young people. First, the FBT-TAY therapist meets for 30 minutes rather than 5– 10 minutes with the young person in order to engage them in the treatment process, in order to work more on building a working relationship with the young person than the younger adolescent, in no small part because they can stop treatment at any time (Le Grange & Lock, 2015; Dimitropoulos et al., 2024). The young person is invited to identify the best method of communicating symptoms and weight changes to the parents/caregivers. Second, the FBT-TAY therapist assesses how much independence the young person has achieved with eating and meals and in other areas of their life (working, driving, socializing outside of the family, financial independence) as well has how much AN has interfered with these processes of autonomy (Hughes et al., 2019). There is also a more deliberate assessment about how much the structure of the family has changed to accommodate AN and to identify the strengths of the family for developing and maintaining behavioural changes in the young person. Third, the FBT-TAY therapist communicates that the young person and the parents/caregivers work as a team against the illness – albeit a team that in the early stages leans heavily on the parents/caregivers to promote normalized eating and weight gain (Lock & Le Grange, 2015). Fourth, developmentally appropriate language and examples for externalizing the illness are used to help mobilize the young person and their parents/caregivers to work together (Le Grange et al., 2010; Lock & Le Grange, 2015). This chapter concludes with a series of leading national ED organizations that work to provide information, resources, and supports for parents/caregivers and families of individuals with EDs.

Chapter Summary

Here are the key points of this chapter:

(1) Session 1 begins by establishing a strong therapeutic alliance with both the young person and their parents/caregivers, creating a foundation of

trust, warmth, and collaboration that honours the young person's growing autonomy.

(2) The therapist works to understand how the AN developed and how it has disrupted physical health, psychological growth, independence, and the young person's ability to move toward adulthood.
(3) Family functioning is explored with curiosity rather than blame, allowing the therapist to identify patterns of communication, autonomy, support, and accommodation that may help or hinder weight restoration.
(4) Externalization is introduced to separate the illness from the young person, reducing guilt and shame while increasing empathy, compassion, and a shared sense of working together against AN.
(5) An "intense scene" is intentionally created to communicate the seriousness and urgency of the illness, helping both the young person and their parents/caregivers recognize the life-threatening nature of AN and the need for immediate action.
(6) The therapist invites the young person and their parents/caregivers to make a clear commitment to work collaboratively on eating, weight restoration, and symptom interruption, emphasizing that parental/caregiver involvement is temporary but essential.
(7) Realistic expectations are set about the challenges ahead, including increased conflict, emotional intensity, ambivalence, and resistance as the ED becomes more "visible" during early change efforts.
(8) The session concludes by preparing everyone for the upcoming family meal, with parents/caregivers selecting a weight-restoring meal and the young person practising the difficult but necessary act of letting their caregivers temporarily take the lead in eating-related decisions.

References

Dimitropoulos, G., Singh, M., Sauerwein, J., Pedram, P., Kimber, M., Pradel, M., Eckhardt, S., Forsberg, S., Keery, H., Allan, E., Bruett, L., & Le Grange, D. (2024). Examining clinicians' perceptions and experiences working with diverse families in family-based treatment: Common adaptations and considerations for treatment engagement. *International Journal of Eating Disorders*, *57*(3), 635–647. https://doi.org/10.1002/eat.24144

Doyle, P. M., Le Grange, D., Loeb, K., Doyle, A. C., & Crosby, R. D. (2010). Early response to family-based treatment for adolescent anorexia nervosa. *International Journal of Eating Disorders*, *43*(7), 659–662. https://doi.org/10.1002/eat.20764

Heywood, L., Conti, J., & Hay, P. (2022). Paper 1: A systematic synthesis of narrative therapy treatment components for the treatment of EDs. *Journal of Eating Disorders*, *10*(1), 1–17. https://doi.org/10.1186/s40337-022-00635-5

Hughes, E. K., Sawyer, S. M., Accurso, E. C., Singh, S., & Le Grange, D. (2019). Predictors of early response in conjoint and separated models of family-based treatment for adolescent anorexia nervosa. *European EDs Review*, *27*(3), 283–294. https://doi.org/10.1002/erv.2668

Le Grange, D., Accurso, E. C., Lock, J., Agras, S., & Bryson, S. W. (2014). Early weight gain predicts outcome in two treatments for adolescent anorexia nervosa. *International Journal of Eating Disorders*, *47*(2), 124–129. https://doi.org/10.1002/eat.22221

Le Grange, D., & Lock, J. (2015). *Help your teenager beat an ED*. Guildford Publications.

Le Grange, D., Lock, J., Loeb, K., & Nicholls, D. (2010). Academy for EDs position paper: The role of the family in EDs. *International Journal of Eating Disorders*, *43*(1), 1–5. https://doi.org/10.1002/eat.20751

Lock, J., & Le Grange, D. (2007). *Treatment manual for anorexia nervosa: A family-based approach* (1st ed.). Guilford Press.

Lock, J., & Le Grange, D. (2012). *Treatment manual for anorexia nervosa: A family-based approach* (2nd ed.). The Guilford Press.

Lock, J., & Le Grange, D. (2025). *Treatment manual for anorexia nervosa: A family-based approach* (3rd ed.). Guilford Press.

Pereira Santos, P. J., Soares, L., & Faria, A. L. (2023). Narrative Therapy as an innovative approach to anorexia nervosa treatment: A literature review. *Journal of Poetry Therapy*, *36*(4), 310–323. https://doi.org/10.1080/08893675.2023.2189532

Chapter 6

Phase 1 – Session 2 (The Family Meal)

(Duration of Session Ranges from 60 to 90 Minutes)

The Goals of Session 2 Are Identical to the Goals Delineated by Lock and Le Grange (2012)

(1) To continue the assessment of the family processes around eating.
(2) To provide an opportunity for the parents/caregivers to begin helping their young person to re-establish healthy eating.
(3) To assess the strengths and challenges for the family and TAY surrounding eating.

To Achieve These Goals, the Therapist Uses the Following Interventions

(1) Discuss the weight and compensatory logs with the young person and their family.
(2) Observe the family patterns around food, food serving, and eating as they relate to the young person and assess their degree of independence with eating.
(3) Encourage collaboration of the young person and their family within the treatment process.
(4) Help the parents/caregivers to assist their young person to eat more than they may believe they are prepared to eat.

As described in the manual by Lock and Le Grange, 2012, ***the following are salient features of the therapeutic meal:***

(1) Observe the family processes to identify any patterns of communicating, interacting, and responding that may interfere or enhance the parents'/caregivers' efforts to facilitate eating in their child.

DOI: 10.4324/9781003463351-7

(2) In a non-judgmental manner, therapists ask questions to help identify how the present family meal is similar or different from meals at home and in other contexts since the young person may be eating with others outside of their family.
(3) Coach the parents/caregivers on how they may work together to help their young person to eat the meal they prepared for this session.
(4) Continue to encourage the young person to work collaboratively with their parents/caregivers and to eat the meal the parents/caregivers prepared/brought to the session.

Weighing the Young Person and Sharing the Weight and Compensatory Log with the Family

As in Session 1, the therapist meets briefly with the young person prior to their family joining the session. The FBT-TAY therapist weighs the young person and records any compensatory symptoms including excessive exercise or vomiting. The individual meeting for this session with the young person is much shorter (5 minutes rather than 30) to signal that the priority is eating in a supportive family climate for the purpose of achieving weight gain and normalization of eating. The FBT-TAY therapist may utilize this opportunity to inquire about what the young person believes has happened to their weight (increased, decreased, or stayed the same). Young people often erroneously assume that their weight has risen considerably since the last session. If weight has decreased, the therapist notes the discrepancy between what the young person thought happened to their weight and the number on the scale. On the other hand, if weight has increased, the amount of weight gained is rarely close to what the young person had feared/anticipated. For individuals who engage in compensatory symptoms, especially laxative abuse, it is important to take into consideration that water retention as a result of these behaviours may initially result in higher weight. The therapist should educate the young person about the side effects of laxative abuse and the potential for weight rebound and encourage them to cease using them. Finally, the therapist documents change in weight and symptoms so they can be presented to the family.

Observe Family Patterns

Assess family patterns and processes related to meals, food choices, food serving, and family discussions about eating as they relate to the young person and assess the degree of independence in the young person with eating. The rationale for why and how to assess family patterns surrounding eating is the same as what has been outlined in the manual for FBT-AN (Lock & Le Grange, 2012, pp. 85–87). FBT-TAY therapists may also observe the degree to which the parents//caregivers and the young person have become entrenched in patterns of interacting and relating surrounding the ED and in other aspects of their relationship. FBT-TAY therapists working with young people must pay special attention to the degree to which the young person has become independent with respect to eating and meal preparation.

Consequently, a slight variation in the family meal session is that the therapist may inquire how many meals the young person has outside of the family home. It is developmentally appropriate that a young person may be eating during school or at work and with their peers. The therapist may further probe with whom the young person is eating their meals outside of their family unit. Are they eating with their peers socially? With whom are they eating while at school (e.g., roommates in a house versus a large cafeteria in residence)? If they are employed, do they eat meals while at work? Are they eating with their co-workers? The degree to which the young person is eating meals outside of the home will be critical to understanding how much re-organizing is needed by the caregivers/family to support with the renourishment process in Phase 1.

As in the FBT manual for AN and BN, the family is asked to begin laying out the meal and the therapist again reiterates that they will not be eating with them. The following questions may be used to assess the structure of meals in a family of a young person:

- How often are you eating together as a family? Does the young person prepare any of the meals? What meals are "sacred" requiring attendance by all?
- What activities/work schedules interfere with family meals?
- How much independence does the young person have with grocery shopping, preparing meals, and eating on their own?
- Does the young person eat any meals outside of the family home? How often do they eat with others like friends, family members, and/or a partner?
- Do they attend secondary school or post-secondary education? Live on or off-campus?
- When/where do they eat when they are at school? With whom do they eat?
- Do they work or volunteer? If yes, do they take breaks to eat a snack or meal? Who prepares the meals for school/part-time work? Probe if the young person brings food from home or purchases food (if any at all) while at work/school.
- How much has the family organized itself around the emerging independence of the young person (and/or the illness) with eating and mealtimes?

The FBT-TAY therapist should also ask questions of the parents/caregivers and the young person about grocery shopping, meal preparation, and the timing of when meals occur. The therapist is particularly interested in hearing how the parents/caregivers may have inadvertently accommodated the illness over time by buying a narrowly prescribed range of foods to appease the ED. Have the parents/caregivers been preparing their meals separately from the young person?

If living together, does the young person insist that their parents/caregivers give them privacy when they are eating their meals? Do parents/caregivers avoid using their kitchen or preparing certain meals and adhere to any ED rules? Therapists observe how the young person eats in the presence of their family. What is the pace (e.g., fast/slow) of young person's eating? Does the young person engage in any ED behaviour (cutting up food in small pieces, eating food in ritualistic way) during the meal? How do the parents/caregivers respond in the presence of disordered eating behaviours (ordering and re-ordering food on their plate, using excessive amounts of condiments, chewing very slowly, spitting out food)? FBT-TAY therapist should elicit this information by asking non-judgmental questions and expressing curiosity about the family and concern about the interference of the illness on all aspects of family life pertaining to food and mealtimes. It is important to note that the discussion is about more than simply identifying where accommodations to the AN have occurred. The goal is to identify how the family and young person can work collaboratively to reverse starvation in a way that feels collaborative. The role of the FBT-TAY therapist is to continue to highlight this need for collaboration and advocate for necessary changes relationally and practically that will be required in Phase 1.

Help the Parents/Caregivers and TAY to Work Together to Eat More than the Young Person Was Prepared to Eat

Another salient goal of the therapeutic meal is to help the parents/caregivers to support the young person to eat more than they previously would have during a meal. The therapist should encourage the parents/caregivers and the young person to think about how they can work together against the power of the illness. To do this, and to maintain trust and alliance with the young person (and their parents/caregivers), the therapist might describe that the illness can be particularly "loud" during these moments and may be critical of the efforts of the young person for eating more food (or eating food that has been avoided). Parents/caregivers are coached to use directive, encouraging, and emotionally supportive statements to help the healthy side of the young person to temporarily give over their control of eating to their parents/caregivers. The FBT-TAY therapist shares that if left up to the young person alone, it would be difficult for them to eat enough to gain weight/address starvation and to increase their intake as needed because AN thinking and behaviours interfere with these processes and their ability to act independently without parents/caregiver support. This is an act of independence by the young person choosing not to give into their illness and agreeing to partner with their parents/caregivers to eat more than they would have without their support. The FBT-TAY therapist also uses this opportunity to address any comments from the parents/caregivers that may sound critical, negative, and punitive by emphasizing that these types of statements only serve to fuel the power of the illness. Equally important, it is paramount that the FBT-therapist intervene if the young person is critical towards themselves and undermines their own capacity for collaboration and self-efficacy. It is important to be as transparent as possible about why this intervention is used in Phase 1 – Session 2. The therapist communicates the following:

> I recognize that it may seem inappropriate to ask you as parents/caregivers to assist your adult child to eat more than they feel they can. What I am asking you to do is no different than what therapists in an ED program would be expected to do with patients during meals. [Turning to the TAY], the difference is that you are agreeing to work with your parents/caregivers who have a history with you and a deep understanding of who you are and the best ways to support you during this difficult time. AN has convinced you and your parents/caregivers that you cannot work together and that the illness is too powerful. Together you are more powerful than this illness and you can find new ways to communicate and work in partnership that is respectful and recognizes the autonomy of the young person (not AN) and the moral authority of you as parents/caregivers to persuade your child to eat more than you thought was possible. [Again facing the young person] I can understand that this must be very difficult for you, but the goal of this session is to work in cooperation with your parents or family to help you recover from this illness.

To assist the parents/caregivers, the FBT-TAY therapist may need to coach the parents/caregivers by asking them questions to help them facilitate this intervention. "Based on what you know of your child, what do you think they need to hear from you right now? How can eating more help your TAY achieve their goals in life? What is the bigger life picture for them?" Similarly, therapists can ask the young person: What may the healthy side of you want right now? What do you hope for yourself in the future? What values are congruent with recovery or AN that you want to change? The therapist should disrupt debates between parents/caregivers and the TAY about the food and eating and discourage any attempts at bargaining with the AN (e.g., delaying eating the food during the meal with the promise of eating more another time or a preferred item). The therapist communicates to the parents/caregivers that their TAY may lose their agency in the moment because of anxiety and fears related to AN resulting in them using several techniques (arguing, bargaining, yelling, threatening, etc.) to divide them as a family and undermine parental/caregiver efforts to help them eat more. As described in the FBT-AN manual (Lock & Le Grange, 2012), therapists should encourage parents/caregivers and the young person to work together to support the latter to eat more than they believe they could without parental/caregiver support. We firmly believe that this discussion will shed light on the degree to which the parents/caregivers and young person can collaborate against the AN. The young person may struggle with relinquishing their independence over eating to others and express their ambivalence about parental/caregiver involvement. The FBT-TAY therapist acts as a consultant to the young person by reinforcing that ambivalence and fears are natural and that autonomous decision-making will be supported and encouraged outside of eating/meals. Conversely, the FBT-TAY therapist encourages the parents/caregivers to convey the importance of their involvement and how they will support refeeding temporarily while supporting agency and respect of their TAY.

Encourage Collaboration of the TAY and the Parents/Caregivers in Recovery

An important task for therapists using FBT-TAY is encouraging and maintaining the cooperation of the young person in the treatment process and their recovery. Young people can choose to leave FBT-TAY at any point in the treatment process and therefore their engagement in treatment is paramount. Consequently, FBT-TAY therapists must continuously assess the level of engagement and willingness of the young person in persevering with the treatment despite the challenges associated with temporarily relinquishing their personal power over to their parents/caregivers. In addition to using the individual time with the young person prior to the family sessions, the therapist must attempt to speak directly to the healthy side of the young person *during* the family sessions. Using their expert knowledge about AN, therapists may directly communicate to the young person that they believe they have the skills to make the necessary changes needed to recover from this life-threatening illness. Therapists must relate to the young person in a firm but warm way about the importance of their parents/caregivers assisting them to eat more food than they may be initially willing to do in the session. A rationale for why we are requesting parents/caregivers to insist on eating needs to be communicated to the young person. A therapist may consider saying:

> I know it may feel as if I am siding with your parents/caregivers against you by encouraging them to help you eat. I can also appreciate that what I am asking them to do may feel unnatural and developmentally inappropriate for a young person. However, I have learned from other young people like you that their parents/caregivers do need to help them temporarily until they can do this on their own. Some of my clients have shared with me that the thought of eating often results in AN [or whatever name has been assigned to AN] beating them down to the point where they feel horrible about themselves. These clients sometimes found it freeing that someone else is making the decision about eating (albeit it may be only temporarily).

In addition to asking parents/caregivers to communicate to the young person that they expect them to eat more, the therapist may also relay messages to elicit their cooperation. For instance, therapists can state that they believe the healthy part of them (no matter how small) wants a life better than the one that AN has given them. Highlight goals of the young person that may be achieved with recovery (i.e., completing high school and starting university/college). If the young person has not identified goals outside of the ED, therapists can communicate that eating now will help them reclaim their independence and autonomy and help them identify other life goals to pursue once they recover from AN. In the family meal and the remainder of Phase 1, parents/caregivers may leverage a fair amount of moral, ethical, and emotional influence over the transition-aged youth which may be helpful in engaging the young person to eat and cease engaging in compensatory behaviours. Additionally, discussions around care, love, responsibility, and support can also work to bond family members in their efforts to support their young person in all phases of treatment and recovery.

Common Challenges, Opportunities, and Ways to Overcome Barriers

Challenge 1: The Young Person and the Family Arrive with Insufficient Food for the Meal

The FBT-TAY therapist may inquire about how decisions were made regarding what food to bring to the session. On the one hand, the young person may have fought vehemently with their parents/families against them bringing food that contradicted their ED rules. On the other hand, sometimes families acquiesce to the ED because of heightened conflict or threats of the young person prematurely leaving treatment. The FBT-TAY acknowledges that despite the influence of the ED, the young person and their family have made a commitment to attend the session and collaborate to systematically address illness behaviours. The therapist reminds the entire family that they will work diligently as their consultant to help them identify how to align with the healthy side of the young person by not accommodating to the illness. The FBT-TAY therapist invites the parents/caregivers to visit the closest cafeteria to purchase a meal or additional food items that they believe is needed for their child to recover from AN. In preparation for similar circumstances like this, therapists often have access to food that they can share with the parents/caregivers that they can add to the family meal. The family meal resumes once sufficient food has been obtained.

Challenge 2: The Young Person and Family Exhibit No Friction, Resistance Nor Difficulties with the Family Meal

Some young people begin FBT-TAY minimizing or denying any problems with food or weight and that AN was an anomaly and the illness no longer has a grip on them. Others may shrug off any probes from the FBT-TAY therapist or their family about how they might experience gaining weight or increasing the quality and quantity of food during treatment. This denial of any concerns may signal a desire to quickly move through Phase 1 to reclaim their independence and resume "normal life." It is important for the FBT-TAY therapist to remind the young person that moving too quickly in an effort to "eat their way out of treatment" can backfire. Unrealistic expectations about recovery can place young people at risk of becoming hopeless when they hit a point in their treatment when eating and the weight gain process becomes difficult. Drawing on their knowledge of their child's temperament and personality, parents/caregivers are invited to consider how they will support their child when they experience challenges during meals and when the illness interferes with their loved one's efforts to expedite treatment.

Conclusions

The FBT-TAY therapist utilizes the information gleaned from the family meal to identify what areas will require greater focus in the remainder of Phase 1 and even Phase 2. Session 2 is an opportunity to simultaneously observe the degree of autonomy and independence in eating- and non-food-related areas of the young person and how much the illness has adversely affected the dynamics and interactions of the family in the eating domain. During the family meal, the FBT therapist also works to assert and re-instate collaboration between the parents/caregivers and the young person to give parents/caregivers control overeating. The therapist communicates directly that this control is temporary and only necessary because of the life-threatening nature of AN. Further, this incursion on the TAY autonomy is directed only on food, eating, and related ED maintaining behaviours and is not meant to suggest caregivers take over all aspects of the developing independence in relationships, work, school, etc. In addition to supporting the parents/caregivers, therapists demonstrate empathy and compassion for the difficult predicament of the young person and the parents/caregivers.

Chapter Summary

Here are the key points of this chapter:

(1) The therapist begins the session by evaluating the young person's weight, compensatory behaviours, and perceptions of weight change to anchor the intervention in accurate clinical data and to correct illness-driven misinterpretations.
(2) The therapeutic meal provides an opportunity for the therapist to closely observe family interactions around food – including serving practices, communication patterns, and behavioural accommodations of the illness – to

assess how these dynamics influence the young person's eating and emerging independence.

(3) The therapist examines how frequently and with whom the young person eats outside the home (school, work, peers) to determine the extent of family restructuring required in Phase 1 to ensure consistent nutritional rehabilitation.
(4) Parents/caregivers are coached in real time to support the young person in eating more than they believe possible, using firm, supportive, and non-critical communication strategies while avoiding statements that inadvertently reinforce AN.
(5) The therapist actively promotes collaboration by validating the young person's ambivalence towards treatment, strengthening the healthy self, and linking meal cooperation to the young person's broader developmental goals, values, and future aspirations.
(6) When challenges arise – such as insufficient food or minimization of symptoms – the therapist intervenes to prevent accommodation of the illness, re-establish treatment structure, and ensure that adequate food is available for the therapeutic meal.
(7) Information gathered from the meal is synthesized to identify entrenched illness-maintaining patterns, relational dynamics, and areas requiring intensified focus in subsequent sessions and phases of FBT-TAY.
(8) The therapist reinforces that parental/caregiver oversight of eating is a temporary, targeted intervention aimed solely at reversing starvation and does not diminish the young person's autonomy in other key developmental domains.

References

Lock, J., & Le Grange, D. (2012). *Treatment manual for anorexia nervosa: A family-based approach* (2nd ed.). The Guilford Press.

Chapter 7

Remainder of Phase 1

Remainder of Phase 1: Session 3–10

The overall goals of the remainder of Phase 1 are similar to the ones described in the manual for adolescents with AN and BN (Lock & Le Grange, 2012, 2007). As noted earlier in this book, therapists work carefully to engage both the young person and their parents/caregivers in the process of achieving the goals of weight restoration and eating rehabilitation. The focus of the therapeutic content in Phase 1 is relentlessly on weight restoration, especially since early and rapid weight gain predicts good outcomes (Doyle et al., 2010).

FBT-TAY Therapists Use the Following Interventions to Meet the Goals of Phase 1, Sessions 3–8

(1) Weigh the young person and collect compensatory behaviour logs when needed.
(2) Direct, re-direct, and focus therapeutic interventions on disrupting all AN maintaining behaviour including rigid food rules, excessive exercise, compensatory behaviours, etc.
(3) Discuss, support, and help the parental/caregiver dyad and the young person to work on weight restoration/normalization, addressing starvation and reducing ED behaviours.
(4) Use externalization to continue to modify parental/caregiver criticism (in and out of sessions) when present and encourage expression of warmth.
(5) Recount and celebrate successful steps that young people and their parents/caregivers have taken that contribute to progress in treatment.

Weigh the Patient and Collect Compensatory Behaviour Logs (When Indicated)

During Sessions 3–8, the FBT-TAY therapist continues to meet individually with the young person for approximately 20– 30 minutes before meeting with the

DOI: 10.4324/9781003463351-8

whole family. Given the often-tenuous involvement of young people who can prematurely leave treatment, this is an important opportunity for the FBT-TAY therapists to build a trusting, collaborative working relationship with the individual and a way to solidify the autonomous decision-making external to the AN. The rationale behind the individual meeting is to simultaneously weigh the young person and support them if needed when distressed by weight changes. Similarly, the FBT-TAY therapist works with the young person to identify and document any compensatory behaviours (e.g., overeating, binge eating, purging behaviours, and excessive exercise that may be employed to control weight or manage emotions related to eating and weight). To elicit engagement of the young person, FBT-TAY therapists directly address any unexpressed or expressed anger that may emerge related to the illness, handing over control of the eating to parents/caregivers and the treatment process itself. In addition, exploration of other feelings related to the illness such as shame must be discussed. Shame usually arises when a young person experiences "failure" to uphold pathological standards of the AN related to weight and eating. At the same time, young people may engage in discussions about this unique stage of life such as interpersonal and communication issues with friends, romantic partners, siblings, parents/caregivers, or professional relationships with co-workers and supervisors or educators if attending school. The young person may also engage in discussions about identity issues (e.g., sexuality, gender, roles, and values), career. and academic aspirations. The FBT-TAY therapist invites this exploration which creates the foundation to strengthen the healthier part of the young person.

At the end of the individual meeting, therapists might typically ask the young person two salient questions: First, what could parents/caregivers specifically do this week to assist with eating and recovery? Second, what can you do differently to illustrate improvements in eating to support increased self-agency and support your recovery? The therapist asks the young person to develop a plan of how they will relay the responses to these questions to their parents/caregivers in the session (prompting of the young person may be needed and should be planned). The therapist should identify and support any evidence of the "healthy" non-AN cognitions/beliefs or behaviours and encourage expression of this in the family meetings by articulating desires and interests that are contrary to the illness.

At the beginning of each family session, the therapist reviews the progress of the young person's weight and changes in AN symptoms. As described in the FBT-AN manual, the rate of weight gain may vary considerably from young person to another (Lock & Le Grange, 2012, pp. 124). Therapists should first highlight all progress and positive changes the family and young person have made that has led to weight gain/normalization or diminished maintaining AN behaviours.

At the same time, FBT-TAY therapists should work with the parents/caregivers to identify the unique barriers within their family context that are hindering them from facilitating weight gain in their child including weight bias. Although not an exhaustive list, the following barriers to weight restoration may be observed:

(1) Parents/caregivers are not on the same page about the seriousness of AN contributing to conflict, arguments, and tensions about the extent to which the young person should withdraw from normative activities (i.e., school, work, and extra-curricular activities).
(2) Parents/caregivers engage in significant conflicts over how best to increase food and support their TAY with eating and normalization of meals.
(3) Parents/caregivers experience significant reluctance about using their parental/caregiver and moral authority because the young person is independent, mature, and self-reliant.
(4) Parents/caregivers are inconsistent in their efforts to support their child because they are unwilling to support weight restoration and the target weight.

As stated by Lock and Le Grange (2012), it may take the parents/caregivers until Session 5 or 6 to find a way to work collaboratively to assist with weight gain (p. 124). However, in young people with a lengthier illness course (developed AN in early to mid-adolescence), it may take parents/caregivers longer to disrupt patterns of interacting surrounding ED symptoms.

At the onset of every family session in Phase 1, the therapist (and young person in Phases 2 and 3) presents the weight chart and compensatory behaviour log to the parents/caregivers. Using a weight chart and/or compensatory log, the therapist documents the direction of the weight with the young person. The therapist and the young person decide together who will share the logs with the parents/caregivers. Either way, the weight chart helps the family to discuss the progress of weight restoration, including the specific progress from the previous week. This objective data can be useful to guide the conversation about what is working/not working related to food intake and symptom management. The FBT-TAY therapist must seek a response from the family about their thoughts regarding the changes in weight. The following types of questions may be posed to the parents/caregivers:

- What are your thoughts about the direction of the weight?
- Who is most/least surprised or worried by the weight change (or lack of weight gain)?
- What changes do you think need to happen based on the information received about the weight?

If the weight is moving upwards, FBT-TAY therapists should spend time focusing on what went well to contribute to the weight changes. The same type of questions should be asked regarding the compensatory behaviour log when needed. Even when weight has increased (and/or compensatory behaviours have decreased), the focus should remain on normalization of eating and weight restoration and avoidance of weight suppression. The therapist should ask the parents/caregivers what level of support they will continue to provide and/or what they intend to undertake differently to keep the momentum moving in the right direction. The following types of questions may be asked:

- What will you add to the meals to promote further weight gain or avoidance of weight suppression?
- Are there any times when the young person will need additional support with eating or eliminating compensatory behaviours?
- Who will provide that support for that specific meal?
- Are there needs to improve variety or range of foods eaten? If so, what specifically can you do to improve or add more variety to the meals?

If the young person loses weight (or increases compensatory behaviours), therapists should ask specific questions of the young person and their parents/caregivers about their understanding of what may have occurred in the previous week that led to the lack of weight gain or increased compensatory behaviours. This line of questioning should not convey disappointment, frustration, and judgment of the young person and parents/caregivers but rather encourage them to recognize that AN is a difficult disorder to overcome. If the rate of weight gain remains slow or stalled, therapists should orchestrate another intense scene about the illness to increase the anxiety of the parents/caregivers and the young person to propel them to work together as a team against the illness. Therapists may need to introduce or reiterate the same information and research discussed in the first session, highlighting the seriousness of this illness and the enormous psychological, medical, social, and academic consequences that arise as this illness progresses further into adulthood. Therapists may also use metaphors or analogies that will work to solidify the commitment to work together to meet the objectives of Phase 1. It may help to use the example of what they would have to do as a parental/caregiver unit if their TAY experienced a serious sports injury that resulted in them becoming severely injured and incapable of caring for them for a prolonged time. Although challenging and disruptive to the family, parents/caregivers would be required to take on responsibilities (bathing, feeding, and assisting with mobility) that may seem developmentally inappropriate but are necessary given the circumstances. In such instances, parents/caregivers would be required to take leaves of absence from work or re-arrange their employment schedules to assist with recovery from an accident or injury or post-surgery.

In the presence of slow weight progress, therapists should inquire about whether parents/caregivers are acquiescing to the fears that their young person cannot tolerate gaining too much weight, too quickly. Another example that can potentially be helpful is to use the example of how the parents/caregivers would respond if an oncologist recommended and prescribed a certain amount of chemotherapy on a weekly basis to their TAY. What would parents/caregivers do if their adult child demanded a less-than-optimal dosage of chemotherapy or radiation every week? Even though the young person can legally decline to receive and continue treatment, how would parents/caregivers respond to this assertion from their adult child? Would they use their parental/caregiver authority and control to insist that the young person pursue and continue with chemotherapy? Would parents/caregivers ever agree to use less chemotherapy in order to help decrease some of the emotional and physical side effects associated with this difficult but life-maintaining treatment? Would a parent/caregivers consider giving a lower dose of chemotherapy because it will help reduce the anxiety/sadness/frustration of their child? Along the same lines, reducing food intake may temporarily dampen intense fears but it will permit the illness to persist and health to deteriorate. If parents/caregivers respond emphatically that they would invariably do everything in their power to ensure that their child (regardless of age) follows through with the treatment prescribed by an oncologist because cancer is lethal but have not expressed the same approach to AN, it may be helpful for the therapist to carefully review the literature on the high morbidity and mortality associated with AN. In such circumstances, therapists should repeat the compelling clinical impacts of AN described in the "intense scene" from Session 1 but incorporate additional examples of the impact of AN on the young person described in the remainder of Phase 1.

Focus on Eating and Maintaining Behaviours

Therapists should direct, re-direct, and focus therapeutic interventions on food, eating behaviours, and management until eating and weight are normalized. Building on the information gleaned from the weight and compensatory behaviours log, the therapist asks specific questions about the quality and the quantity of food eaten in the previous week by working through meals consumed (or not) each day. A discussion about every meal should occur with the young person and the parents/caregivers. The therapist must further ask questions about any potential barriers that made it difficult for parental/caregiver support/management of the eating. It is also important to explore what the young person and the parents/caregivers did to proactively address challenges and reduce ED behaviours. Therapists should ask specific questions about how the parents/caregivers decided upon a particular meal, which parent/caregivers prepared and served the meal and who provided direct meal support and distractions after the meal if purging is a concern. The therapist may ask questions about any meals where the illness was persistent, and the parent(s)/caregiver(s) had difficulties supporting the young person to complete meals.

Questions that are general and vague may prevent therapists and the family from identifying where the ED is most prominent. Therapists should help caregivers to identify what changes will be made to specific meals and what type/amount of food will be included and increased. As described by Lock and Le Grange (2012), these sessions may seem repetitious to the therapist, the young person, and the parents/caregivers, but they are aimed at refining the effectiveness and precision of behavioural changes needed to combat AN. Thus, therapists must remain persistent in their efforts even if it means asking the same questions about food and weight week after week while also working with the parents/caregivers to continue to work together to identify effective ways of problem-solving around how to support eating in the young person.

There are various lines of inquiry that therapists may follow to fully ascertain the degree to which parental/caregiver support of eating during meals was applied. Therapists may inquire about what meals went well, and which meals were most problematic for the parents/caregivers and the young person. Moreover, the therapist may systemically ask about each meal (breakfast, lunch, dinner, and snacks) each day over the last seven days. This deeper inquiry into the specifics about each meals helps to keep the session tightly focused on eating and weight normalization while also allowing for a more refined and detailed plan of action covering all meals. Using their expert knowledge of AN, therapists may act as consultants to the parents/caregivers and the young person by identifying possible strategies for increasing the quality and quantity of food consumed. However, the final decisions about how to alter individual meals are left with the parents/caregivers in Phase 1 with input from the healthy side of the young person.

Supporting Weight Restoration

Therapist should discuss, support, and help the parental/caregiver dyad and the young person to work on weight restoration. It is common for parents/caregivers to require substantial assistance during Phases 1 and 2 to find ways to work together in order to effectively challenge AN. The issues discussed in the manual for treatment of adolescents with AN and BN by Lock and Le Grange (2012) and Lock and Le Grange (2025) are also applicable to young people. However, there are some unique challenges that may interfere with parents/caregivers working together.

First, parents/caregivers may have differing views about how much responsibility young people should have with eating during mealtimes. Parents/caregivers may assign different emphasis on the importance of autonomy, independence, and the appropriateness of supporting a young person with eating. These issues may also arise with younger adolescents, but we assume there are more societal and familial messages about appropriate levels of parental/caregiver involvement in adult treatment for mental health issues. Second, when working with young people, parents/caregivers may be locked in disagreements and tensions especially if the illness has been in the child's life for a longer period. In such cases, parents/caregivers may have greater difficulties finding new ways of working together when patterns of relating and communicating with each other have become habitual.

It is not uncommon for parents/caregivers to raise questions about their role in assisting the young people with meals. Some parents/caregivers may believe that it is no longer appropriate to supervise their 20-year-old child while they eat. The therapist must acknowledge that under different circumstances, the parent/caregiver would not need to step in to provide support that is seemingly age inappropriate. However, parental/caregiver support is appropriate for an illness like AN that it is life-threatening. For instance, the therapist may say:

> I can understand that it does not feel natural to sit with your 20-year-old child to assist with lunch (or any other meal) but this is a temporary solution until s/he can begin to do this independently. There are many instances when an adult needs support. For example, your 20-year-old son was in a car accident and was in a cast for a few months, you would be required similarly to step in to help with preparing meals and sitting with them while he ate.

Therapists should come up with their own analogies and metaphors that they think will work with the parents/caregiver to help them understand the importance of meal support regardless of the age of the young person. It is important to remind the young person and their parents/caregivers that parental/caregiver management of meals/eating is temporary and that this work is not any different from what would happen in an intensive ED program. Therapists communicate that parental/caregiver support with eating has the potential to be far less disruptive than requiring their child to enter an intensive ED hospital program for several months. It is vital that therapists inquire about what may underlie parental/caregiver questions about their involvement in refeeding. Parents/caregivers may be experiencing stress, burden, and frustration with the challenges of assisting with eating and meal support. In this case, the therapist should invite the parents/caregivers to identify how they can support each other to alleviate distress and burnout and to consider involving others who may be able to assist them during the remainder of Phase 1.

In a warm and empathic manner, therapists may share their observations of patterns of interacting that occur continuously and persistently despite decisions to respond differently between sessions. As a case in point, parents/caregivers may become overly accommodating of illness behaviours or avoidant of difficult ED behaviours. Parents/caregivers may vacillate between accommodating and avoiding illness behaviours to reduce conflict or to alleviate the suffering of the young person with AN; however, this wavering ultimately serves to perpetuate AN. Sometimes disagreements within parental/caregiver dyads may arise when one parent/caregiver excessively accommodates while the other unduly overlooks serious ED behaviours because they are distressing or they feel ill-equipped to deal with them. Therapists may consider saying the following to parents/caregivers locked in maladaptive positions:

> I can see that the two of you both love your TAY very much and that you would do anything to assist them with this difficult illness. You have been working together to battle against AN for a very long time. Like a lot of parents/caregivers in similar circumstances, parents/caregivers may at times do things that in the immediate run reduce conflict and tension between them as a couple and with their child, but this only serves to fuel the illness in the long run. I have sometimes noted that the two of you respond very differently to your child when they resist your efforts to help them eat. X, you seem to back away from insisting that your child eats and instead leave the house for many hours. X, you seem to prepare meals to appease the illness such as making a salad rather than the chicken and rice that you had originally planned. How may these responses interfere with you working together as parents/caregivers? This illness has a way sometimes to divide and conquer parents/caregivers because it makes them feel ineffective and it is stronger. Do you think you have become divided as parents/caregivers? What can you do differently? As your consultant, what can I do to support you? Can you think of times when you were able to work together despite it feeling very difficult?

FBT-TAY therapist refrains from prescribing or advising parents/caregivers on how they should behave or respond to their child with AN; in a non-judgmental manner, the therapist works with the parents/caregivers to problem-solve how they can be on the "same page" to diminish the power of the illness over their lives as a family and to better support their child in a warm, compassionate, and collaborative way.

Collaborative Style

In contrast to FBT-AN for adolescents, special attention should be given to developing and strengthening collaborations between young people and their parents/caregivers in Phase 1 because of the older age and increased agency associated with emerging adulthood. A salient goal of FBT-TAY is to assist parents/caregivers and young people to work together on the same team to overcome AN. Due to ambivalence about eating and weight gain in AN (Fairburn, 2008), the ability of young people to collaborate with their parents/caregivers will likely wax and wane throughout the treatment process. In fact, therapists should help normalize ambivalence by emphasizing that many young people with AN seem to want parental/caregiver support one moment while rejecting or declining the need for parental/caregiver involvement the next.

Throughout the first phase, therapists should raise questions of both the young person and their parents/caregivers about how they are managing to prevent or reduce the ambivalence from adversely affecting their collaborative relationship in the treatment process.

Parents/caregivers are acutely aware that the collaborative relationship with the young person is tenuous. This awareness and fears of their child leaving treatment may threaten parental/caregiver empowerment over eating and weight restoration. Consequently, in every session, therapists should directly ascertain from the young person and the parents/caregivers how well they are working together against the power of the AN. In addition to continuously supporting parents/caregivers to work as an effective dyad, every effort should be made to ensure that parents/caregivers are working to align themselves with the healthy side of the young person. Therapists should elevate their knowledge and understanding of how to intervene when the TAY becomes discouraged, hopeless, and distressed by the work required to overcome this life-threatening illness.

Therapists may use an array of interventions for strengthening the collaborative relationship including warmth, empathy, externalization, emphasizing the temporary need for parental/caregiver responsibility over eating, and focusing on building agency in the young person in non-ED areas. First, therapists should model compassion and empathy of the young person and validate their experience when they express ambivalence about engaging in behavioural changes and the involvement of their parents/caregivers in this process. It is important that the young person and the parents/caregivers do not attribute the interventions in FBT as the source of the ambivalence but rather the illness itself. Through modelling and direct support, therapists may work carefully to support the parents/caregivers to communicate their emotional support of their child. Here is a clinical example of therapist/parental warmth/empathy: The therapist says:

> Your parents/caregivers and I can understand that this is a very difficult place for you to be with this illness and treatment. It sounds like you are finding gaining weight (or eating more) very challenging. We understand that you may not be feeling like you want to do this anymore because it is just getting too hard. You are not alone in this treatment even though it may feel that way to you. Your parents/caregivers are doing this with you because they believe in you and that you have the courage and strength to continue to persevere with this treatment.

The therapist turns to the parents/caregivers and asks them directly to share their thoughts/feelings about what it must be like for their child to live with AN and to do this treatment. "What makes them believe that their adult child can do this?" After expressing warmth and hope for the child, therapists may work with the parents/caregivers and the young person to identify when the illness seemed less prominent in their relationship. Therapists should demonstrate curiosity about times when the parents/caregivers and the young person were working well together and when they do not. How were they talking with each other? What were they doing? Weekly sessions are an opportunity to explore these observations and to help families determine if there are additional ways they may communicate their support with recovery.

Modify Parental/Caregiver Criticism

Therapist should continue to modify parental/caregiver criticism (in and out of sessions) and increase parental warmth through the use of externalization. Parental/caregiver management of eating and weight must occur in a climate of support and compassion towards the young person (and the parents/caregivers). FBT-TAY therapists must strike the balance between elevating the anxiety of the parents/caregivers about the illness to sustain their focus on behavioural changes, while also increasing their empathy and understanding of the predicament of the young person with the illness. Therapists should intervene when they hear parental/caregiver criticism, anger, and frustration being expressed towards the young person. Therapists may use a variety of interventions to educate the family about how criticism may worsen AN and decrease the chances of recovery, including discussing research on expressed emotion (Eisler et al., 2000, 2007; Le Grange et al., 1992, 2005; Lock et al., 2005; 2010; Loeb et al., 2007) and the importance of parental/caregiver warmth in improving outcomes (Le Grange et al., 2012).

It is also important for therapists to model an uncritical attitude towards the parents/caregivers. Therapists must avoid becoming judgmental of the parents/caregivers if they have been unsuccessful in supporting their child to eat what is required to gain weight or reduce symptoms. Providing support and compassion towards the parents'/caregivers' models how they can also engage compassionately towards their child when change is slow, ambivalence in their child is high, and the ED symptoms are strong. Along the same lines as the parents/caregivers, therapists must communicate their compassion for the difficult position that the young person is in with the illness.

> The illness sounds like it was very powerful at that meal. What can be learned from this experience? What would you do differently knowing that Ana or ED (possible names for AN to separate it from the young person) can be so persuasive that less food is needed?" The FBT-TAY therapist can also say the following to the young person: I know that this must be very hard for you. It is not easy to relinquish decision making related to eating to other people even when we know their intentions are to be supportive. We are all here to remind me you are not alone in this painful place with your ED. Can you call on the healthy side of you – no matter how small – to help you in this moment?

The therapist should continuously intervene when parents/caregivers are expressing frustration/anger/negativity towards the young person. Using externalization, a therapist can help reframe negative statements about the young person into declarations about the illness. In addition to utilizing externalization to manage parental/caregiver criticism, this intervention may also be employed to enable young people to identify how the illness has interfered with their life trajectory. Through the use of externalization, the therapist can also work with the young person to assert when their thoughts, feelings, and perceptions differ from the illness. For example, a therapist may say, "It sounds like when you are faced with eating a feared food it is as if your brain is hijacked, and your thinking changes, it sounds like you notice that you feel more nervous and are paralyzed from moving forward."

Recounting Success

Using a strengths-focused approach, therapists are persistently expressing their unequivocal belief in the power of families to work together to find effective solutions to support recovery. Any efforts on the part of the young child to eat a "normal meal" with less parental/caregiver support must be celebrated. As described in the FBT-AN manual (Lock & Le Grange, 2012, p. 133), therapists should carve out time to acknowledge the efforts of the healthy part of the young person in increasing their eating, eating previously feared foods, and decreasing symptoms and compensatory behaviours. Therapists must invite each parent/caregiver to identify and acknowledge successful steps that the young person is taking to gain control over their illness and agency in their lives. Similarly, young people should be called upon in every session to describe what they specifically did to diminish the power of the illness in their lives and their relationships with others.

Common Challenges in Phase 1 of FBT-TAY

There are several challenges that may arise in Phase 1. This is not meant to be an exhaustive list.

Challenge 1: The Young Person Struggles to Collaborate or Allow Parents/Caregivers to Take Control

The young person may initially, or throughout Phase 1, struggle to collaborate with their parents/caregivers and the FBT-TAY therapist. It is recommended that this be addressed as it arises and acknowledges that it is natural for young people to fear losing their agency even if temporary. Non-judgmental exploration of this loss of agency and control should be discussed supportively with open-ended and curious questions about the short- and long-term implications of choosing not to work in partnership with their parents/family. Due to the nature of AN, ambivalence, hopelessness, and anxiety can often increase in the early portion of Phase 1, and this can influence a young person's ability to logically and emotionally consider and accept support. Additionally, it is common for many distressing emotions (anger, fear, and mistrust) to also arise during mealtimes. Exploring these observations and using externalization, as well as a return to the values and goals that the young person may have expressed during the pretreatment phase, may aid in shoring them up to accept parental/caregiver involvement in their care again. This can also be an opportunity to explore what is working and not working for the young person in terms of the ED and the support received from their parents/caregivers. Sometimes there may be fears, or ways that support is being offered/delivered that the young person is distressed by. If the young person is able to articulate these fears, this may help with validation and/or problem-solving. It may also help to frame the collaboration with their parents/caregivers over eating as an experiment that can be conducted for a short period of time. Finally, if this becomes a persistent problem with weight and eating remaining unchanged, it may be helpful to review treatment alternate options, including higher level of care or hospitalization.

Challenge 2: Parents/Caregivers Are Hesitant or Refuse to Take Charge of AN Even When the Young Person Is Accepting Their Support

If parents/caregivers are struggling to support their young person because they believe that due to their age, or competencies in other areas of life (school, work, etc.), that the young person is able to eat "on their own," it is important to redirect conversations to early Phase 1 goals, including the rationale for parent/caregiver support, both from the practical/behavioural standpoint as well as their important emotional role. Parental/caregiver reluctance to engage in refeeding may also stem from anxiety and avoidance which are natural responses to a life-threatening illness. Therapists must be sensitive to the high level of distress experienced by parents/caregivers during this treatment. Often fear can be paralyzing, and parents/caregivers report being uncertain about what may occur if they "stand up" to AN. Providing validation to parents/caregivers related to their own emotional response, as well as exploring the treatment goal of disrupting the cycle of restriction that AN perpetuates, and centring parents/caregivers capacity in this role, may help to address parental/caregiver reluctance to support eating in the early stages of treatment.

Challenge 3: Other Comorbid Problems Become the Focus

Throughout this book, we discuss the importance of need for collaborative care between the young person, the parents/caregivers, and the broader interpersonal team. Indeed, this team approach is vital for the support of all young people with AN but becomes particularly critical for young people with comorbid conditions. In order for the FBT-TAY therapist to remain focused on the symptoms related to AN, other providers must address and manage psychiatric comorbidities. Continued conversations, inclusive of the young person and their caregivers, is essential to understanding how comorbidities might be best treated and addressed.

Conclusions

The interventions described in Phase 1 are very similar to those outlined in the Lock and Le Grange (2025) book. Although a relentless focus on eating and weight restoration/normalization is paramount, FBT-TAY therapists should not delay involving other experts who may assist with the amelioration of other impairing mental health problems. Due to the entrenchment of ED behaviours over time, additional effort may be needed to encourage disempowered and reluctant parents/caregivers to develop new strategies for working together in an effective way to support their TAY. When there is evidence of criticism of the young person, using externalization to help the parents/caregivers to separate AN from the young person is needed. Supporting and enhancing the expression of parental/caregiver warmth should also be encouraged. The strengths of both young people and parents/caregivers must be continuously identified and celebrated.

Criteria for Entering Phase 2

- Steady and persistent weight gain or weight maintenance/normalization when in Phase 1.
- Normal eating patterns (three meals and two snacks) and no excessive exercise, binge eating, purging, and/or other unhealthy strategies to maintain low weight.
- Parental/caregiver agreement that the young person can take on increasing responsibility to eat.
- The young person expresses a desire to eat independently and appears to be open to working collaboratively with others on how to achieve this.
- The level of tension, conflict, and anxiety in the family about weight and eating has dissipated and the parents/caregivers are consistently expressing empathy of their TAY.

The young person is able to identify the "healthy" part of themselves more frequently.

Chapter Summary

Here are the key points of this chapter:

(1) Phase 1, Sessions 3–10 continue the intensive focus on renourishment, with the therapist working to keep both the young person and their parents/

caregivers engaged in the difficult but essential work of restoring weight and reducing eating-disorder behaviours.

(2) Each session begins with dedicated individual time for the young person, giving them space to process weight changes; acknowledge or document compensatory behaviours; explore emotions like shame, anger, or fear; and strengthen the healthier parts of themselves that exist outside the illness.

(3) Weekly weight and symptom information is used to guide clear and practical conversations with the family about what contributed to progress, where meals became challenging, and what specific strategies are needed to improve consistency, variety, and parental/caregivers support.

(4) Parents/caregivers often experience uncertainty about how much authority to use or how developmentally appropriate their involvement feels, so the therapist helps them build a unified, collaborative approach that protects the young person even when the work feels uncomfortable.

(5) Externalization continues to play a central role by helping parents/caregivers direct frustration towards the illness rather than the young person, reducing criticism, and improving warmth, empathy, and compassion during high-stress eating situations.

(6) Therapists keep returning to the concrete details of eating throughout the week, even when it feels repetitive, because the precision and consistency of these conversations are essential for reversing starvation and preventing accommodation to the illness.

(7) Collaboration between parents/caregivers and the young person remains delicate during this phase, so the therapist continually supports moments of teamwork, validates ambivalence, and highlights small successes to strengthen motivation and a sense of shared purpose.

(8) Celebrating progress is essential throughout Phase 1, and therapists help families notice even the smallest victories, reinforcing agency, reducing hopelessness, and building confidence that recovery is both possible and already underway.

References

Doyle, P. M., Le Grange, D., Loeb, K., Doyle, A. C., & Crosby, R. D. (2010). Early response to family-based treatment for adolescent anorexia nervosa. *International Journal of Eating Disorders*, *43*(7), 659–662. https://doi.org/10.1002/eat.20764

Eisler, I., Dare, C., Hodes, M., Russell, G., Dodge, E., & Le Grange, D. (2000). family therapy for adolescent anorexia nervosa: The results of a controlled comparison of two family interventions. *Journal of Child Psychology and Psychiatry*, *41*(6), 727–736. https://doi.org/10.1111/1469-7610.00660

Eisler, I., Simic, M., Russell, G. F., & Dare, C. (2007). A randomised controlled treatment trial of two forms of family therapy in adolescent anorexia nervosa: A five-year follow-up. *Journal of Child Psychology and Psychiatry, and Allied Disciplines*, *48*(6), 552–560. https://doi.org/10.1111/j.1469-7610.2007.01726.x

Fairburn, C. G. (2008). *Cognitive behavior therapy and EDs*. The Guilford Press.
Le Grange, D., Binford, R., & Loeb, K. L. (2005). Manualized family-based treatment for anorexia nervosa: A case series. *Journal of the American Academy of Child and Adolescent Psychiatry*, *44*(1), 41–46. https://doi.org/10.1097/01.chi.0000145373.68863.85
Le Grange, D., Eisler, I., Dare, C., & Russell, G. F. (1992). Evaluation of family treatments in adolescent anorexia nervosa: A pilot study. *International Journal of Eating Disorders*, *12*(4), 347–357. https://doi.org/10.1002/1098-108X(199212)12:4<347::AID-EAT2260120402>3.0.CO;2-W
Le Grange, D., Lock, J., Agras, W. S., Moye, A., Bryson, S. W., Jo, B., & Kraemer, H. C. (2012). Moderators and mediators of remission in family-based treatment and adolescent focused therapy for anorexia nervosa. *Behaviour Research and Therapy*, *50*(2), 85–92. https://doi.org/10.1016/j.brat.2011.11.003
Lock, J., Agras, W. S., Bryson, S., & Kraemer, H. C. (2005). A comparison of short- and long-term family therapy for adolescent anorexia nervosa. *Journal of the American Academy of Child and Adolescent Psychiatry*, *44*(7), 632–639. https://doi.org/10.1097/01.chi.0000161647.82775.0a
Lock, J., & Le Grange, D. (2007). *Treatment manual for anorexia nervosa: A family-based approach* (1st ed.). Guilford Press.
Lock, J., & Le Grange, D. (2012). *Treatment manual for anorexia nervosa: A family-based approach* (2nd ed.). The Guilford Press.
Lock, J., & Le Grange, D. (2025). *Treatment manual for anorexia nervosa: A family-based approach* (3rd ed.). The Guilford Press.
Lock, J., Le Grange, D., Agras, W. S., Moye, A., Bryson, S. W., & Jo, B. (2010). Randomized clinical trial comparing family-based treatment with adolescent-focused individual therapy for adolescents with anorexia nervosa. *Archives of General Psychiatry*, *67*(10), 1025–1032. https://doi.org/10.1001/archgenpsychiatry.2010.128
Loeb, K. L., Walsh, B. T., Lock, J., le Grange, D., Jones, J., Marcus, S., Weaver, J., & Dobrow, I. (2007). Open trial of family-based treatment for full and partial anorexia nervosa in adolescence: Evidence of successful dissemination. *Journal of the American Academy of Child and Adolescent Psychiatry*, *46*(7), 792–800. https://doi.org/10.1097/chi.0b013e318058a98e

Chapter 8

Phase 2

(Sessions 11–20)

Phase 2 consists of three main goals:

(1) Transitioning the eating from the family back to the young person.
(2) Helping reduce compensatory behaviours that may be maintaining AN.
(3) Identifying major issues related to emerging adulthood and difficulties in autonomous decision-making with practising eating with an array of individuals and in a variety of contexts.

Lock and Le Grange (2012) state that "*much of the focus in the early part of Phase 2 is on experiments with transitioning control over eating and exercise back to the adolescent child safely*" (p. 179). In FBT-TAY, even more than in younger adolescence, transition of control should be a major focus of Phase 2, encouraging the young person to increasingly gain independence over eating with progressively less parental/caregivers management and support during meals. However, young people may continuously receive support from their parents/caregivers and other important people in their lives as they experiment with eating more independently and in a variety of contexts. Furthermore, it is in Phase 2 that the therapist can decrease frequency of sessions from weekly to biweekly.

In Phase 2 of FBT-TAY Versus FBT-AN

(1) The meeting with the young person prior to the family session is increased from 15 minutes in FBT-AN to 20–30 minutes in FBT-TAY.
(2) Both modalities focus on returning control of age-appropriate eating back to the young person gradually.
(3) FBT-TAY places a greater emphasis on the young person achieving independent eating in a variety of settings outside the home (e.g., school, work, with their partner, or peers), depending on their level of autonomy.

DOI: 10.4324/9781003463351-9

The Therapist Uses the Following Interventions to Meet the Goals of Phase 2

(4) Continue to weigh the young person and complete the compensatory behaviour log.
(5) Introduce the young person to the idea of tracking the quality and quantity of food eaten during each meal.
(6) The young person (not the therapist) introduces the weight and compensatory log on their progress with eating in the beginning of the family meetings.
(7) Help the parent/caregivers and the young person collaboratively decide how to transition control over eating and weight back from the former to the later.
(8) Continuously modify parental/caregivers criticism and self-criticism in the young person.

Monitoring of Weight and Compensatory Behaviours

Continue to Weigh the Young Person and Use the Compensatory Behaviour Log

As described in FBT for AN and BN for adolescents, the therapist continues to weigh and keep track of compensatory behaviours using a log. The amount of time spent with the young person remains the same (20– 30 minutes), but the focus may gradually shift away from weight and food to other issues especially as concerns about the ED symptoms abate. The active role of the therapist in relaying information about the young person's progress to the parents/caregivers also diminishes in this phase. Young people should become increasingly responsible for communicating with their parents/caregivers when they are experiencing improvements but also when they require support from others in their lives.

By Phase 2, a predictable routine has been established between the therapist and the young person regarding weighing and documentation of any compensatory behaviours. At the start of this phase, therapists may communicate to the young person that they will be required to relay changes in their weight and symptoms to their parents/caregivers. A therapist may consider saying the following:

> We are at a point in your treatment where I think it would be important for you to start telling your parents/caregivers what is happening with your weight and other AN maintaining behaviours. It is important for you to develop the skills of communicating to your parents/caregivers your successes and struggles with your weight, eating and symptoms. It will also give you a chance to relate to your parents/caregivers as a young person who is developing more responsibility for her/his recovery and treatment. Of course, I will continue to

support and provide you with assistance in thinking of the best way of letting your parents/caregivers know where you are at with your weight and eating. However, the goal is for you to continue to practice this skill and to be able to do this independently by the end of this phase of the treatment.

During the individual time with the young person, discussions should take place regarding how to transfer the role of communicating weight progress and the binge/purge log from the therapist to the young person. The therapist and the young person should also identify any potential challenges that arise (AN hampers the abilities to accurately relay information about weight and ED behaviours to parents/caregivers) in the family sessions.

This individual time may also be used to address other concerns raised by young people pertaining to the ED and recovery process. For some older adolescents and young people, body image difficulties may continue to persist or escalate as they approach their targeted weight. For individuals who have been ill since adolescence, physiological changes may be distressing to them as they become young adults. Young people may be ashamed of their body changes and may be unlikely to raise these issues unless prompted by an empathetic and supportive therapist. Therapists must find a way to acknowledge the difficulties that may be arising for the young person as they learn to tolerate or become attuned to changes to their body while also reinforcing the advantages of recovery, improved health and mental health, and interpersonal connections.

For other young people, weight may decrease or plateau in Phase 2. If a setback has occurred, the therapist supports the young person and the family to work together to challenge the resurgence of the illness. The therapist will need to bolster the parents/caregivers (and the healthy side of the young person) by emphasizing the medical risks associated with remaining at a weight that is lower than where they need to be, the possibility of AN becoming chronic, and the need for more intensive treatment which would be even more disruptive to the life of the young person. The therapist may also need to increase the sense of urgency in the young person (and the parents/caregivers) about how AN will interrupt their efforts to become independent (e.g., pursue post-secondary education and socialize with their peers). By this stage of the treatment, therapists and parents/caregivers should have developed a wealth of knowledge and examples of what is motivating the young person to continue in the process of recovery. When weight plateaus (and eating becomes disordered), therapists should work with parents/caregivers to highlight all the reasons for recovery that have been discussed in and out of sessions by the young person. These reasons may help reinvigorate the young person to engage in behavioural change.

Self-Monitoring

The FBT-TAY therapist should introduce the young person to the idea of self-monitoring to track the quality and quantity of food eaten during each meal.

This is a significant departure from FBT for adolescents. The rationale for this adaptation is that self-monitoring is a critical component of cognitive behaviour therapy (Mass et al., 2013) and adolescent-focused therapy (Town et al., 2024) that are delivered using an individual format and have been shown to be effective in addressing ED symptoms (Tregarthen et al., 2019). Given that the FBT-TAY provides one-on-one brief sessions with the young person, the skills of self-monitoring are used as a tool to enhance self-awareness and self-efficacy (Dimitropoulos et al., 2014).

By Phase 2, young people should continue to gain increasing responsibility for monitoring their own progress with their own eating. In the individual session, the therapist encourages the young person to reflect on where they may be restricting their eating or eating rigidly/safely. The goals of self-monitoring are twofold: (1) to assist the young person to become responsible for monitoring their eating every day and communicating what meals may be more challenging for them in and outside of the sessions and (2) to learn how to self-monitor their eating in order to develop and practice skills that will assist them in the short and long run to maintain their recovery from AN. As a consultant, therapists leave it entirely up to the young person to decide the best way to monitor their eating. Therapists may provide a range of examples of how to self-monitor including the following:

(1) Initially focus on the exact time and frequency of when they eat their meals and snacks.
(2) Identify with whom they are eating and how much instrumental and emotional support is needed from others.
(3) Assess what helps and interferes with them asking for assistance during eating/meals from their parents/caregivers (and others) when the illness is stronger or ambivalence about change present.
(4) Detailed description of the quality and quantity of food eaten for some or all meals.
(5) Using a monitoring record (see Fairburn, 2008, p. 58) to also monitor feelings, behaviours, and thoughts associated with each meal (Item 5 is typically used by young people who are highly motivated and engaged in the treatment process).

Collaboratively with therapists, young people work to identify which monitoring approach or combination of approaches is beneficial for building skills and promoting recovery. The chief objective is to empower the young person to become simultaneously more self-aware of their eating patterns and to seek assistance from supportive others when they are struggling. A subtle but important shift occurs when a young person rather than their parents/caregivers speak about their struggles with AN. They are required to become responsible for themselves rather than overly reliant on their parents/caregivers to identify problematic eating patterns. It also means that young people are not merely responding to parental/caregiver concerns about restrictive eating but rather are requesting for assistance with meals that they find difficult.

Immediately following the weighing and review of the compensatory behaviour log, the young person will be asked to consider how their eating in the previous week may have influenced the progress of their weight. Depending on the monitoring intervention chosen, therapists may process with the young person what they have learned about their eating and the challenges they face on a day-to-day basis with food and urges to engage in symptoms or compensate for eating and gaining weight. It is important to note that the conversations with the young person are focused and brief with an emphasis on how the therapist may support/prepare them to relay the information to their parents/caregivers in the family session. Therapists may encourage the young person to reflect on occasions when AN thinking was especially challenging and how they combat AN. If they did not ask for parental/caretaker support, what interfered with this request for assistance? Prior to ending the individual meeting, the therapist should request that the young person think about any potentially challenging meals/eating contexts in the upcoming week that they anticipate will require more parental/caregiver support. They will be asked to bring these concerns to their parents/caregivers and specify how they may be helpful.

At the beginning of the family meeting, young people demonstrate the direction of their weight using the weight chart and the compensatory log to note any changes in symptoms. This may initially require considerable support from the therapist, especially in the early stages of Phase 2. Next, young people are to report on how they think their eating/meals may explain the direction of their weight. At this point, the therapist should also solicit the thoughts of parents/caregivers regarding weight changes, compensatory behaviours, and mealtimes in the previous weeks.

Therapists carefully work to promote discussions between the parents/caregivers and the young person by highlighting similarities and differences in what has been discussed. Increased discrepancies between the reporting of the young person and the parents/caregivers suggests that AN continues to be strong and may interfere with accurate reporting. Rather than take sides, therapists merely repeat that the illness manifests itself behaviourally and is evidenced by weight loss, weight stagnation/suppression, and the presence of symptoms/compensatory behaviours. Therapists then summarize the objective data gleaned from the compensatory behaviour log to help reinforce the idea that the parents/caregivers and young person must work more carefully to ensure that eating occurs at every meal without restrictions. Like Phase 1, therapists ask detailed questions about how parents/caregivers worked together (either with or without the healthy side of the young person) during each meal over the previous week. Young people are similarly called upon to identify where they may require support from the family in the upcoming week.

As the young person becomes increasingly autonomous during meals, the parents/caregivers continue to provide emotional support but act like consultants and advisors when the young person is problem-solving about eating. Along the same lines as the therapist, parents/caregivers may ask questions to help encourage the young person to think about the best course of action on how to eat a meal while at work/school/with peers. The young person may need to practice purchasing food at a grocery store with parental/caregiver support and then gradually on their own.

This phase is about transitioning control of eating from the parents/caregiver to the young person. There will be considerable variability in how each family elects to transition control back to the young person and this will likely depend on a number of variables including weight/eating progress, the willingness, and the attitude of the young person to engage independently in the treatment process and parental/caregiver confidence in their ability to accurately assess and then intervene if difficulties arise that exacerbate AN concerns and behaviours. The therapist communicates that they perceive the parents/caregivers and young person as having the skills, knowledge, and experience to decide how best to proceed with the goals of Phase 2. Similarly, therapists acknowledge the strength and courage that the young person has evidenced by their willingness to work with their parents/caregiver against the illness. Given the strengths of the parents/caregivers and the young person, the therapist works carefully to avoid prescribing, leading, and dictating what course of action the parent/caregiver-young person team elect to take to promote greater independent eating in the young person and identify ways to assess/evaluate the progress of the young person in becoming increasingly responsible for eating meals in various contexts.

The young person must have ample opportunity to problem-solve and practice eating at school, with friends and in social settings or variety of contexts. Lock and Le Grange (2025) advocate that the therapist works collaboratively with individuals and their parents/caregivers to develop a plan for how to transition greater independence and control back to the adolescent in an age-appropriate manner. Early in Phase 2 of FBT-AN for adolescents, the emphasis is on eating at home more independently. In the adapted version of FBT for TAY, the focus is on helping the TAY transition to eating independently in a variety of contexts and with various people. The way young people take on more responsibility for eating will be decided upon by them collaboratively with their family, not by the therapist. This may occur by engaging young people in the following types of incremental behavioural changes: preparing their own meal with parental/caregiver monitoring; portioning quantity of food; eating a snack or meal without any parental/caregiver monitoring; eating more meals on their own; grocery shopping, increasing the variety of food; eating meals with others outside of the family; eating at work; and eating at school. The therapist does not direct the specific ways that this transfer of responsibility occurs. However, therapists may use their ED expertise to ensure that the young person and the family make informed decisions about any proposed plans for independent eating. FBT-TAY therapists may do this by promoting discussions between the parents/caregivers and the young person about what the specific steps for eating independently will be over time.

The therapist also encourages the family and the young person to communicate and problem-solve together about mealtimes, meal preparation, and levels of physical activity. The therapist communicates to the family that this phase is about learning how to eat in a multitude of contexts and with various people, with much less instrumental and direct parental/caregiver support. It may be helpful for the therapist to communicate that this process of learning to eat independently will not occur smoothly or in a linear way. As a consultant in the therapeutic process, therapists should invite the parents/caregivers to identify how they will assess if their TAY is eating independently. Equally important, the FBT-TAY therapist engages in discussions with the young person about how they will know when to ask for assistance from others. These are discussions that must be encouraged within the family.

As a consultant, therapists should highlight the importance of using objective measures such as the progress of weight and compensatory behaviour log in addition to other methods agreed upon in the family.

To illustrate these interventions, therapists may say the following:

> You are at a point in the treatment where you can begin to think about how to help Jane [young person] to eat more on her own with less parental/caregiver supervision. As parents/caregivers, you have worked very well together to help X with the weight gain process and eating normally over the last few months. Of course, X deserves a lot of the credit for working extremely hard to make Eddy have less influence over their eating.
>
> Together, you have also found ways to work together very well. As described in the beginning of treatment, Phase 2 is about how best to transition control with eating and over meals from you as parents/caregivers back to X. How and when you do this is entirely up to you as a family. My role will be to continue to act as a consultant and use my expertise about this illness to advise you. I have observed the two of you help your daughter when she was in the depth of despair with Eddy (externalized "name" for AN used by the family). You have the wisdom and the expertise about your daughter to know what the best way is to help her gain independence with eating again. You will also need to think about "red flags" when this plan isn't working very well. I also want you to think about how to become a consultant to your TAY as they move forward to become more independent with their eating and during meals. For instance, X said that she would like to start having evening snacks on her own. What questions do you need to ask her to help her prepare for

eating snacks on her own? What would you like her to consider as she plans to make this change? What information would you like to share to help her make a decision about what snack to elect?

In Phase 2, therapists will increase their efforts at assisting parents/caregivers to become consultants to their TAY. To achieve this objective, therapists may consider asking parents/caregivers what they have learned from this treatment experience that increases their efficacy and expertise about what works well and what interferes with normalized eating and weight gain. Therapists note that parents/caregivers should rely on this wisdom to help their young person in their efforts to make decisions about eating independently.

Modifying Parental/Caregiver Criticism

Continuously modify parental/caregiver criticism and self-criticism in the young person if it arises. Interventions for addressing parental/caregiver criticism have been previously described in Phase 1. Similar interventions may be used if parental/caregiver criticism occurs in this stage of the treatment. Parental/caregiver criticism may occur when a young person falters in their efforts to execute a plan discussed in a family session for eating well on their own. For instance, a young person identifies that they will eat an evening snack on their own. With parental/caregiver support, they select the snack and the time when they will eat the snack. The young person also agrees that they will seek support from their parents/caregivers by calling on them if the illness becomes too challenging for them to deal with on their own. Instead of adhering to this plan, the young person opts to eat a less calorie dense snack and does not ask their parents/caregivers for help. This is the young person's first attempt to eat on their own after months of being supervised by their parents/caregivers. The therapist conveys that this isn't a sign of failure but an opportunity for the parents/caregivers and young person to learn about what to do differently to help with the next snack. If young people have been struggling with AN for a prolonged period, therapists should communicate that it may take considerable time and effort for the young person to practice making behavioural changes (eating snack on their own). This is a skill that can only occur with additional practice and greater planning and support from parents/caregivers. Throughout Phase 2, FBT-TAY therapists should continuously ask parents/caregivers to identify and discuss the progress, strengths, and successes that they have identified in their adult child. Therapists may model this by highlighting how the parents/caregivers and the young person have successfully worked together against the illness.

The FBT-TAY therapist also highlights any efforts that the young person makes towards achieving tasks associated with emerging adulthood (e.g., developing a strong sense of who they are separate from the illness, pursuing post-secondary education, connecting with peers and dating, seeking employment, and developing an identity that is holistic).

Challenges in Phase 2

Challenge 1: The Young Person Tries to Achieve Independence About Eating too Quickly

The young person moves quickly to obtain greater independence with eating and meals. This may occur because the young person is overestimating their readiness to eat and continue gaining weight without the aid of their parents/caregivers and other supportive adults. It is also possible that the young person is pushing for greater independence to engage in restrictive eating and slow down the weight gain process. The therapist uses the weight and compensatory logs as objective evidence of AN re-surfacing and whether independence over eating is moving rapidly in the young person. It is also imperative that therapists observe and communicate with the family if compensatory behaviours are increasing as the young person normalizes eating and approximates the target weight.

Challenge 2: Parent(s)/Caregiver(s) Want to Give Back Control too Quickly

Parents/caregivers are willing to transition control of eating to the young person too quickly or without extensive planning. Parents/caregivers decrease their focus on eating and meal planning when their support is still required to facilitate learning how to eat independently. This may arise for a variety of reasons. Parents/caregivers may believe that it is developmentally appropriate for the young person to eat their meals on their own without their support. Although these sentiments may be present in parents/caregivers of young children, discomfort about continuing to monitor the eating for 16- to 25-year-olds will intensify in Phase 2. As consultants, we relay the message that parental/caregiver support is not only needed for weight gain purposes. Parents/caregivers can play a role in emotionally supporting the young person and working with them to learn how to eat a normal quantity and variety of foods. FBT-TAY therapists should remind parents/caregivers (and the young person) that AN may re-surface, especially with increased autonomy and independence.

Challenge 3: Parental/Caregiver Exhaustion

As discussed in the FBT manual for AN and BN, it is not uncommon for parents/caregivers to become exhausted by the relentless focus on addressing ED symptoms. Parental/caregivers exhaustion and burnout may be a significant issue for parents/caregivers who have been caring for a young person with an illness since adolescence. It is important for therapists to identify and intervene as soon as it becomes apparent that parents/caregivers are having difficulties working together because one parent/caregiver is exhausted. In such cases, therapists should work to identify other family members (grandparents, aunts/uncles/peers of the young person) who may be able to alleviate the sense of burden experienced by this difficult illness.

Challenge 4: Fear and Anxiety

Parents/caregivers are unwilling/unable to relinquish their role in supporting eating. Gripped by fear and anxiety, parents/caregivers may be unable to take the risks associated with giving their child more freedom over food intake. If weight has been increasing steadily, symptoms have decreased, and there are few battles about food and portion sizes, the therapist must work with the parents/caregivers to consider the short- and long-term consequences of not permitting their young person to learn how to eat on their own. Discussions related to safety and tolerating uncertainty can often support these stuck points in clinical treatment.

Conclusions

Phase 2 for young people with AN utilizes many of the same interventions delineated in the manual for adolescents with this illness (Lock & Le Grange, 2012). The only modification is that control over eating may be relinquished over to the young person from the parents/caregivers more quickly than an adolescent. The rationale for this is that the young person likely has greater freedom and independence (outside of the illness) requiring them to practise eating in a variety of contexts (e.g., work and school environment) and with different people (e.g., friends, partner, and colleagues). It is still entirely up to the parents/caregivers and the young person to decide how to transfer this control back to the latter and what methods to utilize to assess progress in this phase. In contrast to young adolescents, young people should also take on the responsibility of sharing their progress weight (and binge/purge symptoms). This provides the young person with the opportunity to communicate their difficulties and successes with recovery directly to their parents/caregivers. In FBT-TAY, young people should also be encouraged to begin monitoring their eating and to communicate any potential challenges with food to their parents/caregivers. This will help them become increasingly aware of their eating patterns and to share with their family when eating has become challenging.

Criteria for Entering Phase 3

- The young person is maintaining their target weight.
- The young person eats a variety of food with an array of people in their social network.
- Cessation of all compensatory behaviours

- The young person eats independently in all settings and contexts without parental/family supervision/monitoring.
- The young people and their parents/caregivers are exploring issues pertaining to late adolescence and emerging adulthood.

We want to emphasize that the completion of Phase 2 does not signal full recovery from AN. In fact, young people may continue to have core cognitions that may contribute to body image difficulties and urges to restrict their eating (Fairburn, 2008; Lock & Le Grange, 2012).

Chapter Summary

Here are the key points of this chapter:

(1) Phase 2 begins when the young person is gaining or maintaining weight, eating regularly without compensatory behaviours, showing more of their healthy self, and when family tension around food has decreased enough for greater independence.
(2) The main goal is to gradually return control of eating to the young person while still tracking weight and symptoms. They begin sharing their own progress with their parents/caregivers, practising adult communication and responsibility.
(3) Self-monitoring helps the young person notice where eating feels easier or harder and identify when they need support. Parents/caregivers shift from hands-on managers to consultants, offering guidance while allowing more autonomy at meals, school, work, and with peers.
(4) Family sessions focus on planning small steps towards independent eating and troubleshooting setbacks, which are expected. The therapist uses objective data to pace independence safely and prevent premature withdrawal of support.
(5) Throughout the phase, warmth and externalization reduce criticism and keep the family aligned with the young person's healthy side. Progress is emphasized to build motivation.
(6) Phase 2 ends when the young person maintains their target weight, eats a variety of foods in multiple contexts, no longer uses compensatory behaviours, and can reliably eat independently while the family begins addressing broader emerging adulthood tasks.

References

Dimitropoulos, G., Le Grange, D., & Lock, J. (2014). *Research manual: Family-based treatment for transition age youth* [Unpublished manuscript].
Fairburn, C. G. (2008). *Cognitive behavior therapy and EDs*. The Guilford Press.

Lock, J., & Le Grange, D. (2012). *Treatment manual for anorexia nervosa: A family-based approach* (2nd ed.). The Guilford Press.

Lock, J., & Le Grange, D. (2025). *Treatment manual for anorexia nervosa: A family-based approach* (3rd ed.). The Guilford Press.

Maas, J., Hietbrink, L., Rinck, M., & Keijsers, G. P. (2013). Changing automatic behavior through self-monitoring: Does overt change also imply implicit change?. *Journal of Behavior Therapy and Experimental Psychiatry*, *44*(3), 279–284. https://doi.org/10.1016/j.jbtep.2012.12.002

Town, R., Hayes, D., March, A., Fonagy, P., & Stapley, E. (2024). Self-management, self-care, and self-help in adolescents with emotional problems: A scoping review. *European Child & Adolescent Psychiatry*, *33*(9), 2929–2956. https://doi.org/10.1007/s00787-022-02134-z

Tregarthen, J., Paik Kim, J., Sadeh-Sharvit, S., Neri, E., Welch, H., & Lock, J. (2019). Comparing a tailored self-help mobile app with a standard self-monitoring app for the treatment of ED symptoms: Randomized controlled trial. *JMIR Mental Health*, *6*(11), 1–15. https://doi.org/10.2196/14972

Chapter 9

Phase 3 – Emerging Adulthood, Relapse Prevention, and Termination of Treatment

In this chapter, we will describe the overall treatment goals of the third and final phase of FBT-TAY, focusing on the period of emerging adulthood including factors impacting the family life cycle over the course of treatment. This chapter will also explore key clinical considerations in developing a relapse prevention and emergency plan with the young person and their parents/caregivers, along with strategies and important factors for implementation in terminating treatment with the family in the third phase of FBT-TAY.

Goals of Phase 3

The following represents the overarching goals of Phase 3 of FBT-TAY:

(1) To review developmental tasks associated with late adolescence and emerging adulthood.
(2) To promote parent/caregiver-child interactions that are not interrupted and dominated by AN concerns.
(3) To develop a relapse prevention and emergency plan with the young person and review these plans with their parents/caregivers and other important support people in their lives.

In meeting these therapeutic goals in Phase 3, the FBT-TAY therapist will use a combination of the following interventions to assist the young person and family to meet the goals of Phase 3:

(1) Delineate and explore issues associated with emerging adulthood and the relationship between young people and parents/caregivers. Prepare the young person for multiple life transitions (e.g., new relationships, gaining employment, and pursuing academic goals) while staying in recovery.
(2) Develop a plan with the young person by identifying high-risk situations (food and non-food related) that may contribute to relapse. The young

DOI: 10.4324/9781003463351-10

person subsequently should work with their parents/caregivers to solidify the prevention plan.

(3) Develop a plan for parents/caregivers to reflect on their learnings as a parental/caregiver dyad or couple and family as a whole. This is an opportunity for the supportive adults to reclaim their lives from the illness, engage in self-care and renew, and resume their own lives.
(4) Review treatment goals and progress and initiate termination of treatment with the young person and parents/caregivers.

This phase officially begins when the young person achieves and maintains their weight target, compensatory behaviours have discontinued, and eating is routine and done independently in all settings and contexts. In this phase, the FBT-TAY therapist should continue to meet with the young person prior to the family meeting for the purposes of weighing them and tracking the emergence of new symptoms. As described in previous chapters, the FBT-TAY therapist should continue to elicit the perspectives of the young person regarding their progress with eating independently and with their parents/caregivers' support when required. The FBT-TAY therapist should work on increasing the amount of time that they spend with the young person to work on relapse prevention plans (two to three sessions) and then meet with the whole family for additional sessions (two sessions). Before discussing relapse prevention plans, the FBT-TAY therapist should review information about adolescent development and emerging adulthood in the first session of Phase 3. In preparation for this session, the therapist may consider inviting the parents/caregivers to reflect on what this time of life was like for them. What was it like for them to move from adolescence to adulthood? What societal and familial expectations were placed on them? Do they think back fondly and/or with regret about this time period in their lives? What are their hopes, expectations, and fears for their child as they become a young person? Although there are no expectations/demands that parents/caregivers share their stories, we invite them to reflect and consider how their values, history, and trajectories may be relevant to the discussions with their child who is embarking on a new stage in their life. In the first session of Phase 3, the FBT-TAY therapist provides a high-level description of the family life cycle and ways to support the young person to achieve their personal life goals and launch into emerging adulthood. In preparation for the session on relapse prevention, we encourage all members of the family to consider how this unique stage in life might protect or pull them back into the AN.

Emerging Adulthood

Since the mid-20th century, a gradual shift has occurred in the transition to adulthood, leading to the beginning of the distinct life stage of emerging adulthood, typically spanning the ages of 18–29 (Arnett, 2015). Unlike earlier generations who married, started families, and entered long-term jobs by their early 20s, young people today experience an extended period of identity exploration, instability, self-focus, and feeling "in-between" adolescence and full adulthood (Arnett et al., 2014).

Emerging adulthood is marked by high hope and optimism, but also uncertainty and anxiety (Kranzler et al., 2019), as individuals navigate a prolonged path to adulthood that is no longer defined by rigid timelines (Gilmore & Meersand, 2023). Psychologically, this period can be both exciting and overwhelming. Emerging adults often explore various paths in relationships, education, careers, and personal values as they attempt to solidify a stable identity (Arnett, 2000). At the same time, this exploration can create instability, with frequent changes in living situations, jobs, and social circles. Emerging adults may prioritize themselves during this stage, focusing on understanding their identity and values as they navigate life (Arnett, 2015).

For young people who have experiences with an EDs, emerging adulthood can present unique challenges. This stage of life often heightens concerns related to identity, autonomy, control, and body image, all of which can contribute to a return to ED behaviours (Gonidakis et al., 2018). As emerging adults face the pressures of transitioning to independence, they may struggle with internalized ideals about success, external achievements, productivity, or appearance, which can be exacerbated by societal expectations (Rice et al., 2023). The ambiguity of this life stage, combined with limited adult responsibilities and high self-focus, can create a breeding ground for disordered eating behaviours to (re)emerge or intensify, particularly for those seeking control or self-worth primarily through their relationship with their bodies and food as a way to deal with new uncertainties (Gonidakis et al., 2018). University or college environments can also be high-risk settings for disordered eating behaviours and EDs due to isolation, academic stress, and an emphasis on appearance and performance (Baranauskas et al., 2022). Starting post-secondary education may accelerate the movement towards greater independence, increased self-reliance on meeting expectations, deadlines, and exposure to new social opportunities. Although this can be an exciting time period for many young people, it is also a vulnerable period for illness behaviours to re-emerge necessitating a proactive transition and relapse prevention plan. In addition, emerging adults may also experience difficulties accessing consistent care, especially as they age out of paediatric services or lose access to university health systems (Nadarajah et al., 2021). The expectation that emerging adults should be independent and self-sufficient can lead to internalized stigma about needing help, delaying treatment or making it difficult to ask for support (Spence et al., 2016). Those without strong family or community ties may also struggle to navigate complex health systems on their own (Wood et al., 2017).

Furthermore, individuals who are in recovery during this period may find it difficult to maintain progress amidst the instability and transitions common in emerging adulthood (Elswick et al., 2018).

However, emerging adulthood also offers powerful opportunities for healing and transformation. The inherent openness and flexibility of this stage can support identity development beyond the ED, as individuals begin to reclaim values, passions, and relationships that align with recovery (Potterton et al., 2021). According to Lane (2015), supportive peer relationships, therapy, and access to appropriate treatment can be especially impactful at this stage. Importantly, interventions must be developmentally attuned, recognizing the unique stressors, social environments, and autonomy needs of emerging adults. Approaches that affirm autonomy, encourage self-reflection, and foster meaningful connection tend to resonate more with emerging adults, as they align with their developmental desire for identity exploration (Nice et al., 2024). Interventions that recognize and respond to these complexities are more likely to engage emerging adults effectively and support long-term recovery and well-being.

The Family Life Cycle

In addition to emerging adults, the whole family system undergoes a period of growth and transformation during this developmental period and beyond. The family cycle, which refers to how families evolve overtime, progresses through a series of distinct and sequential stages across the lifespan. Each stage presents unique challenges, tasks, and opportunities for growth and adaptation. According to McGoldrick et al. (2016), emerging adulthood is a particularly transformative phase for families, marked by increased independence and identity formation for the young person, as well as shifting family roles. This period typically involves significant shifts for both parents/caregivers and young people as they renegotiate roles, routines, and relationships (McGoldrick et al., 2016). Families often experience a mix of pride, freedom, loss, and uncertainty as young people seek greater independence and begin to establish their own identities, careers, and relationships (Hong, 2011). Parents/caregivers often adjust to a new role as consultants rather than caretakers, renegotiating boundaries and routines while supporting their young person's transition into adulthood (McGoldrick et al., 2016).

Stress within the family system tends to peak during transitions between stages of the family life cycle (e.g., D'Amore et al., 2023). The impact of this stress on the physical and mental health of family members depends on the family's adaptability and the availability of internal and external support to help navigate the change (Berge et al., 2012). For young people with EDs, common or expected developmental milestones such as moving out of the family home, pursuing post-secondary education, entering the workforce, and forming intimate relationships can become significantly more challenging (Potterton et al., 2020a, 2025; Safi et al., 2022).

The physical, emotional, and psychological demands of AN can interfere with the young person's ability to function independently, which may create tension within the family system and contribute to feelings of shame, isolation, or failure (Potterton et al., 2020b). As a result, both the young person and their family may experience a sense of being "stuck" in an earlier stage of the family life cycle (Karlstad et al., 2022). When young people are transferred from paediatric to adult care, parents/caregivers may experience conflicting demands on their time and insecurity in their parenting role (Karlstad et al., 2021). Additionally, the reduction in AN treatment resources available at the adult level may require parents/caregivers to maintain their caretaking role into a late stage of the family life cycle (Dimitropoulos et al., 2015b), which can delay the shift to role of consultant for the parent/caregiver.

Taking a family life cycle perspective is important because it allows therapists to look ahead at how individuals and families might grow and change, helping them identify risks early and support planning for relapse prevention. Viewing challenges through a family life cycle lens means looking at symptoms within the broader family system and in relation to culturally defined norms of functioning over time. Therapeutic interventions focus on helping the family regain its forward movement, so each member can continue to grow and develop (e.g., McGoldrick & Carter, 2003; Oren, 2020). This perspective can be particularly valuable when working with young people with AN, as it situates their challenges not only within individual trajectories but also within broader systemic and developmental transitions.

Following this high-level review, the FBT-TAY therapist will discuss challenges associated with the transition from adolescence to adulthood and the resultant changes in the family as interactions between parents/caregivers and the young person are no longer defined by the illness and management of symptoms. As such, the family may discuss how some aspects of young adult development may be lagging in the young person because of the illness and treatment. The FBT-TAY therapist will initially focus on issues regarding autonomy since the illness will have stifled age-appropriate independence in eating and in other areas in the young person's life. The family should be encouraged to think about how parents/caregivers may support the young person to become autonomous, independent, and involved in activities to build relationships that will help create a sense of identity separate from AN and the illness.

Therapists should work collaboratively with the young person and parents/caregivers to identify how the illness has interfered with adolescence and emerging adulthood and from the achievement of critical milestones associated with these stages of life such as identity development. Through this discussion, the young person and their family may consider in what ways the illness has robbed the former from achieving their personal goals and what areas of growth may still be required to progress to adulthood. Since many young people develop AN in adolescence, it is possible that they have not successfully achieved some of the key developmental milestones characteristic of adolescence. Consequently, the FBT-TAY therapist will invite the young person to consider if they are interested in engaging in identity exploration, clarifying their values that will shape their current and future decisions about relationships and academic and career pathways and learn how to individuate and solidify an interdependent relationship with their parents/caregivers and families. As mentioned above and in previous chapters, since older adolescents and young people are likely to be experiencing multiple life transitions including a transfer from paediatric to adult health care providers, FBT-TAY therapists may consider working alongside parents/caregivers and the young person to identify strategies that can be used to access appropriate health and mental health services when required.

It is important to note that this discussion must be strengths-based with the aim of eliciting the skills, experiences, and knowledge the young person has acquired through their recovery from AN that already lays the groundwork for the achievement/exploration of psychological milestones associated with becoming a young person. We need to strike a balance between discussing the adverse impact of AN on the young person and acknowledge all of their efforts to assert and advocate for themselves, demonstrate capacity to live through difficult circumstances, and persevere on their journey to recovery and wellness. FBT-TAY therapists must also approach discussions about adolescence and emerging adulthood with cultural sensitivity recognizing familial values, traditions, historical, religious, and unique contextual factors that may influence how young people and parents/caregivers talk about issues related to becoming an "emerging adulthood." This discussion is not meant to be prescriptive, directive, and value-laden and biased towards favouring one pathway over another for how young people must develop as individuals. The goal is to empower both the young person and family to engage in a respectful, authentic, and supportive discussion about what it means to live a life without AN, develop a positive/healthy sense of self, and find purpose and meaning.

Develop a Prevention Plan

Taking the unique challenges and opportunities of emerging adulthood and the shifting family roles during this developmental period, FBT-TAY therapists must be mindful of the stressors which impede recovery for young people as they transition to the third and final phase of treatment. In particular, the therapist should account for any high-risk stressors (food and non-food related), which may set back the young person on their path to recovery, and work with the young person to identify situations which may contribute to relapse. The young person should also work with their parents/caregivers to solidify a prevention plan to ameliorate the impact of these stressors as they transition out of treatment.

Relapse prevention is an important component of long-term ED recovery. While significant strides can be made in treatment, recovery from EDs is rarely linear (Bowlby et al., 2015; Kenny et al., 2020). Many individuals experience setbacks, known as lapses, along the way (Davis & Smith, 2018; Heal-Cohen et al., 2025). Understanding relapse as a process rather than a single event and learning how to respond to early warning signs is critical for sustaining recovery over time (Melemis, 2015).

Although there currently is no standardized definition of ED relapse that can be applied in both clinical and research contexts (Heal-Cohen et al., 2025), relapse is broadly defined as a return to sustained disordered eating behaviours and cognitive patterns that interfere with daily functioning or health after a period of recovery or symptom improvement (Miskovic-Wheatley et al., 2023). This may involve food restriction, purging, binge eating, or body checking, often accompanied by the re-emergence of rigid food rules, secrecy, and shame (Miskovic-Wheatley et al., 2023).

Relapses are often part of the recovery process and can serve as important learning opportunities when approached with self-awareness and support (Sala et al., 2023). However, relapse prevention strategies can be helpful in reducing the severity of a relapse (Menon & Kandasamy, 2018). Recognizing the nature of relapse is critical for shaping interventions that both reduce its likelihood and support individuals when it occurs (Heal-Cohen et al., 2025).

The combination of life stressors and a lack of internal and external resources and support can contribute to relapse (Heal-Cohen et al., 2025). Research suggests that certain factors increase vulnerability to relapse, including transitional life events (moving, starting university, or changing jobs), interpersonal stress, isolation, co-occurring mental health conditions like anxiety or depression, and a lack of ongoing support (Grilo et al., 2012). Common early warning signs of relapse include increased preoccupation with weight, food, or exercise (National Eating Disorders Association, n.d.); returning to behaviours such as skipping meals, purging, or over-exercising; heightened body dissatisfaction; withdrawing from support systems; or romanticizing past ED experiences (Steinglass et al., 2022). Developing a relapse prevention plan in collaboration with both the young person and their parents/caregivers is a critical in Phase 3 of FBT-TAY. Therapists play an important role in facilitating joint planning that includes not only the individual's goals and coping strategies but also clearly defined roles for family support in the event of relapse (Hibbs et al., 2015; Lock & Le Grange, 2012). As such, FBT-TAY therapists should work closely to support the young person to think about how they can stay well and potential situations that may put them at risk (life transitions, stress associated with school, changes to their bodies, etc.).

A relapse prevention plan should serve as a structured and proactive framework that outlines warning signs, risk factors, and early intervention strategies, tailored to the young person's unique needs and family dynamics (Lock & Le Grange, 2012). Research demonstrates that parents/caregivers continue to provide critical emotional, practical, and financial support for emerging adults with EDs, even into adulthood (Dodge et al., 2024; Geller et al., 2024; Karlstad et al., 2021). This ongoing involvement means that relapse prevention planning in the Phase 3 of treatment should purposefully include parents/caregivers, ensuring they are equipped to recognize warning signs of the young person and offer appropriate support without undermining autonomy. As such, FBT-TAY therapists should facilitate a balanced and collaborative role for parents/caregivers, helping them support recovery while promoting independence in the young person. Collaborative relapse prevention planning clarifies roles and expectations, reduces family conflict, and aligns all parties involved on how to respond should ED behaviours re-emerge (Geller et al., 2024).

Relapse prevention must be thoughtfully integrated into the final phase of FBT-TAY, with attention to both the young person's developing independence and the ongoing supportive role of parents/caregivers (Dimitropoulos et al., 2015a). As described by Dodge et al. (2024), relapse prevention sessions should be brief and focus on reviewing each family member's role, preparing for potential stressors, and clearly marking the transition toward termination. These sessions emphasize that any lapse is the young person's responsibility, while guiding parents/caregivers on how to respond without unintentionally prolonging treatment (Dodge et al., 2024). It is also important that FBT-TAY therapists share information about rates of relapse related to AN and highlight the need for hypervigilance to weight loss, eating restrictions, and a problematic relationship with food and the body. They should work with the young person and their parents/caregivers to review the knowledge, skills, and resources developed throughout Phases 1 and 2, to be utilized to maintain recovery.

FBT therapists typically meet individually with the young person over two to three sessions to develop both a relapse prevention plan and an emergency action plan. The relapse prevention plan involves identifying personal risk factors including academic stress, body image distress, life transitions, interpersonal conflict, or isolation that may increase vulnerability in the coming months. This plan includes careful consideration of the high-risk factors which may arise in the next 6 months, 12 months, and 2 years after FBT. The emergency plan, by contrast, offers concrete steps to take in the immediate aftermath of a slip or resurgence of symptoms, such as returning to structured eating, increasing supervision, or re-engaging with treatment supports. Importantly, FBT-TAY therapists should emphasize that the purpose of planning is not to assume relapse is inevitable, but rather to highlight the resources, coping strategies, and relational supports available if recovery becomes particularly challenging.

In these discussions, FBT-TAY therapists should also guide young people in articulating how their parents/caregivers can be most helpful if concerns arise. This may include clarifying what type of support they are open to receiving (e.g., meal supervision, emotional check-ins, and help contacting providers) and under what conditions that support should be accessed. The young person will then invite their parents/caregivers to review and respond to both plans, creating space for mutual understanding and shared responsibility and offering space for their parents/caregivers to ask questions and raise suggestions for improvement to solidify the plan for recovery. The young person can direct the conversation by sharing information about their recovery process and asking their parents/caregivers to assist with food and non-ED goals. By scaffolding recovery in this way, families can provide emotional and instrumental support without undermining the young person's sense of agency or self-efficacy.

Treatment Review and Termination

As the family transitions out of treatment, it is critical that the FBT-TAY therapist works with the young person and their parents/caregivers to reflect on the progress made over the course of treatment, as well as the new problem-solving and communication skills gained in previous phases of FBT-TAY. During this process, the young person may express resentment, frustration, and/or anger towards parents/caregivers and even the therapist for having limited their independence around food and weight in earlier phases of treatment. FBT-TAY therapists must validate the young person's experience and any unresolved feelings or grievances about the control that was needed to support their recovery from the illness. Conversely, any feelings of gratitude on the part of the young person towards their parents/caregivers for aiding their recovery should be acknowledged. We further invite the parents/caregivers to recognize the tremendous courage the young person has taken to entrust them to aid their recovery including meal support, grocery shopping, and learning to eat with others in their lives. It may also be helpful for the FBT-TAY therapist to review or compare/contrast any materials with the young person and their parents/caregivers which demonstrate progress over the course of treatment, such as the Venn diagram developed in the first phase of treatment (e.g., Lock & Le Grange, 2012).

The FBT-TAY therapist may also consider inviting the parents/caregivers and other supportive adults to consider whether they would like an adult only session to explore their thoughts/feelings/about AN and the treatment itself. This session can be offered just to parents/caregivers if they wish. This is an opportunity for the parent/caregivers and supportive adults to discuss any "trauma" associated with acute periods of the illness where hospitalization or urgent/emergency care was required, regrets or grief about what the illness robbed of their child, each of them, and their family. We can never under-estimate the pain, personal losses, economic costs, and psychological suffering that families experience in their efforts to support their child with AN and with the recovery process. The FBT-TAY therapist works collaboratively with the parents/caregivers to consider ways to reclaim their own lives and engage in their own self-care, healing or pursue professional supports to address physical or mental health issues.

During this phase, the FBT-TAY therapist should invite the family to consider their learnings about one another during treatment. Each member of the family may be asked about their own experiences of treatment. For example, the therapist may say to the young person:

> Your parents/caregivers and I know that this has been a particularly difficult process for you especially the earlier part of the treatment. Some of my clients have shared with me that even though they better understand why their parents/caregivers took a lot of their freedom away from them, they still feel angry with their parents/caregivers for taking away their autonomy. Do you have any feelings towards your parents/caregivers, the treatment and me? What part of the treatment was most difficult for you at the time? Do you feel differently about the treatment now than you did a few months ago?

In this way, a brief discussion about unresolved feelings during treatment, the FBT-TAY therapist, or the young person's parents/caregivers may help accelerate closure on treatment. The FBT-TAY therapist may also encourage the family to recall the skills they have developed and the knowledge gained about their family and illness as they close treatment. If necessary, the FBT-TAY therapist should consider making a referral for systemic family therapy, individual therapy, or other community resources. In the event that the young person requests individual therapy to discuss other concerns (e.g., exploring issues related to sexuality, sexual identity, and intimacy), therapists should recommend an individual therapist who has expertise in working with young people and the issues that the young person would like to explore. Lastly, any outstanding issues within the family system should be addressed through further therapeutic intervention such as general family counselling or other treatment modalities (e.g., emotion-focused therapy, narrative therapy, etc.) most suited to the family.

Challenges in Phase 3

Challenge 1: Aspects of the ED Remain in the Young Person After Treatment

While FBT-TAY is a behavioural intervention, focused on weight restoration, eating rehabilitation, and normalized/healthy eating, it is not uncommon for young people to continue to have ED-related cognitions and thoughts long after FBT-TAY as ceased. Indeed, young people may continue to experience disordered eating/restrictive ED cognitions related to their eating, weight, or body-image preoccupation which may linger after treatment and increase their risk of relapse. FBT-TAY therapists should consider other treatments depending on the level of cognitive distortions and compensatory behaviours exhibited by the young person including CBT and intensive relapse prevention work.

Challenge 2: Presence or Re-Emergence of Other Psychiatric Comorbidities in the Young Person

Young people often come to FBT-TAY with a range of psychiatric comorbidities which may have occurred in parallel, or prior, to their AN. Some of these comorbidities may include, but are not limited to, anxiety, depression, obsessive-compulsive disorder, substance use concerns, suicidality, and self-harm (e.g., Sala et al., 2023). At the end of Phase 3, while the ED behaviours decrease, it is not uncommon for these co-morbidities to resurface in the young person and continue to increase risk of relapse with their AN. In the event that the young person experiences co-occurring psychiatric concerns in Phase 3, the FBT-TAY therapist can facilitate a psychiatric assessment and/or subsequent treatment of their comorbidities. The therapist may also consider referrals for individual therapy to address co-occurring psychiatric concerns.

Challenge 3: Young Person Struggles with Their Identity Outside of the AN

As FBT-TAY therapists initiate treatment termination, develop transition plans for re-integration of the young person to their lives outside of treatment, and engage in planning for relapse prevention, young people may struggle with their identities outside of their AN. Some young people may have struggled with their AN for several months (if not years) and find it difficult to define their sense of identity or sense of self outside of the context of their ED. Young people may also express fear or uncertainty related to "losing" their ED (e.g., Heywood et al., 2022). FBT-TAY therapists should be cognizant to explore issues related to loss of identity or self with the young person in Phase 3 and use other individual therapeutic approaches (e.g., narrative therapy) to explore fear and uncertainty around loss of identity prior to treatment termination.

Conclusion

This chapter provides an overview of the third and final phase of FBT-TAY, including presenting the current evidence and therapeutic considerations regarding emerging adulthood, relapse prevention, and termination of treatment. While the focus in Phases 1 and 2 of FBT-TAY includes a relentless focus on eating and weight restoration, FBT-TAY therapists should involve other experts who may assist with the amelioration of other impairing mental health problems with the young person and family unit. Due to the entrenchment of ED behaviours overtime, greater effort should be made to assist parents/caregivers in developing new strategies for working together in an effective way to support the young person.

In Phase 3, FBT-TAY therapists should also meet individually with the young person to assist them in identifying potential risk factors for relapse and work collaboratively with their parents/caregivers to solidify relapse prevention and emergency plans. Importantly, the family work in Phase 3 should focus on addressing issues related to emerging adulthood and not adolescence.

Chapter Summary

Here are the key points of this chapter:

(1) Phase 3 marks the shift from intensive renourishment to supporting the young person's independence, identity development, and preparation for adulthood, while re-defining family roles beyond illness management.
(2) Emerging adulthood (ages 18–29) is a unique stage marked by exploration, instability, and self-focus; while it brings generative opportunities for growth, it also introduces an array of risks and vulnerabilities for ED relapse due to factors such as identity pressures, transitions, and uncertainty.
(3) Families often face their own transition during this stage, moving from caretakers to consultants and renegotiating roles, which can generate tension, but also critical opportunities to strengthen trust and independence.
(4) Relapse prevention is central to Phase 3; therapists provide support to the young person to identify high-risk situations (academic stress, transitions, isolation, body image concerns) and co-create strategies for staying in the stage of recovery.
(5) Relapse prevention plans should clarify early warning signs, coping strategies, and the supportive roles that both parents and caregivers can play without undermining autonomy, in an effort to balance independence with safety nets.
(6) Emergency planning complements relapse prevention, providing concrete steps if symptoms resurface (e.g., structured eating, increased supervision, re-engaging professional supports).
(7) Termination of treatment involves reflecting on progress, addressing unresolved emotions (e.g., resentment or gratitude), and affirming the practical skills, emotional resilience, and shared successes that the young person and their family built together.
(8) Therapists may identify and recommend ongoing supports systems (e.g., family therapy, CBT, individual therapy for identity/relationship issues) to ensure progress and continuity of growth and to manage any co-occurring conditions or remaining challenges with the young person.

References

Arnett, J. J. (2000). Emerging adulthood: A theory of development from the late teens through the twenties. *American Psychologist*, *55*(5), 469–480. https://doi.org/10.1037/0003-066X.55.5.469

Arnett, J. J. (2015). *Emerging adulthood: The winding road from the late teens through the twenties* (2nd ed.). Oxford University Press. https://doi.org/10.1093/acprof:oso/9780199929382.001.0001

Arnett, J. J., Žukauskienė, R., & Sugimura, K. (2014). The new life stage of emerging adulthood at ages 18–29 years: Implications for mental health. *The Lancet. Psychiatry*, *1*(7), 569–576. https://doi.org/10.1016/S2215-0366(14)00080-7

Baranauskas, M., Kupčiūnaitė, I., & Stukas, R. (2022). Potential triggers for risking the development of EDs in non-clinical higher-education students in emerging adulthood. *Nutrients*, *14*(11), 1–15. https://doi.org/10.3390/nu14112293

Berge, J. M., Loth, K., Hanson, C., Croll-Lampert, J., & Neumark-Sztainer, D. (2012). Family life cycle transitions and the onset of EDs: A retrospective grounded theory approach. *Journal of Clinical Nursing*, *21*(9–10), 1355–1363. https://doi.org/10.1111/j.1365-2702.2011.03762.x

Bowlby, C. G., Anderson, T. L., Hall, M. E. L., & Willingham, M. M. (2015). Recovered professionals exploring ED recovery: A qualitative investigation of meaning. *Clinical Social Work Journal*, *43*(1), 1–10. https://doi.org/10.1007/s10615-012-0423-0

D'Amore, S., Maurisse, A., Gubello, A., & Carone, N. (2023). Stress and resilience experiences during the transition to parenthood among Belgian lesbian mothers through donor insemination. *International Journal of Environmental Research and Public Health*, *20*(4), 1–14. https://doi.org/10.3390/ijerph20042800

Davis, M., & Smith, J. P. (2018). Recovery and beyond: Dealing with triggers and setbacks. In A. Seubert & P. Virdi (Eds.), *Trauma-informed approaches to EDs* (pp. 1–10). Springer.

Dimitropoulos, G., Freeman, V. E., Allemang, B., Couturier, J., McVey, G., Lock, J., & Le Grange, D. (2015a). Family-based treatment with transition age youth with anorexia nervosa: A qualitative summary of application in clinical practice. *Journal of Eating Disorders*, *3*(1), 1–13. https://doi.org/10.1186/s40337-015-0037-3

Dimitropoulos, G., Toulany, A., Herschman, J., Kovacs, A., Steinegger, C., Bardsley, J., Sandhu, S., Gregory, C., Colton, P., Anderson, J., & Kaufman, M. (2015b). A qualitative study on the experiences of young adults with EDs transferring from pediatric to adult care. *EDs*, *23*(2), 144–162. https://doi.org/10.1080/10640266.2014.976106

Dodge, E., Baudinet, J., Austin, A., Eisler, I., Le Grange, D., & Dimitropoulos, G. (2024). Family therapy for emerging adults with anorexia nervosa: Expert opinion on evidence, practice considerations, and future directions. *European EDs Review*, 1–11. https://doi.org/10.1002/erv.3129

Elswick, A., Fallin-Bennett, A., Ashford, K., & Werner-Wilson, R. (2018). Emerging adults and recovery capital: Barriers and facilitators to recovery. *Journal of Addictions Nursing*, *29*(2), 78–83. https://doi.org/10.1097/JAN.0000000000000218

Geller, J., Fernandes, A., Marshall, S., & Srikameswaran, S. (2024). From fixing to connecting: Parents' experiences supporting adult children with EDs. *Journal of Eating Disorders*, *12*(1), 1–9. https://doi.org/10.1186/s40337-024-01140-7

Gilmore, K. J., & Meersand, P. (2023). *Emerging adulthood: A psychodynamic approach to the new developmental phase of the 21st century*. American Psychiatric Association Publishing.

Gonidakis, F., Lemonoudi, M., Charila, D., & Varsou, E. (2018). A study on the interplay between emerging adulthood and ED symptomatology in young adults. *Eating and Weight Disorders*, 23(6), 797–805. https://doi.org/10.1007/s40519-018-0552-8

Grilo, C. M., Pagano, M. E., Stout, R. L., Markowitz, J. C., Ansell, E. B., Pinto, A., Zanarini, M. C., Yen, S., & Skodol, A. E. (2012). Stressful life events predict ED relapse following remission: Six-year prospective outcomes. *International Journal of Eating Disorders*, *45*(2), 185–192. https://doi.org/10.1002/eat.20909

Heal-Cohen, N., Allan, S. M., Gauvain, N., Nabirinde, R., & Burgess, A. (2025). Relapse in EDs: A systematic review and thematic synthesis of individuals' experiences. *Clinical Psychology and Psychotherapy*, *32*(4), 1–19 https://doi.org/10.1002/cpp.70101

Heywood, L., Conti, J., & Hay, P. (2022). Paper 1: A systematic synthesis of narrative therapy treatment components for the treatment of eating disorders. *Journal of eating disorders*, *10*(1), 137. https://doi.org/10.1186/s40337-022-00635-5

Hibbs, R., Rhind, C., Leppanen, J., & Treasure, J. (2015). Interventions for caregivers of someone with an ED: A meta-analysis. *International Journal of Eating Disorders*, *48*(4), 349–361. https://doi.org/10.1002/eat.22298

Hong, G. K. (2011). Exploring the family life cycle: Families with children. *The Family Psychologist*, *27*(2), 4–6. https://www.apadivisions.org/division-43/publications/newsletters/2011/04-issue.pdf

Karlstad, J., Moe, C. F., Adelsten Stokland, R., & Brinchmann, B. S. (2022). "Balancing within a closed family system": A grounded theory study of how family life is affected by having a family member with an ED. *Journal of Eating Disorders*, *10*(1), 1–10. https://doi.org/10.1186/s40337-022-00669-9

Karlstad, J., Moe, C. F., Wattum, M., & Brinchmann, B. S. (2021). The experiences and strategies of parents' of adults with anorexia nervosa or bulimia nervosa: A qualitative study. *BMC Psychiatry*, *21*(1), 1–11. https://doi.org/10.1186/s12888-021-03345-5

Kenny, T. E., Boyle, S. L., & Lewis, S. P. (2020). Recovery: Understanding recovery from the lens of recovery-focused blogs posted by individuals with lived experience. *IJED*, *53*(8), 1234–1243. https://doi.org/10.1002/eat.23221

Kranzler, A., Elkins, R. M., & Albano, A. M. (2019). Anxiety in emerging adulthood: A developmentally informed treatment model. In S. Compton, M. A. Villabø, & H. Kristensen (Eds.), *Pediatric anxiety disorders* (pp. 499–519). Academic Press.

Lane, J. A. (2015). *Counseling emerging adults in transition: Practical applications of attachment and social support research*. The Professional Counselor. https://pdxscholar.library.pdx.edu/cgi/viewcontent.cgi?article=1026&context=coun_fac

Lock, J., & Le Grange, D. (2012). *Treatment manual for anorexia nervosa: A family-based approach*. Guilford publications.

McGoldrick, M., & Carter, B. (2003). The family life cycle. In F. Walsh (Ed.), *Normal family processes: Growing diversity and complexity* (pp. 375–398). The Guilford Press. https://doi.org/10.4324/9780203428436_chapter_14

McGoldrick, M., Preto, N. G., & Carter, B. (2016). The life cycle in its changing context: Individual, family and social perspectives. In M. McGoldrick, N. A. Garcia Preto, & B. A. Carter (Eds.), *The expanding family life cycle: Individual, family, and social perspectives* (pp. 1–44). Pearson.

Melemis, S. M. (2015). Relapse prevention and the five rules of recovery. *The Yale Journal of Biology & Medicine*, *88*(3), 325–332. https://pmc-ncbi-nlm-nih-gov.ezproxy.lib.ucalgary.ca/articles/PMC4553654/

Menon, J., & Kandasamy, A. (2018). Relapse prevention. *Indian Journal of Psychiatry*, *60*(8), 473–478. https://doi.org/10.4103/psychiatry.IndianJPsychiatry_36_18

Miskovic-Wheatley, J., Bryant, E., Ong, S. H., Vatter, S., Le, A., Aouad, P., Barakat, S., Boakes, R., Brennan, L., Byrne, S., Caldwell, B., Calvert, S., Carroll, B., Castle, D., Caterson, I., Chelius, B., Chiem, L., Clarke, S., Conti, J., . . ., Williams, M. (2023). ED outcomes: Findings from a rapid review of over a decade of research. *Journal of Eating Disorders*, *11*(1), 1–25. https://doi.org/10.1186/s40337-023-00801-3

Nadarajah, A., Dimitropoulos, G., Grant, C., Webb, C., & Couturier, J. (2021). Impending transition from pediatric to adult health services: A qualitative study of the experiences of adolescents with EDs and their caregivers. *Frontiers in Psychiatry*, *12*, 1–14. https://doi.org/10.3389/fpsyt.2021.624942

National EDs Association (n.d.). *ED relapse*. https://www.nationaleatingdisorders.org/relapse/?utm

Nice, M. L., Arsh, Dingfelder, R. A., Faris, N. D., Albert, J. K., & Sickels, M. B. (2024). Counseling emerging adults: A phenomenological investigation of professional counselors' lived experiences. *The Professional Counselor*, 14(3), 288–303. https://doi.org/10.15241/mln.14.3.288

Oren, S. (2020). Family therapy with midlife parents: Perceived brief therapeutic intervention. In V. Chis (Ed.), *ERD 2019 – Education, reflection, development, seventh edition* (pp. 452–459). *European Proceedings of Social and Behavioural Sciences*. European Publisher. https://doi.org/10.15405/epsbs.2020.06.45

Potterton, R., Austin, A., Allen, K., Lawrence, V., & Schmidt, U. (2020b). "I'm not a teenager, I'm 22. Why can't I snap out of it?": A qualitative exploration of seeking help for a first-episode ED during emerging adulthood. *Journal of Eating Disorders*, *8*(1), 1–14. https://doi.org/10.1186/s40337-020-00320-5

Potterton, R., Austin, A., Flynn, M., Allen, K., Lawrence, V., Mountford, V., Glennon, D., Grant, N., Brown, A., Franklin-Smith, M., Schelhase, M., Jones, W. R., Brady, G., Nunes, N., Connan, F., Mahony, K., Serpell, L., & Schmidt, U. (2021). "I'm truly free from my ED": Emerging adults' experiences of FREED, an early intervention service model and care pathway for EDs. *Journal of Eating Disorders*, *9*(1), 1–14. https://doi.org/10.1186/s40337-020-00354-9

Potterton, R., Brown, G., & Schmidt, U. (2025). "I thought if my parents got involved, then they'd make me get better": Emerging adults' experiences of support from family and friends during anorexia nervosa. *Journal of Eating Disorders*, *13*(1), 1–13. https://doi.org/10.1186/s40337-025-01260-8

Potterton, R., Richards, K., Allen, K., & Schmidt, U. (2020a). EDs during emerging adulthood: A systematic scoping review. *Frontiers in Psychology*, *10*, 1–16. https://doi.org/10.3389/fpsyg.2019.03062

Rice, K. G., Lopez, F. G., & Wang, Q. (2023). Perfectionism, Goal orientation, and emerging adults' identity processing styles. *Emerging Adulthood*, *11*(4), 815–827. https://doi.org/10.1177/21676968231166715

Safi, F., Aniserowicz, A. M., Colquhoufn, H., Stier, J., & Nowrouzi-Kia, B. (2022). Impact of EDs on paid or unpaid work participation and performance: A systematic review and meta-analysis protocol. *Journal of Eating Disorder*, *10*(1), 1–11. https://doi.org/10.1186/s40337-021-00525-2

Sala, M., Keshishian, A., Song, S., Moskowitz, R., Bulik, C. M., Roos, C. R., & Levinson, C. A. (2023). Predictors of relapse in EDs: A meta-analysis. *Journal of Psychiatric Research*, *158*, 281–299. https://doi.org/10.1016/j.jpsychires.2023.01.002

Spence, R., Owens-Solari, M., & Goodyer, I. (2016). Help-seeking in emerging adults with and without a history of mental health referral: A qualitative study. *BMC Research Notes*, *9*(1), 1–8. https://doi.org/10.1186/s13104-016-2227-8

Steinglass, J. E., Attia, E., Glasofer, D. R., Wang, Y., Ruggiero, J., Walsh, B. T., & Thomas, J. G. (2022). Optimizing relapse prevention and changing habits (REACH+) in anorexia nervosa. *International Journal of Eating Disorders*, *55*(6), 851–857. https://doi.org/10.1002/eat.23724

Wood, D., Crapnell, T., Lau, L., Bennett, A., Lotstein, D., Ferris, M., & Kuo, A. (2017). Emerging adulthood as a critical stage in the life course. In C. B. Forrest, N. Halfon, & R. M. Lerner. (Eds.), *Handbook of life course health development* (pp. 1–21). Springer. https://doi.org/10.1007/978-3-319-47143-3_7

Chapter 10

Contextual Considerations in FBT-TAY

This chapter describes the potential successes and challenges that therapists practising FBT-TAY might face when considering supporting young people transitioning out of paediatric care to private practice. We also discuss how to support those with a late onset disordered eating or AN when they require accessible primary care. To achieve this goal, we describe new and innovative approaches for delivering briefer versions of FBT-TAY in primary care where young people and their families can potentially access care if they present with AN and can access services through primary care. Finally, we introduce Extension for Community Healthcare Outcomes for building capacity in workforce where there are few resources/supports for AN in TAY.

Summary: FBT-TAY Across Multiple Treatment Settings

The treatment of young people with AN takes place across multiple care contexts, from paediatric to adult programs, hospitals, community mental health centres, primary care, and private practice. While there is limited literature focusing on these service settings, this chapter aims to describe some of the ways FBT-TAY may be delivered in non-specialized ED programs and settings.

Factors that may influence where young people are able to access care include long waitlists in specialty clinics, high out of pocket treatment costs, or limited insurance coverage.

Team Building in the Private Practice Context

Across settings, to deliver FBT-TAY, therapists must have opportunities to access training to key clinical materials on emerging adulthood, EDs, and best practices for supporting young people with AN. While not unique to private practice, it is important for private practice and community mental health providers to have the same access to training and materials. While this may represent a cost

DOI: 10.4324/9781003463351-11

concern for a less resourced program, it is a vital component to ensuring fidelity to the model and support for therapists. In our practice, we provide introductory training on the FBT model, plus advanced training for therapists working with TAY. We also supplement this learning with clinic rounds, consultation sessions, and access to the FBT-AN (adolescent) treatment manual as a reference point, as well as to articles written about FBT-TAY. Supporting therapists, ongoing consultation, team meetings, and a community of practice are vital. Team rounds with physicians, dietitians, and other adjunctive team members may aid in providing a forum for communication and discussion of stuck points in treatment.

It is possible in private practice to provide user-friendly weight charts and binge/purge logs, and within treatment questionnaires via a Health Insurance Portability and Accountability Act (HIPAA)-compliant electronic health record system. The use of this online portal allows both clients, their caregivers, and the interdisciplinary team working in the private practice setting access this material in a user friendly and secure manner. Before starting treatment, a phone intake is scheduled with the young person and/or the caregiver. It has been our experience that, for young people, this call can be done jointly between them and their caregiver, by their caregiver seeking preliminary information, or by the young person individually. While all formats of these intake calls can be useful, if the intake is done by a parent/caregiver alone, an additional call with the young person is recommended. This sets an expectation, from the outset, that collaboration and promotion of autonomy and agency of the young person are critical. Like the FBT-AN model, our phone intake focuses on the importance of accurate diagnosis, tailored treatment planning, and conveying the urgency and potential for current/emerging medical or psychiatric crises. It is prudent to defer making specific recommendations for treatment on an phone intake call but important to ensure that young people and their parent/caregivers are aware of the options in the clinic (cognitive behaviour therapy-E, adolescent-focused therapy, FBT-TAY).

Young people with EDs often present with significant co-morbidity, risk for suicide/self-harm, as well as medical risk. Because of this, clear and consistent (regularly scheduled) communication between members of the treatment team aids in supporting the young person and their parents/caregivers in the treatment process. In most private practice settings, a team must be constructed by the FBT-TAY therapist. This can be accomplished by identifying and contacting area therapists that treat AN (psychiatrists, internists, dietitians) to build relationships to support young people in treatment including FBT-TAY. While such relationship building takes time and effort, it is a key component of the treatment process. Whether through team rounds, or email or phone communication, consistent and frequent communication benefits the treatment team and ensures they are on the same page and communicating congruent messages and, ultimately, comprehensive care of the young person. Finally, frequent communication with physicians and utilization of the emergency room, when needed, to assess medical and psychiatric concerns helps therapists in their efforts to mitigate risk in the young person. As is the case with adolescents in FBT, providing treatment for young people must be rooted in a comprehensive, interdisciplinary care model, including collaboration with primary care physicians, dietitians and psychiatrists. This team approach makes it possible to treat medically and psychiatrically compromised individuals on an outpatient basis. The importance of these relationships is paramount, as it allows the team members to remain "on the same page" as clients and their families, while also diminishing professional stress and thereby mitigating clinical burnout.

Treating TAY in Primary Care Settings

Many young people who develop AN later in adolescence or early adulthood may consider pursuing care in a primary care setting. A promising treatment option for young people with a shorter duration of illness presentation is a brief Family-Based Treatment for Primary Care (FBT-PC) which utilizes several core tenants of traditional FBT to create a treatment that can be provided by primary care physicians (PCPs). FBT-PC delivers care to young people with mild to moderate cases of restrictive EDs, including AN and other specificized feeding and EDs (OSFED) (Lebow et al., 2021a, 2021b, 2024a, 2024b, 2025). FBT-PC emphasizes the unique medical expertise of PCPs and pre-existing relationships with families to merge psychological and medical factors at one site, making it an ideal model of treatment for early presentations of EDs (Lebow et al., 2021b, 2024b). There are many obstacles associated with specialized ED treatment that FBT-PC addresses, such as accessibility, time constraints, and stigma (Hahn et al., 2023; Lau et al., 2025; Lebow et al., 2021b, 2024b, 2025. The goal of FBT-PC, informed by traditional FBT, provides an accessible, efficient, and brief intervention for young people with minimally complex restrictive EDs (Hooper et al., 2024; Lebow et al., 2025).

FBT-PC maintains many of the core tenants of FBT including:

> 1) a focus on weight restoration,2) parental/caregiver empowerment, 3) externalization of the AN, 4) the use of metaphors and psychoeducation to communicate the seriousness of the illness, 5) an agnostic stance on the cause of the illness, and 5) reducing guilt and shame within the family (Lebow et al., 2024a, 2024b). However, some modifications have been made to FBT-PC to enhance its efficiency and accessibility including: 1) shorter visits between PCPs and families, 2) PCPs have less specialized training in comparison to traditional FBT-certified psychologists, 3) an increased focus on medical monitoring facilitated by PCPs or nurses, 4) no family meal at the beginning of treatment, 5) siblings are not formally involved throughout treatment, and 6) cross-covered care is used to avoid treatment disruptions (Lau et al., 2025; Lebow et al., 2021b, 2025).

The initial session for FBT-PC lasts approximately 60 minutes (Lebow et al., 2024a). This visit includes both the young person and their parent(s)/caregiver(s) and emphasizes enhancing knowledge surrounding EDs, the crucial role that parents/caregivers play in their child's recovery, and parental/caregiver empowerment (Lebow et al., 2021b). Subsequent sessions are approximately 30 minutes and occur weekly depending on clinical judgement and the patient's symptom improvement (Lebow et al., 2021b, 2025). These later sessions focus on interventions that attain weight restoration such as reviewing meals, assisting parents/caregivers in handling resistance with the AN, and minimizing exercise (Lebow et al., 2021b). In traditional FBT, it is standard for sessions to range from 50 to 60 minutes, and sometimes longer in the initial phase (Lebow et al., 2021b).

FBT-PC is a two-phase model, unlike traditional FBT which consists of three phases (Lebow et al., 2024b; Lock & Le Grange, 2005). Phase 1 of FBT-PC is comparable to Phase 1 of traditional FBT, empowering parents/caregivers to lead the weight restoration process (Lebow et al., 2021b, 2024a). The second phase of FBT-PC is a combination of the elements of Phases 2 and 3 of traditional FBT, including weight maintenance, handing back developmentally appropriate control over eating, and relapse prevention (Lebow et al., 2021b, 2024a). Some studies have evaluated the effectiveness and feasibility of FBT-PC. Through a retrospective clinical cohort study, Lebow et al. (2021a) provided preliminary evidence of the efficiency of FBT-PC by comparing traditional FBT and FBT-PC. Patients in FBT-PC spent roughly half the time in treatment than those in FBT (366.3 minutes compared to 668.7 minutes). While the time spent in treatment differed significantly, both groups revealed a large effect size for increases in their BMI. At the end of treatment, 80% of those in FBT-PC and 87% in FBT had achieved weight restoration. Further, 67% in FBT-PC and 60% in FBT no longer met DSM-5 criteria for an ED. To further demonstrate the efficacy of FBT-PC, Lebow et al. (2021b) ran a pilot study with 15 adolescents receiving FBT-PC. After three months of treatment, patients had gained an average of 6.76 kg, averaging at 0.56 kg per week. This gain is consistent with traditional FBT's recommended weight gain. Additionally, Lebow et al. (2024b) emphasized the capacity of primary care services to enhance accessibility. Through a retrospective chart review comparing FBT-PC to a form of specialized care in an ED clinic, patients in FBT-PC were more racially and socioeconomically diverse. Specifically, there was a greater representation of non-white patients who had government insurance and those who were presenting earlier in the course of their illness, when compared to those in the specialized care clinic (Lebow et al., 2024b). Most recently, Lebow et al. (2025) illustrated not only the weight improvements of patients resulting from FBT-PC, which increased by 1.25 points per week on average, but also the caregiver- and patient-reported ED symptoms and patient quality of life at the end of treatment. These increases feature the ability of PCPs to captivate young people in treatment to break difficult compulsory behaviours.

Further research is required to replicate these findings in other primary care environments to better demonstrate the generalizability of FBT-PC (Lau et al., 2025). Additionally, long-term randomized-control trials are necessary to outline the delayed benefits and definitive evidence for FBT-PC.

FBT-PC is a part of a stepped-care continuum, modified from traditional FBT that can bridge the gap between primary care and specialized ED care (Partain et al., 2023). Preliminary support has demonstrated its potential as an effective treatment for young people with restrictive EDs to reduce the stress of treatment on the healthcare system and families (Lebow et al., 2025). It provides a reliable model for TAY that lives in rural, underserved areas or is away at college.

There are also Guided Self-Help FBT models that are potentially promising resources that can be used by parents/caregivers and families with older adolescents and young people with AN. The approach includes online videos supplemented by written resources and a "coach" to help parents/caregivers navigate these materials. Data suggests the approach is feasible and effective with families of adolescents with AN (e.g., Lock et al., 2017; Wade et al., 2022) and could potentially be used in non-specialty settings such as primary care offices. This is an area of treatment development that could increase access and lower costs for many; however, much work needs to be done to determine whether it is acceptable and feasible with TAY and their families.

Support for Professionals Treating TAY Using FBT in Private Practice

Project for Extension for Community Healthcare Outcomes (ECHO) is a model designed to encourage professional development and continuing education. ECHO uses virtual collaboration to provide specialized training to HCPs and has been designed for numerous illnesses, including EDs (Agley et al., 2021; Bessel et al., 2023; Poulin et al., 2022; Tantillo et al., 2020). Project ECHO-EDs Clinic (PE-EDC) has developed a regional collaborative learning community to bridge the knowledge gap between community-based providers and ED specialists and diminish the barriers of accessibility, time constraints, and lack of resources faced by patients, families, and healthcare professionals (HCPs) (Tantillo et al., 2020).

ECHO works to create interprofessional teams of experts, ranging from nurses, psychiatrists, dietitians, parent/caregiver peer mentors, to young adult peer mentors, who work synchronously in virtual sessions with Health Care Professionals (HCPs; Tantillo et al., 2020). Sessions range in time and frequency depending on the judgement of the team and needs of HCPs (Tantillo et al., 2020). Sessions include three parts: introductions, a didactic presentation, and a case presentation (Project ECHO Ontario Mental Health at CAMH & University of Toronto, n.d.). Didactic presentations are run by subject-matter experts and include interactive activities to stimulate knowledge-building and collaborative discussions (Project ECHO Ontario Mental Health at CAMH & University of Toronto, n.d.). Next is a real, de-identified case presentation, providing the opportunity for participants to work and solve problems collaboratively with guidance from experts (Komaromy et al., 2016; Project ECHO Ontario Mental Health at CAMH & University of Toronto, n.d.).

Tantillo and colleagues (2020) demonstrated the potential of ECHO by developing PE-EDC, a specialized program for enhancing specialized knowledge surrounding EDs. Ninety-nine participants attended sessions that were held twice a month for 90 minutes, synchronously and virtually. Didactic presentations included best practices related to biopsychosocial assessment and diagnosis, patient and family engagement, and medical and behavioural management. Case presentations were facilitated by HCPs and openly discussed. Participating HCPs reported that they were "very" to "highly" satisfied with the PE-EDCs. Key takeaways from participants included the understanding of the complexity of EDs, how to motivate patients for change, and the essential elements of care (e.g., accounting for nutrition, the impact of culture, and planning for the care of patients). Additionally, participants made note of the changes they would make in their practice including improving screening practices, motivating patients for change, and improving treatments.

Recently, the foundations of ECHO were also used to develop a similar program for therapists working with adults with EDs (Bessel et al., 2023). This program included multiple weekly virtual sessions with government employees, state-employed therapists, and primary health care providers. The sessions were designed by a team of specialists and included topics such as assessment, common comorbidities, and developing collaborative treatment plans. At the end of the program, significant increases in self-reported confidence and knowledge surrounding the various topics of EDs were reported.

These outcomes demonstrate the potential for ECHO to develop workforce capacity and enhance specialized knowledge for EDs. However, further research is necessary to better understand limited attendance in sessions and patient outcomes from increased knowledge and capacity in participants (Bessel et al., 2023; Tantillo et al., 2020)

EP-EDC proves a promising, scalable model for bridging the knowledge gap between ED specialists and community-based providers to enhance specialized knowledge. Additionally, it provides a reliable option for better training of primary care situated near post-secondary institutions to support TAY with EDs.

In addition to ECHO, an online training strategy has been developed for therapists that includes online videos on how to implement FBT for AN. Research suggests that this online training approach is acceptable and that therapists learn the basics of FBT using this model. Ongoing studies examining the approach with therapists in private practice will help determine the long-term feasibility of using this type of online training to increase access to FBT training by lowering costs and increasing flexibility and timing of training.

Conclusions

FBT-TAY in private practice faces many of the same challenges as in any other treatment modality; however, building a team, managing insurance, access in non-specialist settings (e.g., primary care offices), and training and support of therapists in these settings are potential additional issues which should be addressed. In closing, treatments in private practice as well as promising low-barrier and accessible interventions in primary care settings suggest feasibility of this model in outpatient care. While not an exhaustive overview of all contexts where young people are treated, we hope this gives a clinical picture of the treatment of TAY in several applications.

Chapter Summary

Here are the key points of this chapter:

(1) Young people with AN access treatment across diverse settings (e.g., paediatric and adult programs, hospitals, community mental health centres, primary care, and private practice), requiring adaptable FBT-TAY approaches when specialized ED services are unavailable.
(2) Implementing FBT-TAY in private practice requires a robust intake process with young people and their parents/caregivers, clear risk communication with other members of the treatment team, and collaborative engagement of young people and their parents/caregivers in instilling autonomy and agency of the young person.
(3) Private practitioners must intentionally build multidisciplinary teams (e.g., physicians, dietitians, primary care providers, and other adjunctive team members) and maintain consistent communication to ensure safe, coordinated care.
(4) Access to quality training and consultation is essential for FBT-TAY therapists to deliver FBT-TAY with fidelity in private practice.
(5) FBT-PC offers a brief, accessible, primary-care–delivered adaptation of FBT that demonstrates strong early outcomes for mild to moderate restrictive EDs.
(6) Guided Self-Help FBT provides a promising low-cost option to increase access to FBT, though more research is needed for TAY-specific applicability.
(7) Project ECHO expands offers scalable virtual training and case-based learning with an interdisciplinary team of nurses, psychiatrists, dietitians, parent/caregiver peer mentors, and young adult peer mentors, who work synchronously in virtual sessions with HCPs. This model adapted for EDs shows promise in increasing workforce capacity and specialized knowledge in EDs.

References

Agley, J., Delong, J., Janota, A., Carson, A., Roberts, J., & Maupome, G. (2021). Reflections on project ECHO: Qualitative findings from five different ECHO programs. *Medical Education Online*, *26*(1), 1–10. https://doi.org/10.1080/10872981.2021.1936435

Bessell, E., Kim, J. S., Chiem, L., McDonald, A., Thompson, D., Glozier, N., Simpson, A., Parcsi, L., Morris, R., & Koncz, R. (2023). Effectiveness of Project ECHO programs in improving clinician knowledge and confidence in managing complex psychiatric patients: A waitlist-controlled study. *Academic Psychiatry: The Journal of the American Association of Directors of Psychiatric Residency Training and the Association for Academic Psychiatry*, *47*(1), 25–34. https://doi.org/10.1007/s40596-022-01701-5

Hahn, S. L., Burnette, C. B., Borton, K. A., Mitchell Carpenter, L., Sonneville, K. R., & Bailey, B. (2023). ED risk in rural US adolescents: What do we know and where do we go? *International Journal of Eating Disorders*, *56*(2), 366–371. https://doi.org/10.1002/eat.23843

Hooper, L., Lebow, J., Gewirtz O'Brien, J. R., Puhl, R. M., & Neumark-Sztainer, D. (2024). Partnerships with primary care providers: Opportunities to prevent EDs and mitigate their progression in young people. *EDs*, *32*(6), 746–762. https://doi.org/10.1080/10640266.2024.2394263

Komaromy, M., Duhigg, D., Metcalf, A., Carlson, C., Kalishman, S., Hayes, L., Burke, T., Thornton, K., & Arora, S. (2016). Project ECHO (Extension for Community Healthcare Outcomes): A new model for educating primary care providers about treatment of substance use disorders. *Substance Abuse*, *37*(1), 20–24. https://doi.org/10.1080/08897077.2015.1129388

Lau, J. S., Kusumoputro, S., Tran, A. T., Fort, V., Lee, H. C., Pierce, L. S., Timm, J. A., Yadav, N., Villarta, M. C., & Lebow, J. (2025). Implementation of Family-Based Treatment for Primary Care in a novel healthcare system: Description of the adaptation process. *EDs*, 1–10. Advance online publication. https://doi.org/10.1080/10640266.2025.2524393

Lebow, J., Billings, M., Mattke, A., Partain, P., Gewirtz O'Brien, J., Narr, C., Breland, R., Jacobson, R. M., Loeb, K., & Sim, L. (2024b). Does embedding pediatric ED treatment in primary care bridge the access gap? *EDs*, *32*(3), 283–296. https://doi.org/10.1080/10640266.2023.2299592

Lebow, J., Mattke, A., Narr, C., Partain, P., Breland, R., Gewirtz O'Brien, J. R., Geske, J., Billings, M., Clark, M. M., Jacobson, R. M., Phelan, S., Harbeck-Weber, C., Le Grange, D., & Sim, L. (2021a). Can adolescents with EDs be treated in primary care? A retrospective clinical cohort study. *Journal of Eating Disorders*, *9*(1), 1–10. https://doi.org/10.1186/s40337-021-00413-9

Lebow, J., Mattke, A., Partain, P., Billings, M., Geske, J., Gewirtz O'Brien, J. R., Narr, C., Breland, R., Schmit, T., Le Grange, D., Loeb, K., Jacobson, R. M., & Sim, L. (2025). Family-Based Treatment for Primary Care: An observational study of a community sample of youth with restrictive EDs. *International Journal of Eating Disorders*, *58*(6), 1085–1095. https://doi.org/10.1002/eat.24416

Lebow, J., O'Brien, J. R. G., Mattke, A., Narr, C., Geske, J., Billings, M., Clark, M. M., Jacobson, R. M., Phelan, S., Le Grange, D., & Sim, L. (2021b). A primary care modification of family-based treatment for adolescent restrictive EDs. *EDs*, *29*(4), 376–389. https://doi.org/10.1080/10640266.2019.1656468

Lebow, J., Sim, L., Redmond, S., Billings, M., Mattke, A., Gewirtz O'Brien, J. R., Partain, P., Narr, C., Breland, R., Soma, D., Schmit, T., Magill, S., Leonard, A., Crane, S., Le Grange, D., Loeb, K., Clark, M., Phelan, S., Jacobson, R. M., Enders, F.,. . ., Leppin, A. (2024a). Adapting behavioral treatments for Primary Care using a theory-based

framework: The case of adolescent EDs. *Academic Pediatrics*, *24*(2), 208–215. https://doi.org/10.1016/j.acap.2023.08.004
Lock, J., Darcy, A., Fitzpatrick, K. K., Vierhile, M., & Sadeh-Sharvit, S. (2017). Parental guided self-help family based treatment for adolescents with anorexia nervosa: A feasibility study. *International Journal of Eating Disorders*, *50*(9), 1104–1108. https://doi.org/10.1002/eat.22733
Lock, J., & Le Grange, D. (2005). Family-based treatment of EDs. *International Journal of Eating Disorders*, *37 Suppl*, S64–S89. https://doi.org/10.1002/eat.20122
Partain, P., Sim, L., Fladager Muth, J., Mattke, A., Billings, M., Jacobson, R., Le Grange, D., & Lebow, J. (2023). The role of Primary Care in bridging adolescents awaiting ED treatment. *Pediatrics*, *152*(5), 1–7. https://doi.org/10.1542/peds.2023-061672
Poulin, P. A., Shergill, Y., Grebowicz, A., Almeida, I., Cantave, R., MacLeod, B., Larocque, T., Garstin, D., Fitzgerald, S. F., & Rash, J. A. (2022). Extension for Community Healthcare Outcomes (ECHO) chronic pain & opioid stewardship in northwestern Ontario: A thematic analysis of patient cases. *Canadian Journal of Pain*, *6*(1), 211–224. https://doi.org/10.1080/24740527.2022.2126754
Project ECHO Ontario Mental Health at CAMH & University of Toronto. (n.d.). *About us*. CAMH ECHO Ontario. https://camh.echoontario.ca/about-us/
Tantillo, M., Starr, T., & Kreipe, R. (2020). The recruitment and acceptability of a project ECHO® EDs clinic: A pilot study of telementoring for primary medical and behavioral health care practitioners. *EDs: The Journal of Treatment & Prevention*, *28*(3), 230–255. https://doi.org/10.1080/10640266.2019.1580125
Wade, T., Byrne, S., Fursland, A., Steele, A., Wilksch, S., Anderson, J., . . ., & Lock, J. (2022). Is guided self-help family-based treatment for parents of adolescents with anorexia nervosa on treatment waitlists feasible? A pilot trial. *International Journal of Eating Disorders*, *55*(6), 832–837. https://doi.org/10.1002/eat.23720

Chapter 11

Post-Secondary Considerations

In this chapter, we explore considerations related to post-secondary education (college, university, and trade school) for young people with AN. Navigating continued education with an active ED, or while receiving care for an ED, poses unique challenges as well as opportunities for active engagement of both parents/caregivers and others in a young person's social support network. This chapter addresses navigating FBT-TAY treatment in post-secondary education environments as well as options related to facilitating and maintaining support networks.

The transition of moving to a new place, whether nearby or across the world from a young person's family, can be an exciting and tumultuous rite of passage for all young people. Factors related to change in routine, availability of preferred foods, increase in courseload, demanding academic expectations, financial concerns, isolation, developing new friendships, among many other issues, can impact health, mood and well-being, and, for some, have a deleterious effect on eating and exercise behaviours and increase body image disturbances. This can be a particularly challenging time for individuals that are recovering from EDs, and for others, this transition period can be a vulnerable time where EDs emerge or lapses or relapses occur.

The 2013 NEDA survey that explored the prevalence of EDs among college students in the United States found that an estimated 10–20% of women in college suffered from an ED, and an estimated 4–10% of men in college suffered from an ED (National EDs Association, 2013). Approximately four out of ten students either had personally experienced an ED or knew someone who had experienced difficulties with such illnesses. According to a more recent study by Alhaj et al. (2022), they found that about 19.7% of university/college students (internationally) screened positive for disordered eating on common screening tools (≈1 in 5), with higher prevalence where sample BMI and the proportion female are larger and with substantial variation by screening instrument and year of study.

Data suggests that the COVID-19 pandemic had a significant impact on the increase in rates of EDs among college students (Devoe et al., 2023;

DOI: 10.4324/9781003463351-12

Luginaah et al., 2025). Pacanowski et al. (2024) studied a large state university in the United States and found that disordered eating was significantly lower in pre-pandemic years compared to pandemic years. Additionally, a study in France, analysing recent ED rates, found that all types of ED increased significantly between 2009 and 2021, except for restrictive ED among men (Tavolacci et al., 2021). In summary, the rates of EDs on college and university campuses suggest that this is a common concern for TAY in these settings.

Access to specialized ED care provides an important safety net for young people transitioning to post-secondary education. Unfortunately, access to such care can be difficult to navigate in post-secondary contexts. According to Grammer et al. (2020), only 60% of surveyed university college counselling centres reported offering year-round access to a counsellor specializing in EDs. Many universities face challenges in offering evidence-based treatment for EDs to the many students in need. Barriers to offering treatment include stigma, the time-intensive nature of in-person interventions, and financial costs of treatment (Grammer et al., 2020). These concerns deter student engagement with in-person care for an ED. Data from Eisenberg et al. (2011) describes that fewer than 20% of university students with EDs receive treatment. This number is even lower for students who belong to an ethnic group or racial minority group. While access to care is problematic for a majority of students, there are also many examples of specialized ED treatment teams on university campuses. One example is based at a US urban university where there is a comprehensive team of ED providers across the student health and Department of Psychiatry (Liu, 2025). Students have access to psychiatrists and medical providers through the student health department and receive referrals for specialized ED psychotherapy through the Department of Psychiatry. Students are seen across these departments where care is coordinated by an ED team. This is one example of how care can be delivered.

Screening is a valuable tool for identifying students that may need support for disordered eating/EDs. According to Grammer et al. (2020), there have been many efforts made to increase screening and connect young people to ED care on college campuses. While gains have been made in the implementation of evidence-based screening, most campuses are not able to tie screening to prevention or ED-specific treatment. Further work is needed to investigate dissemination of evidence-based treatment, particularly in the digital space as these may be more cost-effective, accessible options. While the current data demonstrates significant gaps in accessibility, there are promising changes related to the use of telemedicine, digital interventions, and changes to licensing laws across the United States (PsyPact) that have increased access to care as well as made it easier for young people to retain their treatment team when they move locations temporarily or permanently.

Another important factor in building out assessment and intervention is increasing awareness of EDs on college campuses. The Centre for Innovation in

Campus Mental Health (Ontario) (2025) has developed a campus mental health ED tool kit outlining practical steps to increase staff and faculty's awareness, knowledge, and confidence in supporting students with concerns around EDs. While this toolkit is aimed at campus staff, it may also be useful to young people and their families as a resource to share.

Assessing Readiness for Post-Secondary Education

The process of considering post-secondary education, including applications, decisions, and commitment to a program, often spans over several years. When a young person is still in high school and may be considering post-secondary education, it is vital that the treatment team work with the young person and their family (when available) to determine readiness for independence and transition to a new environment. College readiness has been addressed by Mulheim (2015) in a college readiness checklist, as well as others (Book, n.d.; Gerson, 2023). It is recommended that treatment teams/families assess readiness well in advance of post-secondary attendance and that this is done on an ongoing basis throughout the treatment process. Recovery specific factors to consider include length of behavioural recovery, insight, and opportunities to practice independence prior to transitioning to post-secondary education (Book, n.d.). Factors related to post-secondary options should also be considered (Mulheim, 2015).

These include, but are not limited to, distance from home/family, presence of support, and availability of specialized ED care. The college readiness checklist can be a useful therapeutic tool to determine treatment targets, as well as areas of emerging/sustained recovery. Questions from Mulheim's college readiness checklist include behavioural items related to food, eating, and exercise, as well as insight-oriented questions related to temperament/vulnerabilities related to lapse and relapse. Sample questions include the following: "Has your young person maintained a steady weight in the healthy range (according to childhood growth records) and (if applicable) menstruated consistently for six months?" "Has your young person been free of ED behaviours such as bingeing, purging, laxative use, and excessive exercise for six months?" "Is your young person able to independently and consistently prepare and choose meals that contain enough energy-dense foods to maintain this weight?" and "Does your young person openly acknowledge their ED and have insight into the need to construct a life and schedule that supports recovery?"

Given that the timeline for post-secondary education is sometimes misaligned with an individual's treatment trajectory, there can be an opportunity to leverage trial runs with eating on campus and in cafeterias, or a gradual exposure of independence with decision-making regarding meal preparation, grocery shopping, and eating away from family. For example, young people may choose to live at home for a semester or take classes at a commuter school, community, or other local college. This may help them better understand gaps, as well as areas of competency/strength in their own level of readiness related to independence. Allowing space in the treatment to discuss beliefs around college readiness, timelines, and comparison may be of utility in clinical conversations related to post-secondary education. Discussion of readiness, potential barriers, and future goals must happen at various times during the application process as there can be a high level of pressure to apply and attend college on the timeline of the young person's academic cohort. Creating clinical space to talk about the unique needs of the individual related to treatment, recovery, and choosing a post-secondary environment that will help support and sustain their recovery and development is an important goal of treatment with the young person especially in Phase 3.

Developing a Treatment Team

While the young person, family, and treatment team are determining the feasibility of a transition to a post-secondary education environment, constructing an "on-campus" treatment team becomes an important goal. Establishing a care team requires first understanding the options on campus/near campus. It is recommended that young people/families evaluate the options on campus in terms of medical, psychiatric, and specialized ED care. Then, families can evaluate the options related to off-campus providers. This information can be located on post-secondary education websites, through support of school counsellors, school psychologists, and from the referral networks of treating providers. Given that many young people change geographic location during this time, navigating providers and their availability can sometimes be an arduous and time-consuming process.

Informed consent is an ongoing part of the treatment process and should be revisited as members join the interdisciplinary team. It is recommended that there is a balanced discussion with the young person and their treatment team to determine how information will be shared with parents/caregivers while the young person is on campus and seeking care in student mental health services or in the broader community. Due to privacy laws across the world, this written consent will be necessary for parents/caregivers to receive information from the college treating providers. Discussion should include information related to what information is shared, how often it is shared, and with whom information it is shared (parents/caregivers, primary care provider at home, and home therapist). We would like to highlight how the home team and campus team may work together to bridge services as the young person travels between home and their college/university. When constructing the treatment team, discussions related to periodic check-ins regarding treatment progress and ongoing treatment sessions inclusive of family/support members should also be discussed. These conversations should be considerate of a young person's stage of development and concerns that they may have related to privacy, individuation, and sharing of confidential information including related to AN or other mental health concerns.

Embedding a focus on support and relational care can be useful in maintaining these clinical conversations during stuck points. It is also important for young people to have choice in what information is shared, understanding that within the FBT-TAY framework, all information related to weight, food, and ED symptoms is important to include in conversations with everyone involved in the care of young people, including providers and the young person's parents/caregivers (Dimitropoulos et al., 2018a).

The process of establishing a care team should be done with as much advance planning as possible and in partnership with the young person (and their parents/caregivers or other supportive adults). In the process of crafting the outpatient campus team, investigating options related to urgent care, emergency psychiatric care, as well as other higher level of care options help young people and their support team to build a comprehensive suite of treatment options (whether plentiful or not). Logistical concerns related to cost, location, transportation, hours, and fit to academic schedule (school year vs. summer/holidays) should be considered. Finally, while building an outpatient team that particular attention is paid to securing release of information/consent for information to be shared with the young person and their support team. Within the FBT-TAY model, inclusion of parent/s, cargiver/s, and/or other support team members is important (Dimitropoulos et al., 2018b).

On-Campus Support

During this stage of development, it is common for peers/peer groups to take on an important role in a young person's recovery. Peers (and romantic partners) become a new support system, alongside or rather than parents/caregivers, when the young person is away at university. In a small qualitative study completed by Paul and colleagues (2018), the authors explored how college students' disordered eating behaviours affected their peers. In this study, peers engaged in a variety of different behaviours including protective, confrontational, and "do nothing" behaviours in relation to their peers' ED. Peers also demonstrated support related to helping their friend seek care and supported obtaining professional care. This study demonstrated reactions including denial, curiosity, negative reaction, determination to maintain the relationship, and self-consciousness emerged as miscellaneous themes. While this study represents a small study sample, it parallels clinical experience from this book's authors and represents important clinical issues to discuss with clients in ED care in terms of seeking support from peers on campus.

Additionally, while limited data is published in this area, according to Doney et al. (2023), sorority/fraternity housing also failed to predict ED-risk. Greek Life Affiliation is not associated with greater ED risk among US college students (Doney et al., 2023). It is critical to work with young people to help them determine who in their support network (peers, clergy, roommates, resident assistant/

dorm parents, family, etc.) will be on their support team. It is recommended that this is done at the beginning of the treatment process as a way to both evaluate the suitability of individuals that a person relies on for support more generally, as well as related to the ED, and determine who may play a pivotal role in FBT-TAY. This can be done in a variety of ways including creating a sphere of a support map, or through questions about the individuals that the person may turn to for emotional, financial, physical, logistical, and spiritual support. Adapted from Family and Social Circles Activity in Marriage and Family Therapy, the therapist can work with the young person and their caregivers (based on preference of the young person) to assess their important connections. Questions regarding close versus extended family, other trusted adults (coaches, teachers, and neighbours), virtual/online support, and professional support can be assessed by open-ended questioning. These questions could include the following: "Who do you turn to in times of joy, celebration, difficulties, stressors, etc.?" "Who do you spend time with for holidays, for fun, exploring hobbies?" "Tell me about people you work with, go to school with, live near . . . how would you describe your relationship?" While this activity does not need to include an artistic component, some young people find value in mapping this out with them at the centre, and circular rings moving outward. Each ring represents a level of "closeness" to the young person. This activity can also be explored verbally with no mapping required.

Specific tasks throughout the course of FBT-TAY include, but are not limited to, weighing, meal support, coordination and payment of appointments, and emotional support (Dimitropoulos et al., 2015b). Identifying how the following areas may be addressed is central to FBT-TAY interventions at different phases of treatment (Dimitropoulos et al., 2018a). Within the FBTTAY framework, it is important to consider the mandatory parts of treatment including weighing and direct decision-making around food/eating and meal support in Phase 1. These are not optional parts of treatment, but there are a variety of ways that these tasks can be addressed. This affords young people, and their treatment team, an opportunity to discuss who may be best able and available to support these roles. Weighing can be completed by the on-campus therapist or medical provider in the student health program, or by another provider on campus. While there may be many options for who can complete the weighing, the important component would be sharing this weight with the FBT-TAY therapist, who in turn would share with the young person and their parents/caregivers. It is important to balance what is necessary (weekly weighing in Phase 1, with what can be a choice point, how the weight is taken, and whom). While this is not an exhaustive list of options, it outlines the problem-solving stance that is essential in the FBT-TAY framework.

Meal support/decision-making is also a key component to the FBT-TAY framework (Gorrell et al., 2019). During Phase 1, meal support is typically determined collaboratively between the young person and their parents/caregivers, but during Phase 2, Phase 3, and beyond, there are many individuals that may occupy this role, including friends and classmates (Dimitropoulos et al., 2015a). Typically, in Phase 1, meal support would be done in person, and the young person may return home, or family members may join the young person in an off-campus apartment, or other living arrangement to provide support. As treatment progresses, the option for some virtual meal support may become more feasible. It is important to consider that while post-secondary education can be a positive and developmentally appropriate environment for a young person, the core tenets of the FBT-TAY approach should not be compromised. For example, in Phase 1, it would not be appropriate for a young person to be eating meals on their own without support. Throughout the treatment process, it is important to understand who the young person may feel comfortable asking for support. This is an ongoing conversation throughout the treatment process and can be revisited across the phases of treatment. For example, in Phase 2, some young people may involve their roommate or significant other for more frequent meal support, whereas in Phase 1, they may have been used in more of an emotional support capacity. Finally, when considering emotional support, the opportunities are endless. Young people are not limited to only people in physical proximity to them, and considerations should be made regarding ways to connect to friends and family and other supportive communities (religions, hobby-based, and athletics). Clinical experience suggests that many young people rely on their parents/caregivers for the coordination and payment of services (if applicable). A parent/caregiver taking over scheduling and coordination of appointments, particularly at the beginning of treatment, can be a way to unburden the young person from additional tasks during a stressful time. This should be approached with clear communication from the treating providers, as it is seen as a form of support, rather than parent/caregivers dictating or controlling treatment. As treatment progresses, there is often a developmentally consistent handover of logistics of tasks. Payment of sessions (if applicable) should also be discussed at this time. Care should be paid related to the instances when the person who is paying for treatment is not providing any care/support during the treatment. While this is an infrequent occurrence, when this is the case, a separate Release of Information (ROI) for financial purposes only should be signed. Because the bill typically includes diagnosis, treatment codes, and frequency of visits, the young person must be aware of, and agree to, this information being shared.

Discussion related to the opportunity for non-uniformity in sharing information or occupying support roles may aid in the conversation of identifying support people. Simply put, not all information needs to be shared with all people; however as stated above, it is important that those providing direct support to the young person (treatment team and parents/caregivers) be included in information sharing about weight, food, and ED symptoms. Friends, classmates, professors, and others in the support network may be utilized for different supportive roles while the young person is on campus but do not need to have access to highly confidential information. Clarifying these roles will help the young person and their treatment team determine what information may need to be shared to best support the young person's treatment goals. When signing Release of Information forms (ROI), it is vital that a separate form is filled out for each person that is involved in treatment, explicitly outlining the information that is to be shared.

Common Challenges in FBT-TAY in Post-Secondary Education Environments

(1) The FBT-TAY treatment team and on-campus support team are not on the same page.
(2) The young person is isolated at college and lacks significant support.
(3) Parents/caregivers are concerned that young person is not able to return to/stay on campus during treatment.

Challenge 1: FBT-TAY Treatment Team and On-Campus Support Team Are Not on the Same Page

It is very common for communication issues to arise in teams. As outlined in this book, multiple providers are usually required to be part of the young person's team due to the psychological and physical effects of AN and the presence of comorbid diagnoses. Thus, "remaining on the same page" becomes a vital task of not just the young person and their family, but the providers as well. It is recommended that teams establish consistent and reliable communication frameworks. Typically, this requires medical providers and therapists (and/or other providers) checking in with each other after every visit verbally or in writing, as well as communicating any treatment plan changes internally, as well as with the young person and their parents/caregivers. This can be achieved through phone calls, emails, or note sharing. Maintaining a collegial relationship, and consistent communication, supports a proactive rather than reactive clinical style and promotes collaboration, information sharing, and continuity of care. In situations in which the treatment team is not aligned, we recommend that an internal conversation take place to rectify any misunderstandings or to ensure that a unified front is presented to avoid confusion and alienation of the young person and their family. Common dilemmas might include disagreements about weight goals, distress tolerance related to weight gain, and difficulties related to self-injury and suicidality.

Challenge 2: The Young Person Is Isolated at Post-Secondary and Lacks Significant Support

AN can severely disrupt a young person's developmental trajectory, as well as their ability to navigate changing social landscapes. While there have been some recommendations made in this chapter regarding exploration of social networks, it may, sometimes, be useful for the young person and their parent/caregiver, alongside the FBT-TAY therapist to explore ways to expand the former's social network. AN thrives in a socially isolated environment, where maintaining behaviours may remain undetected and unchallenged. Social connection helps to quiet the voice of AN and provides distraction, pleasure, and alternative behaviours to help facilitate recovery.

Therapeutic discussions may include exploring social groups, clubs, and affinity groups on campus, continuing to maintain social connections with friends at home or with extended family members/friends (e.g., cousins, aunts/uncles, siblings, etc.) as well as suggesting other ways for young people to connect virtually. Clinical experience has shown that sometimes it is not the quantity of social connections but the strength and consistency of relationships with a few key people.

Challenge 3: Parents/Caregivers Are Concerned That Young Person Cannot Return To/Stay on Campus During Treatment

Recovery is usually not a linear process in any treatment of AN. Due to the complicated nature of this illness, relapse/lapse and stuck points in treatment are common especially in those who have been ill for some time. Therapists may find that anticipating these common concerns may help young people experience less judgement and shame when they, inevitably, hit these bumps in the road. When possible, conversations earlier on in treatment that point to the normalcy of "trial and error" and learning from experience can help support the young person and their caregivers to normalize such experiences. If a "bump in the road" is assessed by the parent/caregivers and the treatment team to be a larger issue, than this becomes a key intervention point for discussion with the young person. Much like in FBT for adolescents, health and safety of the young person are of paramount importance throughout treatment. If returning to or staying on campus would result in a significant risk to a young person's health (e.g., low weight, bradycardia, and suicidality), then it would be advised that the therapist provide clear direction to the young person and their support network to prioritize addressing the AN and delay post-secondary educations. These recommendations would typically be to return home for a medical follow-up or in some cases visit the student health centre or emergency department for a medical evaluation. In some other circumstances, that may represent a need for more frequent visits home, or to the campus by the parents/caregivers, increasing virtual meal support and regular and frequent medical visits to ensure medical stability.

Conclusions

In closing, the application of FBT-TAY in a post-secondary education affords young people and their providers an opportunity to apply "real world" independence and challenges within ED treatment and beyond. In this chapter, we explored the prevalence of EDs on campus, screening tools, and building awareness of EDs on campus, establishing care teams, as well as clinical recommendations regarding building support networks.

Chapter Summary

Here are the key points of this chapter:

(1) Post-secondary transitions may heighten vulnerability to AN symptoms due to shifts in routine, academic pressure, food access, and changes with peers and other social networks.
(2) EDs are common on campuses, with the prevalence rates of EDs rising significantly post-COVID, demonstrating that EDs are a common concern among TAY.
(3) Access to consistent specialized ED care during the transition to post-secondary is challenging for young people, requiring navigation of campus services, sourcing specialized community providers, and exploring digital options for care.
(4) Readiness for post-secondary education must be assessed in the young person early and repeatedly, focusing on behavioural stability with their ED, independence with eating and decision-making, and fit with the post-secondary environment. FBT-TAY therapists may consider using a college readiness checklist (Mulheim, 2015) to assess for the young person's capacity to transition into post-secondary.
(5) FBT-TAY requires building a coordinated, multi-site, and interdisciplinary care team, with clear communication channels between providers and intentional consent processes with young people. FBT-TAY therapists should consider leading a balanced discussion with the young person and the care team to determine if and how information about the young person will be shared with their parents/caregivers while they receive treatment on campus.
(6) Mapping a support network with the young person, including peers, roommates, partners, family, and other trusted adults, is essential in determining the care plan for young people receiving FBT-TAY in post-secondary contexts. Mapping exercises using concentric rings to determine level of "closeness" of their support network to the young person is recommended.
(7) Core FBT-TAY tasks (weighing, meal support, symptom monitoring) remain essential for young people receiving care in post-secondary, though they may be delivered creatively. For example, the FBT-TAY therapist may consider bringing in other on-campus providers to assist with weighing the young person or identify members of their support network (e.g., peers, roommates) to assist with meal support.
(8) Common challenges, such as team misalignment, social isolation, and concerns about campus safety, require proactive communication with the young person, normalization of setbacks, and clear clinical decision-making on the part of FBT-TAY therapists.

References

Alhaj, O. A., Fekih-Romdhane, F., Sweidan, D. H., Saif, Z., Khudhair, M. F., Ghazzawi, H., Nadar, M. S., Alhajeri, S. S., Levine, M. P., & Jahrami, H. (2022). The prevalence and risk factors of screen-based disordered eating among university students: A global systematic review, meta-analysis, and meta-regression. *Eating and Weight Disorders: EWD*, *27*(8), 3215–3243. https://doi.org/10.1007/s40519-022-01452-0

Book, K. (n.d.). *Transitioning to college with an ED: Are you ready*? National EDs Association. https://www.nationaleatingdisorders.org/transitioning-college-eating-disorder-are-you-ready/

Centre for Innovation in Campus Mental Health. (2025, March). *EDs toolkit*. https://campusmentalhealth.ca/wp-content/uploads/2025/03/CICMH-Eating-Disorder-Toolkit.pdf

Devoe, D. J., Han, A., Anderson, A., Katzman, D. K., Patten, S. B., Soumbasis, A., Flanagan, J., Paslakis, G., Vyver, E., Marcoux, G., & Dimitropoulos, G. (2023). The impact of the COVID-19 pandemic on EDs: A systematic review. *International Journal of Eating Disorders*, *56*(1), 5–25. https://doi.org/10.1002/eat.23704

Dimitropoulos, G., Freeman, V. E., Allemang, B., Couturier, J., McVey, G., Lock, J., & Le Grange, D. (2015a). Family-based treatment with transition age youth with anorexia nervosa: A qualitative summary of application in clinical practice. *Journal of Eating Disorders*, *3*(1), 1–13. https://doi.org/10.1186/s40337-015-0037-3

Dimitropoulos, G., Landers, A. L., Freeman, V. E., Novick, J., Cullen, O., Engelberg, M., Steinegger, C., & Le Grange, D. (2018b). Family-based treatment for transition age youth: Parental self-efficacy and caregiver accommodation. *Journal of Eating Disorders*, *6*, 13. https://doi.org/10.1186/s40337-018-0196-0

Dimitropoulos, G., Landers, A. L., Freeman, V., Novick, J., Garber, A., & Le Grange, D. (2018a). Open trial of family-based treatment of anorexia nervosa for transition age youth. *Journal of the Canadian Academy of Child and Adolescent Psychiatry*, *27*(1), 50–61, 1–12. https://link.springer.com/article/10.1186/s40337-015-0037-3

Dimitropoulos, G., Lock, J., Le Grange, D., & Anderson, K. (2015b). Family therapy for transition youth. In *Family therapy for adolescent eating and weight disorders* (pp. 250–275). Routledge.

Doney, F. M., Lee, J., Sarkisyan, A., Compte, E. J., Nagata, J. M., Pedersen, E. R., & Murray, S. B. (2023). ED risk among college sorority and fraternity members within the United States. *EDs*, *31*(5), 440–449. https://doi.org/10.1080/10640266.2023.2188005

Eisenberg, D., Nicklett, E. J., Roeder, K., & Kirz, N. E. (2011). ED symptoms among college students: Prevalence, persistence, correlates, and treatment-seeking. *Journal of American College Health: J of ACH*, *59*(8), 700–707. https://doi.org/10.1080/07448481.2010.546461

Gerson, M. (2023, May 30). College readiness and ED recovery. *Psychology Today*. https://www.psychologytoday.com/ca/blog/the-road-to-recovery/202305/college-readiness-and-eating-disorder-recovery

Gorrell, S., Loeb, K. L., & Le Grange, D. (2019). Family-based treatment of eating disorders: A narrative review. *The Psychiatric Clinics of North America*, *42*(2), 193–204. https://doi.org/10.1016/j.psc.2019.01.004

Grammer, A. C., Fitzsimmons-Craft, E. E., Laing, O., Pietro, B., & Wilfley, D. E. (2020). EDs on college campuses in the United States: Current insight on screening, prevention, and treatment. *Current Psychopharmacology*, *9*(2), 91–102. https://doi.org/10.2174/2211556009999200416153022

Liu, Y. (2025). *Eating concerns support and assessment*. UChicago Student Wellness. https://wellness.uchicago.edu/mental-health/eating-concerns-support-and-assessment/

Luginaah, N. A., Dhillon, S., Batung, E. S., Ziegler, B. R., & Luginaah, I. (2025). The impact of the COVID-19 pandemic on children and adolescents EDs: A systematic review. *Children and Youth Services Review, 171*, 1–20. https://doi.org/10.1016/j.childyouth.2025.108190

Muhlheim, L. (2015, October 10). *Is your young adult with an ED ready for college? ED Therapy LA*. https://www.eatingdisordertherapyla.com/is-your-young-adult-with-an-eating-disorder-ready-for-college/

National EDs Association. (2013, February). *EDs on the college campus*.

Pacanowski, C. R., Skubisz, C., Borton, D., & Ryding, R. (2024). Prevalence and correlates of disordered eating at a large state university before and after the onset of the COVID-19 pandemic. *Journal of Eating Disorders, 12*(1), 1–12. https://doi.org/10.1186/s40337-024-01056-2

Paul, E. C., Pazienza, R., Maestro, K. J., Flye, A., Mueller, P., & Martin, J. L. (2018). The impact of disordered eating behavior on college relationships: A qualitative study. *Journal of College Counseling, 21*(2), 139–152. https://doi.org/10.1002/jocc.12093

Tavolacci, M.-P., Ladner, J., & Dechelotte, P. (2021). COVID-19 Pandemic and Eating Disorders among University Students. *Nutrients, 13*(12), 4294. https://doi.org/10.3390/nu13124294

Chapter 12

FBT-TAY for Diverse Families

In this chapter, we explore how diverse families, who often bring multiple sociocultural, economic, practical, and systemic considerations, interface with FBT-TAY. This chapter provides an overview of how to work with diverse young people and their families in FBT-TAY, to ensure that this treatment remains clinically responsive for *all* families, regardless of ethnicity, gender, socioeconomic status, and/or geographic location.

FBT in Diverse Populations: Treatment Access, Engagement, and Treatment Adaptations

Evidence from FBT studies conducted in Singapore, China, Japan, and Brazil suggest that FBT has cross-cultural efficacy in non-Western contexts. In Singapore, Wong and colleagues (2019) compared FBT to adolescent-focused therapy and found that young people receiving manualized FBT achieved remission more quickly (median: 5 vs. 16 months), had higher remission rates at one- and two-year follow-up, and had roughly a 30-day reduction in hospital stay within inpatient care compared to those in adolescent-focused therapy. Similarly, Chew and colleagues (2020) employed a retrospective consecutive-cohort design comparing FBT to treatment as usual for adolescents with AN and reported that those in FBT exhibited higher per cent-median-BMI at every follow-up point across the study (6, 12, and 24 months post-treatment) and achieved weight restoration more rapidly than adolescents within the treatment as usual cohort (median: 7 vs. 19 months).

In China, Chen and colleagues (2020) demonstrated how FBT could be integrated into an inpatient-ED system by introducing a series of minor modifications to the core model, including shortening treatment sessions, modifying meals to align with local dietary guidelines, and embedding parental/caregiver coaching during hospital stays. These authors identified several clinical considerations for therapists implementing FBT within the Chinese context, including subverting traditional roles of therapists and medical professionals

DOI: 10.4324/9781003463351-13

as "saviours" and reframing their relationship with families as collaborators working to empower parents/caregivers to take responsibility of their child's refeeding in treatment. Similarly, in Japan, Iguchi and colleagues (2020) introduced FBT during inpatient hospitalization for adolescents with AN which resulted in a reduction in total number of hospitalizations, a shorter time frame for achieving weight restoration, and patients achieving discharge criteria rapidly. These authors highlighted that cultural norms surrounding gender roles and the social positions of mothers and fathers within Japanese families necessitated a re-evaluation of the involvement of *both* parents and caregivers within FBT – working with fathers in a way that was aligned with traditional Japanese culture (i.e., putting mothers in charge of their child's renourishment, while fathers provided emotional support to their partner and child) during the implementation of FBT.

Beyond Asian contexts, in Brazil, a prospective observational study conducted by Turkiewicz and colleagues (2010) demonstrated significant improvements in BMI and reductions in ED symptoms from baseline through to the end-of-treatment and six-month follow-up for adolescents with AN receiving FBT, supporting the feasibility and efficacy of FBT in the South American context. Overall, these studies including retrospective cohort designs, descriptive chart reviews, program evaluations, and observational research demonstrate that FBT's core principles and therapeutic interventions translate effectively when therapists accommodate to local cultural norms and implementation contexts.

Social Determinants of Health in FBT

FBT continues to be the leading evidence-based model for adolescents with EDs (e.g., Borges et al., 2024; Dimitropoulos et al., 2015, 2018, 2019, 2024; Lock & LeGrange, 2015; Wong et al., 2019), yet many young people and their families may experience social and economic hardships making it difficult for them to access and fully participate in treatment (Kourgiantakis et al., 2023). Young people and their families may experience multiple negative social determinants of health (SDH; Sauerwein et al., 2025; Simone et al., 2022) – the array of social factors which influence one's overall health outcomes (World Health Organization, 2024) – which may interfere or impede with timely, appropriate, and equitable care (Chunara et al., 2024) including FBT-TAY. Examples of SDH may include, but are not limited to, histories of colonization, racism, housing instability, food insecurity, immigration stress, trauma, disability, access to education and healthcare, social support networks, and/or unstable paid employment (Monroe et al., 2023). Indeed, evidence suggests that SDH may reduce accessibility and engagement in FBT (Bailey-Straebler et al., 2024; Crest et al., 2024; Dimitropoulos et al., 2024; Egbert et al., 2024; Gall et al., 2025; Mikhail & Klump, 2020; Sauerwein et al., 2025).

In addition to experiences with negative SDH, diversity reinforces how an individual occupies intersecting identities and structural locations which inform what they may or may not have access to within the context of the social institutions they interact with and inhabit (e.g., schooling, housing, health services, employment, and administration of law; Crenshaw, 1991; Sherman et al., 2023; Vohra-Gupta et al., 2023). Within treatment, diverse service users can include, but are not limited to, racialized, Indigenous, non-English speaking, sexual and gender diverse, neurodivergent, under-resourced, multigenerational, and low-income young people and families who are vulnerably positioned to encounter one or many SDH (Chen et al., 2020; Doyle et al., 2009; Duffy et al., 2025; Moradi et al., 2024; Urban et al., 2023). Addressing these inequities may require significant accommodations when implementing the key components of FBT-TAY (i.e., caregiver empowerment, externalization of the illness, behavioural focus on interrupting ED symptoms, and a collaborative, non-authoritarian therapeutic stance); FBT-TAY therapists need to be attuned to how, when, and where to enforce flexibility in the timing, delivery, and format of the model to mitigate the unique SDH that young people and their supportive networks may experience when in treatment.

Evidence suggests that the incidence and prevalence of EDs in diverse populations (including racially/ethnically diverse, sexual/gender diverse, and socioeconomically disadvantaged individuals) either meet or exceed that of their dominant counterparts – White, cisgender/heteronormative, and those in higher socioeconomic strata (e.g., Burke et al., 2023; Cheng et al., 2019; Nagata et al., 2024, Sharpe et al., 2023). There is a growing recognition that ED therapists across the continuum of care must work diligently to recognize and prioritize equity to ensure that all young people and their families have access to FBT-TAY. Attention to equity will ensure that all young people receive timely, low-barrier, and financially viable care that might require adaptations to the frequency of appointments, how sessions are delivered (primarily virtual or via a hybrid approach), and the integration of case or service management to support families in navigating prospective income supports, food banks, and grocery subsidy programs that would facilitate access to the high-cost calorie-dense foods required for weight restoration (Accurso et al., 2021; Sauerwein et al., 2025; Urban et al., 2023).

In addition, research demonstrates that ED care typically assumes a specific service user profile: flexible schedules, two caregivers (often heterosexual), adequate transportation to and from treatment, disposable income, comprehensive insurance, and geographic proximity to specialty services (Bailey-Straebler et al., 2024; Crest et al., 2024; Egbert et al., 2024; Moreno et al., 2023). In the context of FBT-TAY, therapists need to be mindful of implicit assumptions held towards diverse young people and families' readiness and ability to engage in and comply with treatment, as these factors may be attributable to socioeconomic factors (e.g., income, steady employment) and broader structural/systemic considerations (e.g., access to quality healthcare, economic stability, social and community context) rather than motivation and readiness to engage in treatment alone (Egbert et al., 2024; Sauerwein et al., 2025). Without directly acknowledging and addressing structural and systemic barriers within FBT-TAY, young people and families with the least number of resources but the greatest burden of illness risk disengaging from treatment (Accurso et al., 2021; Borges et al., 2024; Egbert et al., 2024).

Intersectionality and Cumulative Adversity in FBT

Intersectionality demonstrates how multiple SDH factors cumulatively interact ("intersect") to uniquely (and potentially, adversely) shape the identities and experiences of diverse families, including what they must overcome to access, remain in, and successfully complete evidence-based treatments including FBT-TAY (Wilkins et al., 2025). Two qualitative studies examining the perceptions and experiences of FBT therapists working with diverse families globally – conducted by Dimitropoulos and colleagues (2024) and Sauerwein and colleagues (2025) – emphasized that intersecting SDH including historical/ongoing trauma, housing and employment precarity, immigration status, insufficient insurance coverage, food insecurity, language barriers, and low socioeconomic status directly influenced how FBT therapists adapted or modified the model in practice. For example, FBT therapists who worked with predominantly racially/ethnically diverse parents and families experiencing economic challenges that were unable to meet the resource- and time-intensive demands of FBT often adjusted the length, duration, or frequency of appointments in one or multiple phases of treatment. FBT therapists shared that they made these adjustments to accommodate families who were unable to take renumerated leaves of absence from work or did not have sufficient insurance coverage to cover the total costs of treatment (Dimitropoulos et al., 2024; Sauerwein et al., 2025). Overall, therapists adhered to the model as described in the manual, however, these types of minor adjustments were made to FBT to accommodate the intersecting needs of diverse families in routine clinical practice (Dimitropoulos et al., 2024; Sauerwein et al., 2025). It is important to note that FBT for AN and BN is not prescriptive allowing for some modifications of the model insofar as the guiding principles remain the same. That said, we strongly recommend that FBT-TAY therapists continue to be responsive to the unique circumstances of the young person and their families with whom they work while aligning their work with the core tenets of the model.

Diversity-Specific Considerations in FBT

Socioeconomic Marginalization and Food Insecurity

Qualitative, prospective cohort, and longitudinal studies consistently demonstrate that socioeconomic marginalization strongly influences the feasibility, duration, and course of evidence-based treatments (Moreno et al., 2023). Publicly-insured populations, who are statistically lower-income and racially/ethnically diverse individuals, face the highest barriers to accessing high-quality evidence-based care (Huryk et al., 2021; Moreno et al., 2023); therapists working with these populations frequently report differences in continuity of care, care coordination, and supportive infrastructure for publicly-insured families, even when family engagement and willingness to participate in treatment is high (Crest et al., 2024; Moreno et al., 2023). Accurso and colleagues (2021) conducted an implementation study adapting FBT for racially/ethnically diverse and low-income families receiving publicly funded care within the United States; the authors reported that therapists made modifications to the model by flexibly engaging extended family members if caregivers were unable to be present for all meals and continuing treatment despite inconsistent or irregular attendance from one or both caregivers due to inflexible work hours or extensive family obligations. Similarly, Borges and colleagues (2024) conducted a qualitative study with FBT therapists practising with Medicaid-insured adolescents within publicly funded care in the United States and found that therapists reported addressing broader concerns related to financial instability, food insecurity, and housing earlier in treatment and sometimes *before* focusing on ED symptoms and weight restoration. These therapists also highlighted flexible scheduling and early problem-solving around family concerns related to availability for appointments due to shift work and lack of reliable transportation (e.g., cars) to maintain engagement in treatment (Borges et al., 2024).

Food insecurity is another factor shown to impact the ability of parents/caregivers to monitor meals and procure calorically dense foods required for weight restoration during treatment (Sauerwein et al., 2025; Urban et al., 2023). In a large longitudinal cohort study examining the treatment characteristics of 729 adolescents receiving FBT, Urban and colleagues (2023) reported that young people who experienced food insecurity while receiving FBT showed a non-linear symptom trajectory, with initial improvement, worsening of symptoms at mid-treatment, and then later decline – highlighting that inconsistent access to nutritious and calorie-dense foods required for weight restoration significantly disrupts treatment progress and outcomes.

Sauerwein and colleagues (2025) further described the disruptive nature of food insecurity on diverse families' participation in Phase 1 of FBT; therapists reported caregivers feeling intense pressure to accommodate calorically dense foods within their child's meal plan with limited financial means and/or highlighted concerns that diverse families may have about their therapists not appreciating the challenges that come with refeeding when they simply cannot afford food. Taking both studies into consideration, FBT-TAY therapists must support families experiencing food insecurity by helping parents/caregivers identify alternative food options and a range of resources and best ways to utilize these to support refeeding.

Non-Traditional Family Structures

FBT has also demonstrated efficacy across diverse family structures, developmental stages, and clinical profiles, largely supported by case reports, retrospective comparisons, and qualitative therapist accounts. Aspen and Boutelle (2014), using a detailed case analysis, documented successful weight restoration for a foster youth receiving FBT in a group home where rotating staff acted as their caregivers in charge of renourishment; this study found increases in weight for the foster youth from 76% to 87% IBW over nine months, demonstrating that FBT can be implemented effectively when caregiving responsibilities are clearly structured even without a traditional family unit. Doyle et al. (2009), in a retrospective comparison of single- versus two-parent households, found no differences in symptom reduction or attendance, indicating that FBT does not require a two-parent structure.

Furthermore, the seminal RCTs in FBT (Lock & Le Grange, 2005; Lock et al., 2006) included single-parent and divorced families, and although these families often required a longer course of treatment, they ultimately demonstrated comparable outcomes and "caught up" to those in two-parent intact households over time.

Patients with Histories of Trauma

With regard to families experiencing historical or ongoing trauma, Kimber et al. (2019a, 2019b) and Brewerton (2019), based on therapist case reviews and qualitative reports, emphasized that when interpersonal partner violence, emotional abuse, trauma, or self-harm is present within the young person or the family system, FBT therapists must incorporate safety planning, regular risk assessments, and trauma-informed modifications alongside the primary goal of refeeding. These studies demonstrate that FBT treatment outcomes, even with non-traditional family structures and/or families with histories of trauma or self-harm, can be achieved with minor adjustments throughout treatment and with adequate structure and safety practices.

Diverse Families in FBT-TAY: Modifications by Phase

Within FBT-TAY, minor adjustments or modifications can be made to the core model to better suit and meet the needs of diverse young people and families in treatment. The following outlines the most common adjustments made in practice, informed by the literature synthesized above.

The primary goal of Phase 1 is to empower the young person and their parents/caregivers to collaboratively work together to relentlessly focus on renourishment to achieve weight restoration and restore healthy eating. FBT-TAY therapists may choose to invest more time at the start of this phase to establish trust, build rapport, or address structural or systemic barriers where historical or ongoing discrimination has eroded confidence in healthcare, adjusting the family meal for cultural acceptability, accommodating inflexible schedules by determining adjusted session frequency, or allotting more time for interpreters to join sessions (e.g., Dimitropoulos et al., 2025). For publicly insured or low-income families, FBT-TAY therapists will need to prioritize identifying affordable, calorie-dense options and linking young people and their parents/caregivers to a variety of community resources (Sauerwein et al., 2025). If young people are placed in foster or group homes, identifying and mobilizing non-parent caregivers or supportive carers to act as the primary caregiver unit for the purposes of renourishment will be a top priority for FBT-TAY therapists (e.g., Aspen & Boutelle, 2014). In addition, FBT-TAY therapists must continue to reinforce trauma-informed principles of safety, collaboration, choice, and sensitivity when working with young people and their families who have experienced historical or ongoing trauma (Brewerton, 2019).

During Phase 2, the focus on gradually returning responsibility of eating back to the young person remains unchanged; however, the frequency and duration of this phase can be adjusted to better suit the needs of young people and their families facing insurmountable social and economic barriers. For example, FBT-TAY therapists may invite the young person and family members to consider lengthening the intervals between sessions or reducing session length to accommodate travel to sessions and potential income loss, provided that the treatment trajectories of the young person remain focused on practising eating with greater independence (Dimitropoulos et al., 2024). During this phase, FBT-TAY therapists must also pay careful consideration of family or cultural values around independence which may influence the rate or level of autonomy "handed back" to the young person. For instance, collectivist cultures value family cohesion and interdependence over individuation from the family (e.g., Lansford et al., 2021), requiring FBT-TAY therapists to determine how best independence with eating will be achieved with the young person while preserving core family and/or cultural values.

The goals of Phase 3, which includes relapse prevention, developmental re-engagement in various social settings (school, work, and relationships), and treatment termination, remain unchanged; however, the duration of this phase may be compressed, lengthened, or, in some cases, offered virtually or eliminated when attendance becomes poor due to the cost of attending sessions or competing challenges for the young person and their parents/caregivers facing economic demands and constraints. FBT-TAY therapists may consider weaving relapse-prevention planning into the later part of Phase 2 to prepare the young person and family to determine early warning signs of relapse and how best to integrate community support systems and care. These support systems can include, but are not limited to, short-term transition workers or psychiatry liaison teams to support the transition from care provision to independent management (Dimitropoulos et al., 2024).

Practice Considerations for FBT-TAY Therapists

The primary goal for FBT-TAY therapists when working with diverse young people and families is to ensure that this treatment is accessible by removing barriers that are often centred around SDH.

(1) FBT-TAY therapists may consider using consultation and supervision to consider how cumulative adversity and concrete structural barriers may be impeding progress in the young person and their family throughout all phases of treatment but especially in Phase 1.
(2) FBT-TAY therapists may also ask young people and their families if they would like to invite other supportive carers or community leaders in treatment, such cultural liaisons, religious leaders, or Elders* (e.g., Lavender, 2020).
(3) When food insecurity, transportation challenges, childcare demands, insurance constraints, or inflexible work schedules are present, FBT-TAY therapists should engage other members of their team to assist the young person and family to access formal or informal community resources and government supports to facilitate access to food, housing, and other SDH that may influence their success in treatment.
(4) FBT-TAY therapists may consider using virtual sessions via tele-health or home-based sessions especially for young people and their families who live in rural and remote communities and face transportation challenges in commuting to large urban centres or locations that are difficult to access due to geography. Session spacing in Phase 2 and Phase 3 may be increased cautiously to reduce cost; however, when progress diminishes, intervals should be tightened promptly (Steinberg et al., 2023; Goldschmidt et al., 2023; Dimitropoulos et al., 2024).

***An important note:** Many racialized and Indigenous communities hold longstanding and well-justified suspicions towards healthcare and mental healthcare systems. These concerns are rooted in historical and ongoing experiences of racism, discrimination, coerced treatment, and unethical medical experimentation, as well as contemporary encounters with culturally invalidating practices and racially informed stereotypes within care settings (e.g., Cooke & Shields, 2024; Stewart & Gonzalez, 2023; Williams et al., 2024). As a result, some families may approach ED treatment with fear, distrust, or avoidance, which can significantly shape how they engage with FBT-TAY. Hesitation from these families is not always indicative of resistance to treatment but rather may be a protective response grounded in collective histories of harm. At the start of treatment, FBT-TAY therapists should dedicate a session or more to addressing anxiety, mistrust, or ambivalence on the part of these families by actively acknowledging the discrimination, prejudice, and historical harm they may have experienced within healthcare settings or in ED treatment. FBT-TAY therapists may consider building a safety plan in collaboration with these families, which details how the therapists will work to address any power imbalances throughout the course of treatment, and empower families to make decisions around refeeding and renourishment for the young person devoid of authoritative clinical practice. To that end, FBT-TAY therapists should also work with their clinical and administrative teams to create transparent, culturally safe, and collaboratively oriented treatment practices to support meaningful engagement and mitigate historical harm for these families in FBT-TAY.

Training and Supervision for Equity-Centred FBT-TAY

We would recommend developing training opportunities to prepare FBT-TAY therapists to support diverse youth and families. Given this, FBT-TAY therapists would greatly benefit from structured training on how to work with families that may be reluctant to engage in any evidence-based treatments due to mistrust, historical and current violence, and colonization and misalignment with their cultural traditions. Mentorship and supervision of FBT-TAY therapists are further needed to identify ways to support those who may be disempowered due to systemic inequities making it challenging to fully engage in refeeding and independence building in the young person.

Where these opportunities do not already exist, we recommend FBT-TAY therapists advocate for equity training opportunities with their team leaders, clinical decision-makers, and/or program administrators to better prepare them to support diverse young people and families in practice. To that end, therapists would also benefit from structured training focused on engaging families who may be hesitant to participate in evidence-based treatments due to mistrust, colonization, ongoing violence, and misalignment between Western clinical models and their cultural traditions. Supervision and mentorship are also essential to help therapists recognize how structural inequities, racism, poverty, and migration stress may limit a family's ability to fully engage in refeeding and independence-building with the young person. Training content should draw on established frameworks related to structural competency, anti-oppressive practice, trauma- and violence-informed care, Indigenous cultural safety, and culturally responsive approaches to ED treatment.

Key resources to ground training content:

- Equity considerations in ED treatment
    - Becker, A. E. (2018). Culture and EDs. In D. Bhugra & K. Bhui (Eds.), *Textbook of cultural psychiatry* (pp. 304–316). Cambridge University Press.
    - Becker, A. E., Hadley Arrindell, A., Perloe, A., Fay, K., & Striegel-Moore, R. H. (2010). A qualitative study of perceived social barriers to care for EDs: Perspectives from ethnically diverse health care consumers. *International Journal of Eating Disorders*, *43*(7), 633–647.

   - Hambleton, A., Le Grange, D., Touyz, S., & Maguire, S. (2025). Advancements in family-based treatment of adolescent anorexia nervosa: A review of access barriers and telehealth solutions. *Nutrients, 17*(13), 1–18.
   - Keitel, M. A., Cummings, M. P., & Park-Taylor, J. (2025). *Counseling individuals with EDs: An intersectional approach.* Emerald Group Publishing.

- Trainings and other resources
   - *Academy for EDs* – articles, blogs, and other text centring around equity, diversity, and inclusion
   - *National EDs Association (NEDA)* – culturally competent care, referral directories, webinars
   - *Mental Health Academy* – micro-credentials on working in EDs, with a focus on culturally competent care

Conclusions

FBT-TAY can be used with diverse young people and their families across a variety of contexts. It is critical that attention be given to cumulative adversity, historical mistrust, and systemic inequities in Phase 1 to ensure that young people and families can participate in this treatment. When pacing in Phase 2 is calibrated and adjusted to acknowledge affordability, transportation realities, financial constraints, and food-access limitations, young people and their families are better able to sustain progress, with the timely and appropriate transfer of independence of eating to the young person. In Phase 3, the FBT-TAY therapists may consider the how the young person can continue to address and effectively respond to environmental stressors that may contribute to slips and relapses while also celebrating their successes in overcoming adversities in their lives.

Chapter Summary

Here are the key points of this chapter:

(1) Young people and their families who participate in FBT-TAY are diverse: their histories, resources, social locations, and lived realities shape how treatment can be delivered and what is possible.
(2) Therapists must consider how best to support young people and their families in FBT-TAY when they struggle with food and housing insecurity in order to maximize their ability to participate in this treatment.
(3) FBT-TAY therapists must work to build safety and trust when working with young people and families who have experienced historical and current challenges and trauma accessing and participating in treatments.
(4) Workforce training should be advocated for by FBT-TAY therapists or other clinical team leaders, decision-makers, and/or program administrators to

support therapists working with diverse young people and their families in practice.

(5) FBT-TAY should be delivered in a way that recognizes and honours the realities of diverse young people, their families, and other supportive networks. For instance, FBT-TAY therapists can accommodate schedules, demonstrate flexibility in who attends and supports the refeeding process, and facilitate the identification of resources that will help the family meet the nutritional needs of their young person in ways they can access and afford food.

References

Accurso, E. C., Mu, K. J., Landsverk, J., & Guydish, J. (2021). Adaptation to family-based treatment for Medicaid-insured youth with anorexia nervosa in publicly funded settings: Protocol for a mixed methods implementation scale-out pilot study. *Journal of Eating Disorders*, *9*(1), 1–11. https://doi.org/10.1186/s40337-021-00454-0

Aspen, V., & Boutelle, K. (2014). Family-based treatment without a family: Case report of an adolescent with anorexia nervosa. *Eating and Weight Disorders*, *19*(1), 119–123. https://doi.org/10.1007/s40519-013-0070-7

Bailey-Straebler, S., Glasofer, D. R., Ojeda, J., & Attia, E. (2024). Equitable access to evidence-based treatment for EDs for patients with low-income: Identifying barriers and exploring solutions. *Cognitive Behaviour Therapist*, *17*, 1–17. https://doi.org/10.1017/S1754470X24000023

Borges, R., Crest, P., Landsverk, J., & Accurso, E. C. (2024). Adaptations to family-based treatment for Medicaid-insured adolescents with anorexia nervosa. *Frontiers in Psychology*, *15*, 1–13. https://doi.org/10.3389/fpsyg.2024.1389652

Brewerton, T. D. (2019). An overview of trauma-informed care and practice for eating disorders. *Journal of Aggression, Maltreatment & Trauma*, *28*(4), 445–462. https://doi.org/10.1080/10926771.2018.1532940

Burke, N. L., Hazzard, V. M., Schaefer, L. M., Simone, M., O'Flynn, J. L., & Rodgers, R. F. (2023). Socioeconomic status and ED prevalence: At the intersections of gender identity, sexual orientation, and race/ethnicity. *Psychological Medicine*, *53*(9), 4255–4265. https://doi.org/10.1017/S0033291722001015

Cooke, M., & Shields, T. (2024). Anti-indigenous racism in Canadian healthcare: A scoping review of the literature. *International Journal for Quality in Health Care*, *36*(3), 1–12. https://doi.org/10.1093/intqhc/mzae089

Chen, J., Guo, L., Gu, L., & Han, H. (2020). The introduction of treatment and the cultural adaptability of western psychotherapies for EDs in China. *International Journal of Eating Disorders*, *54*(1), 102–106. https://doi.org/10.1002/eat.23437

Cheng, Z. H., Perko, V. L., Fuller-Marashi, L., Gau, J. M., & Stice, E. (2019). Ethnic differences in ED prevalence, risk factors, and predictive effects of risk factors among young women. *Eating Behaviors*, *32*, 23–30. https://doi.org/10.1016/j.eatbeh.2018.11.004

Chew, C. S. E., Kelly, S., Tay, E. E., Baeg, A., Khaider, K. B., Oh, J. Y., Rajasegaran, K., Saffari, S. E., & Davis, C. (2020). Implementation of family-based treatment for Asian adolescents with anorexia nervosa: A consecutive cohort examination of outcomes. *International Journal of Eating Disorders*, *54*(1), 107–116. https://doi.org/10.1002/eat.23429

Chunara, R., Gjonaj, J., Immaculate, E., Wanga, I., Alaro, J., Scott-Sheldon, L. A. J., Mangeni, J., Mwangi, A., Vedanthan, R., & Hogan, J. (2024). Social determinants of health: The need for data science methods and capacity. *The Lancet Digital Health, 6*(4), e235–e237. https://doi.org/10.1016/S2589-7500(24)00022-0

Crenshaw, K. (1991). Mapping the margins: Intersectionality, identity politics, and violence against women of color. *Stanford Law Review, 43*(6), 1241–1299. https://doi.org/10.2307/1229039

Crest, P., Vendlinski, S. S., Borges, R., Landsverk, J., & Accurso, E. C. (2024). Interdisciplinary perspectives on accessing specialty evidence-based treatment for Medicaid-insured adolescents with EDs. *Journal of Eating Disorders, 12*(1), 1–12. https://doi.org/10.1186/s40337-024-01124-7

Dimitropoulos, G., Freeman, V. E., Allemang, B., Couturier, J., McVey, G., Lock, J., & Le Grange, D. (2015). Family-based treatment with transition age youth with anorexia nervosa: A qualitative summary of application in clinical practice. *Journal of Eating Disorders, 3*(1), 1–13. https://doi.org/10.1186/s40337-015-0037-3

Dimitropoulos, G., Landers, A. L., Freeman, V. E., Novick, J., Cullen, O., Engelberg, M., Steinegger, C., & Le Grange, D. (2018). Family-based treatment for transition age youth: Parental self-efficacy and caregiver accommodation. *Journal of Eating Disorders, 6*(1), 1–11. https://doi.org/10.1186/s40337-018-0196-0

Dimitropoulos, G., Landers, A. L., Freeman, V., Novick, J., Cullen, O., & Le Grange, D. (2019). Family-based treatment for transition age youth: The role of expressed emotion and general family functioning. *EDs, 27*(5), 419–435. https://doi.org/10.1080/10640266.2018.1529472

Dimitropoulos, G., Nicula, M., Krishnapillai, A., Austin, A., Singh, M., Lee, J., Webb, C., Scott, S., de Almeida, A. C. V., Bergmann, C., Vander Steen, H., Kimber, M., Mushquash, C., Norman, L., Sauerwein, J., Keshen, A., Boachie, A., Toulany, A., Levinson, A., . . ., Couturier, J. (2025). Transitions for youth and young adults with EDs and/or other mental health conditions: A Canadian guideline. *Journal of Eating Disorders, 13*(1), 1–27. https://doi.org/10.1186/s40337-025-01343-6

Dimitropoulos, G., Singh, M., Sauerwein, J., Pedram, P., Kimber, M., Pradel, M., Eckhardt, S., Forsberg, S., Keery, H., Allan, E., Bruett, L., & Le Grange, D. (2024). Examining clinicians' perceptions and experiences working with diverse families in family-based treatment: Common adaptations and considerations for treatment engagement. *International Journal of Eating Disorders, 57*(3), 635–647. https://doi.org/10.1002/eat.24144

Doyle, A. C., McLean, C., Washington, B. N., Hoste, R. R., & le Grange, D. (2009). Are single-parent families different from two-parent families in the treatment of adolescent bulimia nervosa using family-based treatment? *International Journal of Eating Disorders, 42*(2), 153–157. https://doi.org/10.1002/eat.20584

Duffy, F., Peebles, I., Clark, E., Loomes, R., Thomson, L., Maloney, E., & Nimbley, E. (2025). Clinicians' experiences of ED focused family therapy with autistic young people. *European EDs Review, 33*(4), 637–646. https://doi.org/10.1002/erv.3173

Egbert, A. H., Irizarry, B., Lualdi, E., Tortolani, C. C., Donaldson, D. L., & Goldschmidt, A. B. (2024). A qualitative assessment of provider-perceived barriers to implementing family-based treatment for anorexia nervosa in low-income community settings. *Journal of Eating Disorders, 12*(1), 1–10. https://doi.org/10.1186/s40337-024-01008-w

Gall, Z., Smith, H., Grant, G., Kunaratnam, K., Lee, C., Kerslake, F., & Gall, A. (2025). Culturally responsive recommendations for ED prevention and management for First Nations peoples in Australia: A policy scoping review. *Journal of Eating Disorders, 13*(1), 1–15. https://doi.org/10.1186/s40337-025-01243-9

Goldschmidt, A. B., Tortolani, C. C., Accurso, E. C., Dunbar, E.-M. P., Egbert, A. H., Donaldson, D., & Donaldson, A. A. (2023). Adapting family-based treatment for adolescent anorexia nervosa delivered in the home: A novel approach for improving access to care and generalizability of skill acquisition. *Journal of Eating Disorders*, *11*(1), 1–12. https://doi.org/10.1186/s40337-023-00850-8

Huryk, K. M., Drury, C. R., & Loeb, K. L. (2021). Diseases of affluence? A systematic review of the literature on socioeconomic diversity in EDs. *Eating Behaviors: An International Journal*, *43*, 1–16. https://doi.org/10.1016/j.eatbeh.2021.101548

Iguchi, T., Miyawaki, D., Harada, T., & Ogiwara, K. (2020). Introduction of family-based treatment to Japan with adaptations to optimize the cultural acceptability and advance current traditional treatments of adolescent anorexia nervosa. *International Journal of Eating Disorders*, *54*(1), 117–119. https://doi.org/10.1002/eat.23405

Kimber, M., McTavish, J. R., Couturier, J., Le Grange, D., Lock, J., & MacMillan, H. L. (2019a). Identifying and responding to child maltreatment when delivering family-based treatment – A qualitative study. *International Journal of Eating Disorders*, *52*(3), 292–298. https://doi.org/10.1002/eat.23036

Kimber, M., McTavish, J. R., Luo, C., Couturier, J., Dimitropoulos, G., & MacMillan, H. (2019b). Mandatory reporting of child maltreatment when delivering family-based treatment for EDs: A framework analysis of practitioner experiences. *Child Abuse & Neglect*, *88*, 118–128. https://doi.org/10.1016/j.chiabu.2018.11.010

Kourgiantakis, T., Markoulakis, R., Lee, E., Hussain, A., Lau, C., Ashcroft, R., . . ., Levitt, A. (2023). Access to mental health and addiction services for youth and their families in Ontario: Perspectives of parents, youth, and service providers. *International Journal of Mental Health Systems*, *17*(1), 1–15. https://doi.org/10.1186/s13033-023-00572-z

Lansford, J. E., Zietz, S., Al-Hassan, S. M., Bacchini, D., Bornstein, M. H., Chang, L., . . ., & Alampay, L. P. (2021). Culture and social change in mothers' and fathers' individualism, collectivism and parenting attitudes. *Social Sciences*, *10*(12), 1–20. https://doi.org/10.3390/socsci10120459

Lavender, K. R. (2020). Rebooting "failed" family-based treatment. *Frontiers in Psychiatry*, *11*, 1–6. https://doi.org/10.3389/fpsyt.2020.00068

Lock, J., Couturier, J., Bryson, S., & Agras, S. (2006). Predictors of dropout and remission in family therapy for adolescent anorexia nervosa in a randomized clinical trial. *International Journal of Eating Disorders*, *39*(8), 639–647. https://doi.org/10.1002/eat.20328

Lock, J., & Le Grange, D. (2005). Family-based treatment of EDs. *The International Journal of Eating Disorders*, *37*(S1), S64–S67. https://doi.org/10.1002/eat.20122

Lock, J., & Le Grange, D. (2015). *Treatment manual for anorexia nervosa: A family-based approach* (2nd ed.). Guilford.

Mikhail, M. E., & Klump, K. L. (2020). A virtual issue highlighting EDs in people of black/African and Indigenous heritage. *International Journal of Eating Disorders*, *54*(3), 459–467. https://doi.org/10.1002/eat.23402

Monroe, P., Campbell, J. A., Harris, M., & Egede, L. E. (2023). Racial/ethnic differences in social determinants of health and health outcomes among adolescents and youth ages 10–24 years old: A scoping review. *BMC Public Health*, *23*(1), 1–14. https://doi.org/10.1186/s12889-023-15274-x

Moradi, M., Salehian, R., Bozorg, B., & Bozorg, M. (2024). The effectiveness of family-based treatment and pharmacotherapy in an adolescent with anorexia nervosa and intellectual disability: A case report. *Advances in Mental Health and Intellectual Disabilities*, *18*(4), 141–148. https://doi.org/10.1108/AMHID-10-2023-0037

Moreno, R., Buckelew, S. M., Accurso, E. C., & Raymond-Flesch, M. (2023). Disparities in access to EDs treatment for publicly insured youth and youth of color: A retrospective cohort study. *Journal of Eating Disorders*, *11*(1), 1–10. https://doi.org/10.1186/s40337-022-00730-7

Nagata, J. M., Stuart, E., Hur, J. O., Panchal, S., Low, P., Chaphekar, A. V., Chou, C. P., & Lavender, J. M. (2024). EDs in sexual and gender minority adolescents. *Current Psychiatry Reports*, *26*(7), 340–350. https://doi.org/10.1007/s11920-024-01508-1

Sauerwein, J., Austin, A., Singh, M., Pedram, P., Allan, E., Bruett, L., Eckhardt, S., Forsberg, S., Keery, H., Kimber, M., Pradel, M., Accurso, E. C., Le Grange, D., & Dimitropoulos, G. (2025). "FBT is for the rich": A qualitative study examining clinicians' experiences and perceptions of treatment access and engagement for diverse families in family-based treatment. *International Journal of Eating Disorders*, *58*(3), 554–563. https://doi.org/10.1002/eat.24351

Sharpe, S. L., Adams, M., Smith, E. K., Urban, B., & Silverstein, S. (2023). Inaccessibility of care and inequitable conceptions of suffering: A collective response to the construction of "terminal" anorexia nervosa. *Journal of Eating Disorders*, *11*(1), 1–9. https://doi.org/10.1186/s40337-023-00791-2

Sherman, A. D. F., Febres-Cordero, S., Johnson, K. B., Clark, K. D., Klepper, M., Duroseau, B., Lin, Y., Zhang, W., Coleman, M., Prakash, D., Daniel, G. A., Chand, A. T., Kalu, U., Tarter, R., Allgood, S., Cohen, S., Kelly, U., & Balthazar, M. (2023). Intersectionality in nursing research: A scoping review. *International Journal of Nursing Studies Advances*, *5*, 1–25. https://doi.org/10.1016/j.ijnsa.2023.100155

Simone, M., Slaughter-Acey, J., Hazzard, V. M., Eisenberg, M., & Neumark-Sztainer, D. (2022). Exploring the intersection of multiple social determinants of health and disordered eating behaviors in a population-based sample in the United States. *International Journal of Eating Disorders*, *55*(11), 1589–1602. https://doi.org/10.1002/eat.23795

Steinberg, D., Perry, T., Freestone, D., Bohon, C., Baker, J. H., & Parks, E. (2023). Effectiveness of delivering evidence-based ED treatment via telemedicine for children, adolescents, and youth. *EDs*, *31*(1), 85–101. https://doi.org/10.1080/10640266.2022.2076334

Stewart, T. J., & Gonzalez, V. M. (2023). Associations of historical trauma and racism with health care system distrust and mental health help-seeking propensity among American Indian and Alaska Native college students. *Cultural Diversity & Ethnic Minority Psychology*, *29*(3), 348–357. https://doi.org/10.1037/cdp0000587

Turkiewicz, G., Pinzon, V., Lock, J., & Fleitlich-Bilyk, B. (2010). Feasibility, acceptability, and effectiveness of family-based treatment for adolescent anorexia nervosa: An observational study conducted in Brazil. *Revista Brasileira de Psiquiatria*, *32*(2), 169–172. https://doi.org/10.1590/S1516-44462010005000001

Vohra-Gupta, S., Petruzzi, L., Jones, C., & Cubbin, C. (2023). An intersectional approach to understanding barriers to healthcare for women. *Journal of Community Health*, *48*(1), 89–98. https://doi.org/10.1007/s10900-022-01147-8

Urban, B., Jones, N., Freestone, D., Steinberg, D. M., & Baker, J. H. (2023). Food insecurity among youth seeking ED treatment. *Eating Behaviors: An International Journal*, *49*, 1–8. https://doi.org/10.1016/j.eatbeh.2023.101738

Williams, K. K., Baidoobonso, S., Lofters, A., Haggerty, J., Leblanc, I., & Adams, A. M. (2024). Anti-Black racism in Canadian health care: A qualitative study of diverse perceptions of racism and racial discrimination among Black adults in Montreal, Quebec. *BMC Public Health*, *24*(1), 3152. https://doi.org/10.1186/s12889-024-20636-0

Wilkins, J., Ahmed, M., Allen, K., & Schmidt, U. (2025). Intersectionality in help-seeking for EDs: A systematic scoping review. *Journal of Eating Disorders*, *13*(1), 1–12. https://doi.org/10.1186/s40337-025-01202-4

Wong, L., Goh, L. G., & Ramachandran, R. (2019). Family-based therapy for anorexia nervosa: Results from a 7-year longitudinal Singapore study. *Eating and Weight Disorders*, *24*(6), 1215–1219. https://doi.org/10.1007/s40519-019-00654-3

World Health Organization. (2024). *Social determinants of health*. https://www.who.int/health-topics/social-determinants-of-health#tab=tab_1

Chapter 13

FBT-TAY for Young People Without Family Involvement

While FBT-TAY emphasizes collaboration of young people and their parents/caregivers to support weight restoration and greater independence with meals and eventually practising eating with a variety of individuals and contexts (Dimitropoulos et al., 2018a, 2018b; Dodge et al., 2024; Gorrell et al., 2019; Le Grange et al., 2012). Even with the best intentions, not all parents nor caregivers can actively participate in FBT-TAY. Moreover, some young people may be unable to engage parents/caregivers in treatment because of strained or precarious relationships due to historical injuries and ongoing conflicts. In this chapter, we will explore how FBT-TAY therapists can support young people to meaningfully engage siblings and other supportive adult carers while preserving the core therapeutic principles of the model.

Finally, we will briefly introduce other evidence-based models that can be employed when FBT-TAY is not a viable option for young people, and their preferred treatment is for an individualized approach or a treatment that is more intensive.

FBT-TAY in the Absence of Parental/Caregiver Support

FBT-TAY leverages parental/caregiver empowerment, unity, and consistency, which are central to facilitating recovery from AN in young people (Dimitropoulos et al., 2018b; Le Grange et al., 2012; Lock & Le Grange, 2012). As mentioned in the previous chapter, it is not always feasible for families to assume the responsibility for refeeding/weight restoration (Waage et al., 2025; Pedersen et al., 2025) and a strong drive for autonomy and living independently from family may require a fundamentally different conceptualization of whom to involve in treatment for EDs (Dodge et al., 2024).

There are several findings in the literature that provide preliminary support for including a broader network of individuals in FBT-TAY during treatment:

- When parents/caregivers are inconsistently involved, overburdened, or unavailable, therapists can incorporate extended family, siblings, partners,

DOI: 10.4324/9781003463351-14

friends, or roommates to help bridge caregiving gaps (Egbert et al., 2024; Goldschmidt et al., 2023; van Langenberg et al., 2018).

- Caregiver fatigue – especially for parents/caregivers who have undergone previous treatment with their adolescent – can produce feelings of exhaustion or disempowerment (Conti et al., 2021; Dodge et al., 2024; Wufong et al., 2019). This may necessitate a reduced role of parents/caregivers in treatment, even for a short period of time, allowing for other supportive carers to take on this role (Dodge et al., 2024).
- Research demonstrates that weight restoration in FBT is achievable through the implementation of structure, practical support, and consistent external scaffolding by supportive adults/people who are regularly available throughout treatment (Chen et al., 2016; Matthews et al., 2023).

Some Young People Have Limited Family Involvement in Treatment

Young people who have experienced estrangement, volatile family dynamics, and a history of child maltreatment are unlikely to identify their parents/caregivers as candidates for FBT-TAY (Jewell et al., 2016; Soler et al., 2013). Other young people are structurally separated from caregivers through immigration or displacement, geographic distance, or separated living arrangements, making standard session attendance and family meals significantly more challenging to implement (Couturier et al., 2013; Egbert et al., 2024; Goldschmidt et al., 2023). Many families also face overwhelming caregiving demands, financial constraints, or severe mental or physical illnesses such as receiving cancer care making it difficult to consistently participate in FBT and adequately be present to support with refeeding (Dimitropoulos et al., 2024; Egbert et al., 2024; Matthews et al., 2023; Sauerwein et al., 2025; Scarborough, 2018).

Furthermore, some young people prefer a therapeutic focus on recovery centred on self-agency rather than a strict reliance on parental/caregiver involvement in assisting with meals and weight restoration (Baudinet et al., 2024; Medway et al., 2019; Dodge et al., 2024). Service- or system-level factors such as limited availability of FBT-trained therapists and young people's concerns overly rigid family requirements for FBT may exacerbate treatment delays (Couturier et al., 2013; Gorrell et al., 2019; Scarborough, 2018).

Building a Caregiving Network

The broader carer literature (Treasure et al., 2021), family therapy models for emerging-adults (Dodge et al., 2024), and studies of siblings and other adult supports (Fjermestad et al., 2020; van Langenberg et al., 2018; Withers et al., 2014) suggest building a caregiving network in FBT when traditional family involvement is lacking. FBT-TAY therapists can work with the young person to identify who in their life can reliably and safely take on core caregiving functions such as meal support, emotional containment, boundary-setting, care coordination, and relapse-prevention support in treatment (Dimitropoulos et al., 2015; Goldschmidt et al., 2023). For example, these roles can be carried out in collaboration with roommates, close friends, extended family members (e.g., aunts, uncles, grandparents), mentors, etc. Supportive carers can be effective when provided with clear guidance, knowledge, and strategies by therapists to manage ED behaviours and modulate emotional responses without accommodating the illness (Treasure et al., 2021); similarly, significant others and partners can fulfil supportive roles with young people in treatment when their involvement is flexible and clearly articulated and revised as needed throughout the recovery process (e.g., based on the young person's need, risk, level of independence) (Dodge et al., 2024).

Establishing the Caregiving Network

In building the caregiving network, FBT-TAY therapist can work with the young person to map out who can be invited into a supportive role during treatment when there is no family involvement.

Key questions that can guide this assessment include:

- Who does the young person turn to when distressed?
- Who has shown consistent and reliable care or concern for the young person in the past and present?
- Are there siblings, extended relatives, significant others, close friends who would be willing to be included as temporary caregivers?
- What boundaries, confidentiality, and privacy needs does the young person want to maintain throughout treatment, and how might this vary with different supportive individuals?

The young person's preferences about whom to involve, how, and in what capacity will shape the FBT-TAY treatment plan. The young person will define the scope and role(s) of supportive people, clarify concrete expectations around meal supervision, and discuss appropriate boundaries in treatment, such as avoiding unnecessary surveillance with meals, and rapidly returning autonomy over refeeding to the young person as soon as weight restoration is achieved. A contract detailing the parameters of emotional, relational, and instrumental support, information sharing, and the degree of participation of supportive adults in the different phases of FBT-TAY must be carefully delineated in partnership with the young person. Ongoing consent and collaboration with the young person and their supportive adult/person are also critical (Treasure et al., 2021; Dodge et al., 2024). Finally, it is incumbent upon FBT-TAY therapists to routinely assess the supportive adult/person's capacity to assume caregiving responsibilities in order to minimize burnout (Matthew et al., 2023).

In addition, siblings, can be utilized as powerful supports with adequate coaching and therapeutic guidance (Downs & Blow, 2011; Maon et al., 2020; Schuman et al., 2025). Both van Langenberg et al. (2018) and Withers et al. (2014) describe siblings taking on quasi-parental tasks during FBT, encouraging eating, monitoring behaviours, and offering emotional support. However, siblings may experience long-term emotional and relational consequences of living with a sibling with AN and report experiencing a mixture of worry, guilt, isolation, and frustration towards their sibling with an ED (Fjermestad et al., 2020; Dimitropoulos et al., 2009). Consequently, siblings may want to maintain active involvement in the young person's care yet may feel uncertain about how best to help and require assistance with boundary setting (Dimitropoulos et al., 2009). Therefore, FBT-TAY therapists should prioritize structured psychoeducation for siblings around the illness and treatment goals, while accounting for, and actively accommodating, their emotional and psychosocial needs in treatment. As described above, a contract between the young person and their sibling(s) must be collaboratively established covering the following areas: Which meals will be prepared by the sibling? Will the sibling be present for all of the meals, or will meal support be shared with other supportive adults (peers and partners) in the young person's life? What topics or activities are encouraged or discouraged during meals? Scheduling regular (daily, weekly) meetings to proactively assess and address when siblings and the young person with AN are not working towards the same goals in a supportive and collaborative way and to explicitly identify when sibling involvement in meal support and treatment is no longer working for both parties. As FBT-TAY therapists progress through treatment with the young person and their supportive adult/person, the goals and central tenets of each phase (weight restoration and symptom interruption, gradual return of responsibility of eating to the young person, and relapse prevention and outstanding developmental concerns) remain unchanged whether working with siblings, peers, or extended family.

Alternative Options for Treatment

In instances where FBT-TAY may not be appropriate or feasible for a young person and family, therapists should share the following treatment models as therapeutic alternatives.

Adolescent-Focused Therapy

Adolescent-focused therapy (AFT) is an individual treatment that seeks to enhance young people's autonomy, self-efficacy, and capacity to facilitate their recovery from an ED (Lock et al., 2010; Lock, 2020; Medway et al., 2019; Stewart & Baumann, 2024). Like FBT, AFT consists of three phases

(Fitzpatrick et al., 2009). Building on a strong therapeutic relationship in Phase 1, the AFT therapist assesses psychological concerns and motivation, setting target weights based on historical growth charts, establishing explicit behaviour-goals, and fostering responsibility for addressing eating-related challenges (Lock et al., 2010). Phase 2 encourages self-efficacy and autonomy of the young person and builds on their capability to tolerate negative affect surrounding meals and weight changes (Lock et al., 2010). Lastly, Phase 3 focuses on supporting young people to review and terminate from the treatment (Lock et al., 2010). Collateral parent/caregiver meetings occur throughout the three phases to provide progress updates (Fitzpatrick et al., 2009). AFT has proved to be a promising alternative treatment to FBT (Lock et al., 2010; Lock, 2020; Nice, 2004).

Dialectical-Behavioural Therapy

Dialectical-Behavioural Therapy (DBT) is another alternative treatment option to FBT-TAY. DBT is commonly used with clinical populations experiencing interpersonal ineffectiveness, emotional dysregulation, and skill deficits in emotion regulation (Federici et al., 2012).

Multidiagnostic ED DBT (MED-DBT) has been created to treat these treatment interfering deficits (TIBs) while concurrently tackling the ED and comorbid conditions (Federici et al., 2012; Federici & Wisniewski, 2013). MED-DBT is outpatient, intensive skills-based treatment that is delivered employing a combination of group sessions and individual meetings with DBT therapists, psychiatrists, and dietitians (Federici et al., 2012). Throughout the course of treatment, emphasis is placed on flexibility, individual accountability, commitment building, and acknowledgement and disruption of treatment and life interfering behaviours (Federici & Wisniewski, 2013). Through case series and comparative studies, MED-DBT has demonstrated efficacy for young people with ED presentations that have responded poorly to traditional ED treatments (Federici & Wisniewski, 2013; Pennell et al., 2019). Results have shown improvements in weight gain, medical stability, ED-related symptoms, and suicidal and self-injurious behaviours (Federici & Wisniewski, 2013). Therapists have also reported reductions in hospital admissions, frequency of treatment interfering behaviours, and, importantly, young people's enhanced willingness to participate in treatment (Federici & Wisniewski, 2013).

Day Treatment or Partial Hospitalization

Day-treatment programs, also known as partial hospitalization, are in-person or virtual treatment options that do not necessitate that a young person remain overnight within a hospital or treatment facility (Baudinet & Simic, 2021). Day programs provide intensive group-based interventions while permitting young people to remain connected with family, friends, and their broader social environments (Herpertz-Dahlmann, 2017). Most day programs provide supervised meal support and group-based therapy with some individual psychiatric support; however, there is significant variation among programs in the content of the treatment and the populations treated (Baudinet & Simic, 2021). Day-treatment programs have demonstrated promising outcomes from the achievement of weight restoration and eating rehabilitation (Herpetz-Dahlmann et al., 2014). Day programs offer an effective alternative to inpatient programs – addressing ED symptoms, comorbid conditions, and restoring body weight – for those requiring a less or more intensive treatment program (Baudinet & Simic, 2021; Krishnamoorthy et al., 2023).

Residential Care

Residential and in-patient care programs are the most intensive form of ED treatment, offering 24-hour care by an interdisciplinary team (Rieneck et al., 2024). These programs are highly variable but typically offer highly structured and supervised meals, group- and individual-based therapy, and supportive interventions (Derenne, 2019). Residential (RES) care is an intensive treatment option that is typically offered to individuals that are medically stable but may require interventions to disrupt ED symptoms (Derenne, 2019). Settings represent homes, rather than medical centres; however, care is still delivered by nurses and certified counsellors (Derenne, 2019).

Conclusions

The origins of FBT-TAY and FBT position parents/caregivers as the primary agents of change, yet the clinical realities of "families" in practice may not always lend to traditional two-parent/caregiver households and family systems. Supportive carers, including siblings, peers, mentors, and extended family members, can meaningfully contribute to recovery when they receive appropriate guidance and support from FBT-TAY therapists on how to effectively manage refeeding and weight restoration, and negotiate clear and defined roles about who will assume which specific caregiving responsibilities throughout the course of treatment. When FBT-TAY is not a viable option, other evidence-based treatments must be shared with the young person which include AFT to inpatient care.

Chapter Summary

Here are the key points of this chapter:

(1) FBT-TAY therapists may work with young people to identify supportive people in their lives such as siblings, peers, roommates, mentors, and other

health professionals or practitioners to assist with refeeding, weight restoration, and other treatment goals.

(2) Prior to starting FBT-TAY, therapists should work with the young person and their preferred identified supportive adults/people to clarify roles, boundaries, and expectations.

(3) Other treatments, such as AFT and DBT, are available for young people and families for whom FBT-TAY may not be the right fit. FBT-TAY therapists may consider a variety of treatment options for these families, including those that are more intense – day-treatment programs, residential, and in-patient care – when compared to outpatient offerings.

References

Baudinet, J., Eisler, I., Konstantellou, A., Simic, M., & Schmidt, U. (2024). How young people perceive change to occur in family therapy for anorexia nervosa: A qualitative study. *Journal of Eating Disorders*, *12*(1), 1–14. https://doi.org/10.1186/s40337-024-00971-8

Baudinet, J., & Simic, M. (2021). Adolescent eating disorder day programme treatment models and outcomes: A Systematic Scoping Review. *Frontiers in Psychiatry*, *12*, 1–12. https://doi.org/10.3389/fpsyt.2021.652604

Chen, E. Y., Weissman, J. A., Zeffiro, T. A., Yiu, A., Eneva, K. T., Arlt, J. M., & Swantek, M. J. (2016). Family-based therapy for young adults with anorexia nervosa restores weight. *International Journal of Eating Disorders*, *49*(7), 701–707. https://doi.org/10.1002/eat.22513

Conti, J., Joyce, C., Natoli, S., Skeoch, K., & Hay, P. (2021). "I'm still here, but no one hears you": A qualitative study of young women's experiences of persistent distress post family-based treatment for adolescent anorexia nervosa. *Journal of Eating Disorders*, *9*(1), 1–17. https://doi.org/10.1186/s40337-021-00496-4

Couturier, J., Kimber, M., Jack, S., Niccols, A., Van Blyderveen, S., & McVey, G. (2013). Understanding the uptake of family-based treatment for adolescents with anorexia nervosa: Therapist perspectives. *International Journal of Eating Disorders*, *46*(2), 177–188. https://doi.org/10.1002/eat.22049

Derenne, J. (2019). The role of higher levels of care for EDs in youth. *Child and Adolescent Psychiatric Clinics of North America*, *28*(4), 573–582. https://doi.org/10.1016/j.chc.2019.05.006

Dimitropoulos, G., Klopfer, K., Lazar, L., & Schacter, R. (2009). Caring for a sibling with anorexia nervosa: A qualitative study. *European EDs Review*, *17*(5), 350–365. https://doi.org/10.1002/erv.937

Dimitropoulos, G., Landers, A. L., Freeman, V., Novick, J., Garber, A., & Le Grange, D. (2018a). Open trial of family-based treatment of anorexia nervosa for transition age youth. *Journal of the Canadian Academy of Child and Adolescent Psychiatry*, *27*(1), 50–61. https://pubmed.ncbi.nlm.nih.gov/29375633/

Dimitropoulos, G., Landers, A. L., Freeman, V. E., Novick, J., Cullen, O., Engelberg, M., Steinegger, C., & Le Grange, D. (2018b). Family-based treatment for transition age youth: Parental self-efficacy and caregiver accommodation. *Journal of Eating Disorders*, *6*(1), 1–11. https://doi.org/10.1186/s40337-018-0196-0

Dimitropoulos, G., Singh, M., Sauerwein, J., Pedram, P., Kimber, M., Pradel, M., Eckhardt, S., Forsberg, S., Keery, H., Allan, E., Bruett, L., & Le Grange, D. (2024).

Examining clinicians' perceptions and experiences working with diverse families in family-based treatment: Common adaptations and considerations for treatment engagement. *The International Journal of Eating Disorders*, *57*(3), 635–647. https://doi.org/10.1002/eat.24144

Dimitropoulos, G., Toulany, A., Herschman, J., Kovacs, A., Steinegger, C., Bardsley, J., Sandhu, S., Gregory, C., Colton, P., Anderson, J., & Kaufman, M. (2015). A qualitative study on the experiences of young adults with EDs transferring from pediatric to adult care. *EDs*, *23*(2), 144–162. https://doi.org/10.1080/10640266.2014.976106

Dodge, E., Baudinet, J., Austin, A., Eisler, I., Le Grange, D., & Dimitropoulos, G. (2024). Family therapy for emerging adults with anorexia nervosa: Expert opinion on evidence, practice considerations, and future directions. *European EDs Review*, 1–11. https://doi.org/10.1002/erv.3129

Downs, K. J., & Blow, A. J. (2013). A substantive and methodological review of family-based treatment for EDs: The last 25 years of research. *Journal of Family Therapy*, *35*(1), 3–28. https://doi.org/10.1111/j.1467-6427.2011.00566.x

Egbert, A. H., Irizarry, B., Lualdi, E., Tortolani, C. C., Donaldson, D. L., & Goldschmidt, A. B. (2024). A qualitative assessment of provider-perceived barriers to implementing family-based treatment for anorexia nervosa in low-income community settings. *Journal of EDs*, *12*(1), 1–10. https://doi.org/10.1186/s40337-024-01008-w

Federici, A., & Wisniewski, L. (2013). An intensive DBT program for patients with multidiagnostic ED presentations: A case series analysis. *International Journal of Eating Disorders*, *46*(4), 322–331. https://doi.org/10.1002/eat.22112

Federici, A., Wisniewski, L., & Ben-Porath, D. (2012). Description of an intensive dialectical behavior therapy program for multidiagnostic clients with EDs. *Journal of Counseling & Development*, *90*(3), 330–338. https://doi.org/10.1002/j.1556-6676.2012.00041.x

Fitzpatrick, K., Moye, A., Hostee, R., Lock, J., & Le Grange, D. (2009). Adolescent focused therapy for adolescent anorexia nervosa. *Journal of Contemporary Psychotherapy*, *40*(1), 31–39. https://doi.org/10.1002/eat.24252

Fjermestad, K. W., Rø, A. E., Espeland, K. E., Halvorsen, M. S., & Halvorsen, I. M. (2020). "Do I exist in this world, really, or is it just her?" Youths' perspectives of living with a sibling with anorexia nervosa. *EDs*, *28*(1), 80–95. https://doi.org/10.1080/10640266.2019.1573046

Goldschmidt, A. B., Tortolani, C. C., Accurso, E. C., Dunbar, E.-M. P., Egbert, A. H., Donaldson, D., & Donaldson, A. A. (2023). Adapting family-based treatment for adolescent anorexia nervosa delivered in the home: A novel approach for improving access to care and generalizability of skill acquisition. *Journal of Eating Disorders*, *11*(1), 1–12. https://doi.org/10.1186/s40337-023-00850-8

Gorrell, S., Loeb, K. L., & Le Grange, D. (2019). Family-based treatment of EDs: A narrative review. *The Psychiatric Clinics of North America*, *42*(2), 193–204. https://doi.org/10.1016/j.psc.2019.01.004

Herpertz-Dahlmann, B. (2017). Treatment of EDs in child and adolescent psychiatry. *Current Opinion in Psychiatry*, *30*(6), 438–445. https://doi.org/10.1097/YCO.0000000000000357

Herpertz-Dahlmann, B., Schwarte, R., Krei, M., Egberts, K., Warnke, A., Wewetzer, C., Pfeiffer, E., Fleischhaker, C., Scherag, A., Holtkamp, K., Hagenah, U., Bühren, K., Konrad, K., Schmidt, U., Schade-Brittinger, C., Timmesfeld, N., & Dempfle, A. (2014). Day-patient treatment after short inpatient care versus continued inpatient treatment in adolescents with anorexia nervosa (ANDI): A multicentre, randomised, open-label, non-inferiority trial. *The Lancet (British Edition)*, *383*(9924), 1222–1229. https://doi.org/10.1016/S0140-6736(13)62411-3

Jewell, T., Blessitt, E., Stewart, C., Simic, M., & Eisler, I. (2016). family therapy for child and adolescent EDs: A critical review. *Family Process*, *55*(3), 577–594. https://doi.org/10.1111/famp.12242

Krishnamoorthy, G., Shin, S. M., & Rees, B. (2023). Day Programs for children and adolescents with EDs: A systematic review. *European EDs review: The Journal of the EDs Association*, *31*(2), 199–225. https://doi.org/10.1002/erv.2953

Le Grange, D., Lock, J., Agras, W. S., Moye, A., Bryson, S. W., Jo, B., & Kraemer, H. C. (2012). Moderators and mediators of remission in family-based treatment and adolescent focused therapy for anorexia nervosa. *Behaviour Research and Therapy*, *50*(2), 85–92. https://doi.org/10.1016/j.brat.2011.11.003

Lock, J. (2020). *Adolescent-focused therapy for anorexia nervosa: A developmental approach*. Guilford Press. https://www.guilford.com/books/Adolescent-Focused-Therapy-for-Anorexia-Nervosa/James-Lock/9781462542840?srsltid=AfmBOop8nkqdqYxo4_ilHqkh29ksUopnsnlTJ08849mofWXw6IdVkc-7

Lock, J., & Le Grange, D. (2012). *Treatment manual for anorexia nervosa: A family-based approach* (2nd ed.). Guilford Press.

Lock, J., Le Grange, D., Agras, W. S., Moye, A., Bryson, S. W., & Jo, B. (2010). Randomized clinical trial comparing family-based treatment with adolescent-focused individual therapy for adolescents with anorexia nervosa. *Archives of General Psychiatry*, *67*(10), 1025–1032. https://doi.org/10.1001/archgenpsychiatry.2010.128

Maon, I., Horesh, D., & Gvion, Y. (2020). Siblings of individuals with EDs: A review of the literature. *Frontiers in Psychiatry*, *11*, 1–11. https://doi.org/10.3389/fpsyt.2020.00604

Matthews, A., Bruening, A. B., Aarnio-Peterson, C. M., & Kramer, R. (2023). Predictors of caregiver burden before starting family-based treatment for adolescent anorexia nervosa and associations with weight gain during treatment. *Eating and Weight Disorders*, *28*(1), 1–10. https://doi.org/10.1007/s40519-023-01553-4

Medway, M., Rhodes, P., Dawson, L., Miskovic-Wheatley, J., Wallis, A., & Madden, S. (2019). Adolescent development in family-based treatment for anorexia nervosa: Patients' and parents' narratives. *Clinical Child Psychology and Psychiatry*, *24*(1), 129–143. https://doi.org/10.1177/1359104518792293

National Institute for Clinical Excellence. (2004). *EDs: Core interventions in the treatment and management of anorexia nervosa, bulimia nervosa, and binge ED.*

Pedersen, S. H., Bay, S., Bentz, M., & Midtgaard, J. (2025). Straight, bumpy, or detoured: Three roads through family-based treatment for anorexia nervosa–a qualitative study of parents' experiences. *Psychotherapy Research*, 1–13. https://doi.org/10.1080/10503307.2025.2554891

Pennell, A., Webb, C., Agar, P., Federici, A., & Couturier, J. (2019). Implementation of dialectical behavior therapy in a day hospital setting for adolescents with EDs. *Journal of the Canadian Academy of Child and Adolescent Psychiatry*, *28*(1), 21–29. https://pubmed-ncbi-nlm-nih-gov.ezproxy.lib.ucalgary.ca/31001348/

Rienecke, R. D., Blalock, D. V., Duffy, A., Johnson, C., Riddle, M., Le Grange, D., Mehler, P. S., & Brandt, H. A. (2024). Does 24/7 care result in better outcomes for adults with eating disorders? A comparison of inpatient/residential care to partial hospitalization/intensive outpatient care for patients at low BMIs. *Journal of Eating Disorders*, *12*(1), 1–8. https://doi.org/10.1186/s40337-024-01150-5

Sauerwein, J., Austin, A., Singh, M., Pedram, P., Allan, E., Bruett, L., Eckhardt, S., Forsberg, S., Keery, H., Kimber, M., Pradel, M., Accurso, E. C., Le Grange, D., & Dimitropoulos, G. (2025). "FBT is for the rich": A qualitative study examining clinicians' experiences and perceptions of treatment access and engagement for diverse families in family- based treatment. *International Journal of Eating Disorders*, *58*(3), 554–563. https://doi.org/10.1002/eat.24351

Scarborough, J. (2018). Family-based therapy for pediatric anorexia nervosa: Highlighting the implementation challenges. *The Family Journal, 26*(1), 90–98. https://doi.org/10.1177/1066480717754280

Schumann, A., Vatne, T. M., Dalton, L., Rapa, E., & Fjermestad, K. W. (2025). "It's like a car that doesn't like gasoline" – a qualitative study of siblings' understanding of anorexia nervosa in childhood: Perspectives from siblings and parents. *Journal of Eating Disorders, 13*(1), 1–13. https://doi.org/10.1186/s40337-025-01263-5

Soler, J., Soriano, J., Ferraz, L., Grasa, E., Carmona, C., Portella, M. J., Seto, V., Alvarez, E., & Pérez, V. (2013). Direct experience and the course of EDs in patients on partial hospitalization: A pilot study. *European EDs Review, 21*(5), 399–404. https://doi.org/10.1002/erv.2224

Stewart, M. P., & Baumann, O. (2024). The effectiveness of adolescent-focused therapy and family-based therapy for anorexia nervosa. *Psychological Reports, 0*(0), 1–22. https://doi.org/10.1177/00332941241226687

Treasure, J., Parker, S., Oyeleye, O., & Harrison, A. (2021). The value of including families in the treatment of anorexia nervosa. *European EDs Review, 29*(3), 393–401. https://doi.org/10.1002/erv.2816

van Langenberg, T., Duncan, R. E., Allen, J. S., Sawyer, S. M., Le Grange, D., & Hughes, E. K. (2018). "They don't really get heard": A qualitative study of sibling involvement across two forms of family-based treatment for adolescent anorexia nervosa. *EDs, 26*(4), 373–387. https://doi.org/10.1080/10640266.2018.1453632

Waage, D., Bryde, A., Bentz, M., & Micali, N. (2025). Family life and caregiving during family-based treatment (FBT) for anorexia nervosa: Parent, patient, and clinician perspectives. *Journal of Eating Disorders, 13*(1), 1–11. https://doi.org/10.1186/s40337-025-01367-y

Withers, A., Mullan, B., Madden, S., Kohn, M., Clarke, S., Thornton, C., Rhodes, P., & Touyz, S. (2014). Anorexia nervosa in the family: A sibling's perspective. *Advances in Eating Disorders, 2*(1), 53–64. https://doi.org/10.1080/21662630.2013.839187

Wufong, E., Rhodes, P., & Conti, J. (2019). "We don't really know what else we can do": Parent experiences when adolescent distress persists after the Maudsley and family-based therapies for anorexia nervosa. *Journal of Eating Disorders, 7*(1), 1–18. https://doi.org/10.1186/s40337-019-0235-5

Book Summary and Conclusions

In this book, we have presented an evidence-informed FBT model for TAY (ages 16–25) with AN, their parents/caregivers, and families. Building upon the previously validated FBT model for AN in younger adolescents (ages 12–18), this book comprehensively details the empirical and clinical considerations of FBT-TAY, including how the model can be uniquely applied to a variety of young people with AN across tertiary care contexts, those experiencing multiple and concurrent clinical and life transitions, and within other non-specialized settings including post-secondary institutions, primary care, and private practice. This book also includes detailed adaptations to the core principles and clinical interventions of FBT-TAY.

We start by providing a detailed overview of the evidence for AN, the transition challenges present for young people with EDs in treatment, and the key neurocognitive processes and developmental challenges that are disrupted due to AN. Next, we provide an introduction to FBT-TAY, including its key principles, tenets, and phases of treatment. We review the scientific evidence supporting FBT-TAY, providing compelling support for its acceptability, feasibility, and effectiveness, and describe the developmental processes in late adolescence and young adulthood which impact the delivery of FBT-TAY. Thereafter, we include a detailed account of how FBT-TAY therapists set up treatment, including the pre-treatment evaluation processes to assess young people and their families prior to the onset of FBT-TAY. We explore key assessments, measures, and other targeted areas for nutritional, medical, andpsychological/psychiatric expertise to be incorporated within the evaluation process. We then comprehensively describe the goals, key interventions, adaptations, clinical considerations, and applications of employing Phase 1, Phase 2, and Phase 3 of treatment. Evidence detailing the period of emerging adulthood and factors impacting the family unit throughout these phases are also described. Subsequently, we discuss the key evidence, successes, and challenges that FBT-TAY therapists may encounter when implementing the model in primary care, private practice, or in post-secondary contexts. Finally, we describe how diverse young people and

DOI: 10.4324/9781003463351-15

families may interface with FBT-TAY, including the clinical factors and considerations in accounting for their unique and intersecting identities in practice, and end with describing how FBT-TAY therapists can engage supportive carers outside of the parent/caregiver dyad in treatment and explore other evidence-based models when FBT-TAY is not a good fit.

Finally, this book offers the theoretical, empirical, and clinical foundations, considerations, dilemmas, solutions, and applications of FBT-TAY with young people, their parents/caregivers, families, and supportive carers. We recognize that emerging adulthood represents a unique, sometimes challenging, yet opportunistic, developmental period for therapists to apply FBT to fit the needs of TAY with AN. Parents/caregivers, families, and other supportive carers also play a critical role in advancing recovery for their child while working to centre autonomy and independence of the young person as developmentally appropriate and in collaboration with the therapist throughout treatment. Ultimately, we hope that this book provides therapists, program administrators, healthcare providers, and other key professionals involved in the care of EDs with the clinical tools needed to implement FBT-TAY in practice, taking into the account the unique and varying needs of TAY and their families in treatment.

Index

Note: Page numbers in *italics* indicate a figure, and page numbers in **bold** indicate a table on the corresponding page.

Accommodation and Enabling Scale for EDs – Revised (AESED-R) 74–75
accommodation of illness 74–75, 176, 190; parents/caregivers 29, 32–33, 46, 99, 104–105, 117–118; young people 47, 108
Accurso, E. C. 178
adolescent-focused therapy (AFT) 129, 154, 174, 191–192
agnosticism 26, 31, **36**, **37**, 45, 89, 155; parents/caregivers 27–28; young people 28–29
Agras, W. S. 48
Alhaj, O. A. 162
ambivalence 7, 11, 26, 29, 32, 69, 94, 95, 107, 118, 120–121, 181
anger 92, 112, 120, 122, 146
anorexia nervosa (AN) 2–4; brain development and 4–5; chronic 8–9; developmental disruption 169; diagnosis criteria 74; effect on treatment-seeking behaviours 5–6; medical consequences 2–3; mental health conditions and 3–4; morbidity and mortality associated with 2–4, 92, 115; recovery 107–108, 170; relapse rates 145; restricting type 2–3; symptoms 55, 88, 112, 122–123; transition-age youth with 6; weight criteria 74
anxiety 3, 6, 8, 26, 33, 53, 58, 77, 92, 106, 114–115, 120–122, 135, 140, 144, 148, 181
Arcelus, J. 3
Aspen, V. 179
assessment process 70–72
autonomy 9–11, 13, 29, 56, 71, 76, 85–88, 99, 108, 116, 131, 140–141, 145, 154, 188, 191–192; decision-making 33–34, 107, 112, 126; diminished 66, 78; emerging 25; emotional 54; lack of 44–45; over refeeding 190; social 54; supportive approach 50
awareness of EDs 163–164

Beat Eating Disorders (UK) 98
binge-eating 2–4, 13, 77, 86, 123, 144, 164
body mass index (BMI) 47–49, 156, 162, 174–175
borderline personality disorder 3
Borges, R. 178
Boutelle, K. 179
Brewerton, T. D. 179
Buhren, K. 3
bulimia nervosa (BN) 1, 12–13, 35, 86, 88–89, 104, 111, 116, 127, 134, 177
burden 177; fear of being 30–32, 68, 93; parents/caregivers 29, 33, 117, 135; of partner 59; young people 30–32, 93, 95–96
burnout 8, 33, 92, 96, 117, 134, 155, 191

cardiac problems 3, 76
caregiving network 189–191

care team 78, 165, 166
celebrating progress 121
central coherence 5–6
Centre for Innovation in Campus Mental Health (Ontario) 163–164
Chen, E. Y. 47–48
Chen, J. 174
Chew, C. S. E. 174
cognitive abilities 47, 52–54, 59, 136, 144; early and middle adolescence 55; ED-related 48, 147; late adolescence and young adulthood 56–57
cognitive behavioural therapy (CBT) 96, 129, 154
Cognitive Behavioural Therapy for Young Adults (CBT-YA) 48–49
cognitive inflexibility 5–6
collaboration 9, 25, **36**, **37**, 45, 47, 67, 154–155, 158, 169; decision-making 13, 31–32; parents/caregivers-young person 12, 27, 29, 32, 88–89, 92–94, 105–108, 111, 112–113, 118–120, 142, 144–145, 167, 179–182; reduced 69; sibling 190–191; therapist-parents/caregivers 131, 146; therapist-young person 34, 72, 91, 129, 131, 199; virtual 157
college readiness checklist 164–165
comorbidities 3–4, 122–123, 148, 158; heart failure 3; *see also specific entries*
compensatory log 86, *87*, 102–103, 111–113, 127–128, 130, 134
confidentiality 35, 65
consultative and collaborative approach 27, 31–32, **36**, **37**
COVID-19 pandemic 162–163
criticism 27, 30, 72; parental/caregiver 92, 111, 120–121, 133; self-criticism 133
cross-covered care 155
cumulative adversity 177

day-treatment programs 91, 192–193
depression 77, 144, 148; major depressive disorders 3; moderate to severe 47; symptoms 4
developmental re-engagement 145, 180
Dialectical-Behavioural Therapy (DBT) 192
distress 4, 8, 29, 33, 46, 69, 77, 112, 117–119, 122, 128, 145, 169
diverse families 174–175; diversity-specific considerations 177–179; modifications by phase 179–180; practice considerations for therapists 181–182; social determinants of health 175–177; training and supervision for equity-centred FBT-TAY 182–183
Dodge, E. 145
Doney, F. M. 166
Doyle, A. C. 179

Eating Attitudes Test (EAT-26) 74–75
eating behaviours 7, 28, 31, 68, 70, 105, 115–116, 140, 144, 166
Eating Disorder Foundation (Colorado, USA) 98
eating disorders (EDs) *see* anorexia nervosa (AN); bulimia nervosa (BN)
eating rehabilitation 7, 32, 35–36, **36**, **37**, 44, 85, 111, 147, 193
ED Examination Questionnaire (EDE-Q) 74–75
ED Programs (EDPs) 9–10, 44, 66, 68, 106, 117, 153
Eisenberg, D. 163
emerging adulthood 88, 118, 126, 133, 138–143, 153, 198–199
emotion: abuse 179; autonomy 54; avoidance 6; awareness 55, 57; duress 33; dysregulation 192; expression 55; maturity 11; outbursts 57; regulation 6, 52–55, 192; stability 7; starvation and 55
emotional support 105, 122, 167–168; family 95; parents and caregivers 10, 58, 119, 131, 134, 144; siblings 191; therapists 88, 190
empathy 30, 90, 109, 117, 119–120, 128
empowerment **36**, **37**; disempowerment 8, 90, 95, 182; parental/caregiver 8, 12, 25–27, 29, 32, 45, 79, 86, 119, 143, 155–156, 175–176, 179, 182, 188; young person 12, 25–27, 29–30, 33, 35, 129, 143, 179
equity 182–183
exhaustion 92, 96, 134–135
externalization 27, 30–31, 33, **36**, **37**, 57, 70, 89–91, *91*, 99, 111, 119–122, 155, 176; strategies for 45, 57; weight stigma 68–70

Families Empowered and Supporting Treatment for EDs (F.E.A.S.T) 98
Family and Social Circles Activity in Marriage and Family Therapy 167
family-based treatment (FBT) 1–2, 12–13; FBT-TAY *vs.* 25–27, **36**, **37**
Family-Based Treatment for Primary Care (FBT-PC) 155–157
family-based treatment for transitional age youth (FBT-TAY) 1–2, 13–14, 25, 38–39; barriers to implementation 69; caregiving network in 189–191; challenges 32–33; in diverse populations 174–179; *vs.* FBT 25–27, **36**, **37**; Guided Self-Help FBT 35, 157; intersectionality and cumulative adversity in 177; key principles of **36**, **37**; phases 35–36; social determinants of health in 175–177; support for professionals treating TAY using 157–159; *see also specific entries*
family functioning, history of 88–89, **90**
family life cycle 138–139, 141–143
family meal 48, 78, 94–95, 102–104, 108–109, 155, 180, 189
family members 9, 34–35, 46–48, 49, 72, 165; evaluation session with 73; in event of relapse 144; family meeting 26, 36, 112, 130, 139; greeting 86–88; strategies 97; taking history **90**; during transfer of care 10–11; *see also* parents/caregivers
family of choice 34–35
family patterns 103–105
FBT related approach adapted for young adults (FT-YA) 48–49
fear 8, 69, 73, 106–107, 114, 121–122, 135, 139, 148, 181; about being burden 31–32, 68; about being with others 58; intense 95, 115; of losing control 78; parents/caregivers 29, 33, 92, 95–96; of reprisal 33; of weight gain 2, 77
food choices 94–95
food insecurity 175, 177–178, 181
friend support 6–7, 34, 52, 57–58, 72, 112, 131, 166–168, 170, 190, 193
frustration 32, 58–59, 92, 114–115, 117, 120, 146, 191

gender 52, 57, 174; diversity 176; roles 175
Grammer, A. C. 163
Guided Self-Help FBT 35, 157
guilt 26–30, 89, 155, 191

healthcare professionals (HCPs) 157–158
Health Insurance Portability and Accountability Act (HIPAA) 154
help-seeking 4–7, 66, 68–69

identity 7, 56–57, 71, 76, 89, 176–177, 188; exploration 140–142; issues 112; loss of 148; social 55, 57
Iguchi, T. 175
impulse control disorders 3–4
independence 9, 11–13, 33, 54, 56–59, 72, 86, 108, 116; eating 26, 29, 36, 45, 102–107, 123, 126, 131–134, 139–142, 146, 180, 182, 188, 199; emerging adults 140–141; loss of 44–45; readiness for 164–165; restricted 85
informed consent 65, 165
in-patient care program 193
InsideOut Institute for Eating Disorders (Australia) 98
intense scene 86, 92–93, 114–115
interpersonal partner violence 179
intersectionality 177
isolation 4, 58, 97, 140–141, 144–145, 162, 191; intense 30; self-isolation 6

Kelty Mental Health Resource Centre (Canada) 97
Kimber, M. 179

Lane, J. A. 141
Lebow, J. 156

maintaining behaviours 12, 58, 99, 115–116, 170
major depressive disorders 3
maladaptive coping strategies 6
McGoldrick, M. 141
meal support 7, 94, 98, 115, 117, 146, 167–168, 170, 190–191, 193
mistrust 122, 181–183
mood disorders 3, 53, 77, 162
mortality rates 2–4, 92, 115
motivation 7, 11, 28, 30, 45, 76, 89, 92, 128, 158, 177, 192
Muhlheim, L. 165
multidiagnostic ED DBT (MED-DBT) 192

Nadarajah, A. 10
National ED Information Centre (NEDIC, Canada) 97
National EDs Collaboration (NEDC, Australia) 98–99
National Initiative for EDs (NIED, Canada) 97
negative emotions 6, 27
neurocognitive development 76, 198
non-AN cognitions 112
non-authoritarian therapeutic stance **36**, **37**, 45
non-suicidal self-injury 3
non-traditional family structures 179
nutritional and medical assessments 76–78

obsessive-compulsive disorder (OCD) 3–4, 77, 148
on-campus support 166–169
open trial 45–46
over eating 33, 95, 106, 119, 122, 126, 134, 156

Pacanowski, C. R. 163
parent-focused therapy (PFT) 12, 34–35, 72
parents/caregivers: absence of 188–193; accommodation 29, 32–33, 46, 99, 104–105, 117–118; agnosticism 27–28; ambivalence 26, 32, 94, 107; anorexia nervosa, impacts of 7–8; burden 29, 33, 117, 135; burnout 8, 33, 92, 96, 117, 134, 155, 191; collaborative care (*see* collaboration); confidence 131; control 44–45, 94, 115; convincing request to 79; criticism 92, 111, 120–121, 133; dyad 111, 116–118, 199; emotional support 10, 58, 119, 131, 134, 144; empowerment (*see* empowerment); exhaustion 92, 96, 134–135; fear 29, 33, 92, 95–96; hesitant/refusal to take charge of 122; management of eating 115, 117, 120, 126; monitoring 131; perception of illness 7; questions posed to 113–114; reluctance 122; resources for 97–99; support 7–8; taking history **90**; during transfer of care 8–12; transition of control to young person 36, 126–127, 131–132, 134, 180; urgency of involvement 92
Parents Versus Anorexia Scale (PVA) 74–75
partial hospitalization *see* day-treatment programs
partners support 6, 34, 57–59, 72, 105, 112, 166, 188, 190–191
Paul, E. C. 166
peer mentors 157
peer support 5, 26, 30, 34, 55, 57–58, 68, 70, 75, 96–98, 104, 131, 141, 157, 166, 191
perfectionism, maladaptive 3
post-secondary education 13, 33, 141, 162–163; assessing readiness for 164–165; challenges in 169–170; on-campus support 166–169; treatment team development 165–166
Potterton, R. 7, 68
primary care physicians (PCPs) 155–156
Project ECHO-EDs Clinic (PE-EDC) 157–158
Project for Extension for Community Healthcare Outcomes (ECHO) 157–159
psychoeducation 29, 45, 70–71, 76, 78, 92, 96, 155, 191
purging 2–4, 13, 71, 86, 115, 123, 144, 164

race/ethnicity 156, 163, 174–178, 181–182
recovery 107–108, 170
refeeding 13, 25, 27, 32–33, 59, 71–72, 76–77, 104, 107, 117, 122, 175, 178–180, 182, 188–190
relapse 29, 38, 68, 162, 164, 170; prevention 11, 36, 45, 97, 138–140, 142–148, 156, 180, 190–191; risk factors for 147–148
Release of Information (ROI) 166, 168–169
renourishment *see* refeeding
residential (RES) care program 91, 96, 193
resilience 11, 54
restricting type AN 2–3
roommates support 6, 34, 168, 189–190

Sauerwein, J. 177–178
SCOFF 74–75
self-advocacy 9
self-agency 112, 189

self-blame 26–29, 33, 89
self-confidence 27
self-criticism 133
self-determination 25, 33, 56, 71, 85
self-efficacy 46, 50, 74–75, 106, 129, 146, 191–192
self-harm 3, 148, 154, 179
self-isolation 6
self-management 55
self-monitoring 128–129
self-reflection 57, 141
self-reliance 140
self-report 46, 74–75, 158
self-starvation 58
self-worth 57, 140
sense of self 57, 143, 148
set-shifting ability 5–6, 54
sexual diversity 176
shame 4, 6, 8, 26, 28–30, 68, 70, 89, 112, 141, 155, 170
siblings support 6, 35, 70, 72, 75, 78, 95, 112, 155, 188–191
Smith, A. R. 3
social connection 55, 170
social determinants of health (SDH) 175–177
social functioning, impact on 169–170
social media 58
socioeconomic status 156, 174, 176–178
standardized mortality ratio (SMR) 3–4
starvation 4–5, 27, 53, 58, 105
stigma 6, 8, 28, 67, 98, 155, 163; internalized 140; weight 68–70
stress 8, 28, 54, 78, 99, 117, 140, 143–145, 155, 157, 175, 182
substance use disorders 3, 148
suicidality 3–4, 46, 148, 154, 169, 192
symptoms 55, 88, 112, 122–123
systemic family therapy (SyFT) 48–49

Tantillo, M. 158
TAY *see* transition-age youth (TAY)
team approach, externalization and 30–31
team building 153–155, 165–166, 169
termination of treatment 38, 138–139, 145–148, 180, 192
therapeutic alliance 12, 26, 45, 66, 71
therapeutic stance 31, **36**, **37**
therapist training 153–154
transfer of care 8–10, 67–68; family support during 10–11
transition-age youth (TAY) 1; with AN 6; brain development 4–5; emotional difficulties 6; therapist's experience with 12–13; treatment-seeking behaviours in 5–6; *see also specific entries*
transition of control 36, 126–127, 131–132, 134, 180
Transition Readiness Assessment Questionnaire (TRAQ) 67
trauma 7, 54, 69, 146, 175, 177, 179–180, 182
treatment review 146–147, 192
Turkiewicz, G. 175

uncertainty intolerance 5
Understanding and Assessing for Refeeding Syndrome in Severe EDs 76–77
Urban, B. 178

van Langenberg, T. 191
Voswinkel, M. M. 31

warmth 30, 32, 86, 90, 119–120
weighing 85–86, *87*, 111–115, 127–128, 167
weight chart 26, 86, *87*, 102–103, 113, 127–128, 130, 134, 154
weight restoration 5, 12, 26–27, 35, 114, 119, 147, 155–156, 174–176, 179, 189–190, 193; barriers to 113; calorie-dense foods for 178; FBT for 46–47; parents/caregivers–young person collaboration for 92–94, 111; partner role in 59; supporting 116–118; SyFT for 48
weight stigma 68–70
Withers, A. 191
Wong, L. 174

Youth EDE-Q (Y-EDE-Q) 75

For Product Safety Concerns and Information please contact our EU representative GPSR@taylorandfrancis.com
Taylor & Francis Verlag GmbH, Kaufingerstraße 24, 80331 München, Germany

www.ingramcontent.com/pod-product-compliance
Ingram Content Group UK Ltd.
Pitfield, Milton Keynes, MK11 3LW, UK
UKHW022353190926
475702UK00015B/2265
* 9 7 8 1 0 3 2 7 0 4 7 9 1 *